ワンオペ JOKER

one operation joker   vol. 1

Written by Satoshi Miyagawa
Drawn by Keisuke Gotou
Translations by Sheldon Drzka
Lettering by Wes Abbott

CONTENTS

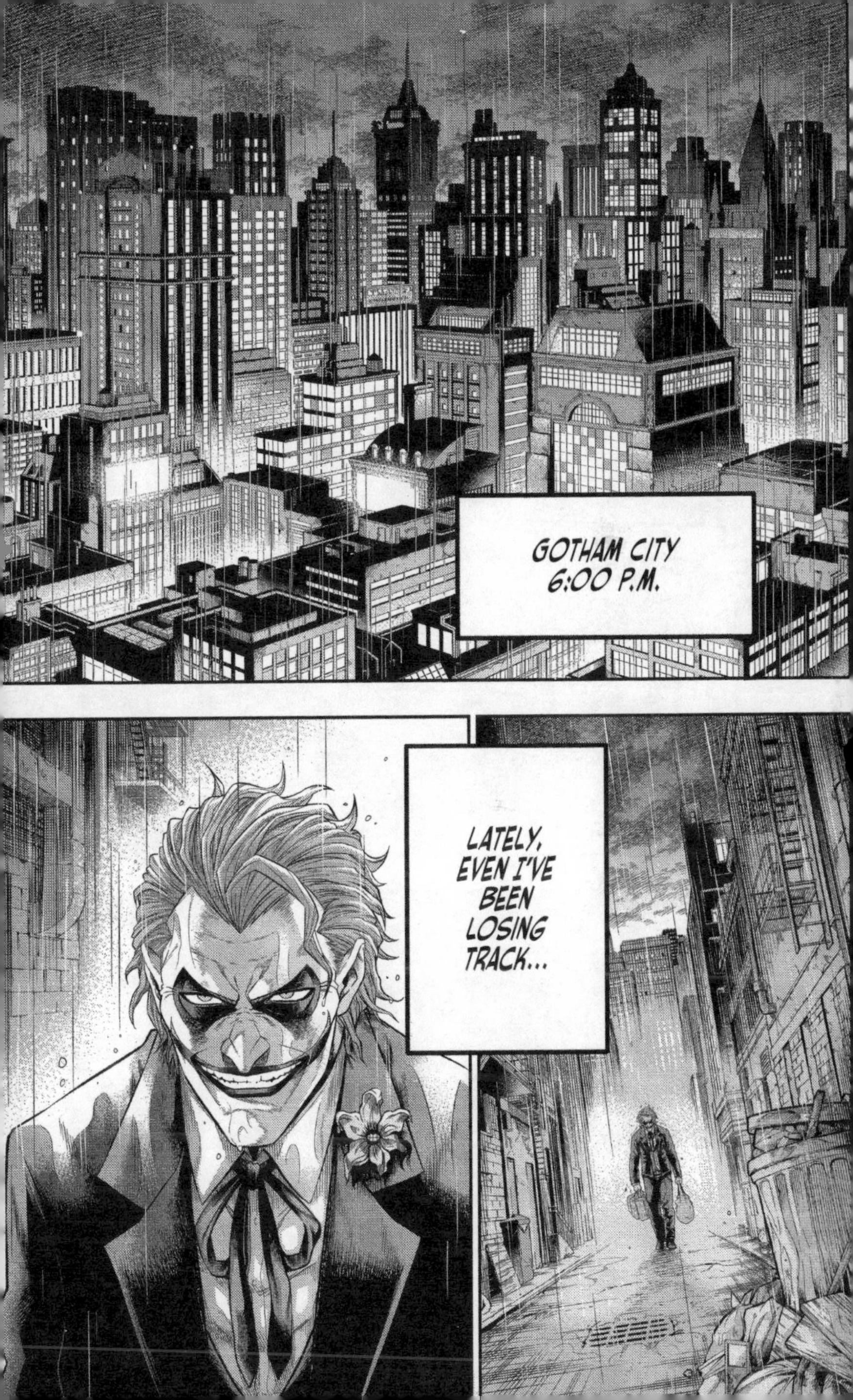
GOTHAM CITY 6:00 P.M.
LATELY, EVEN I'VE BEEN LOSING TRACK...

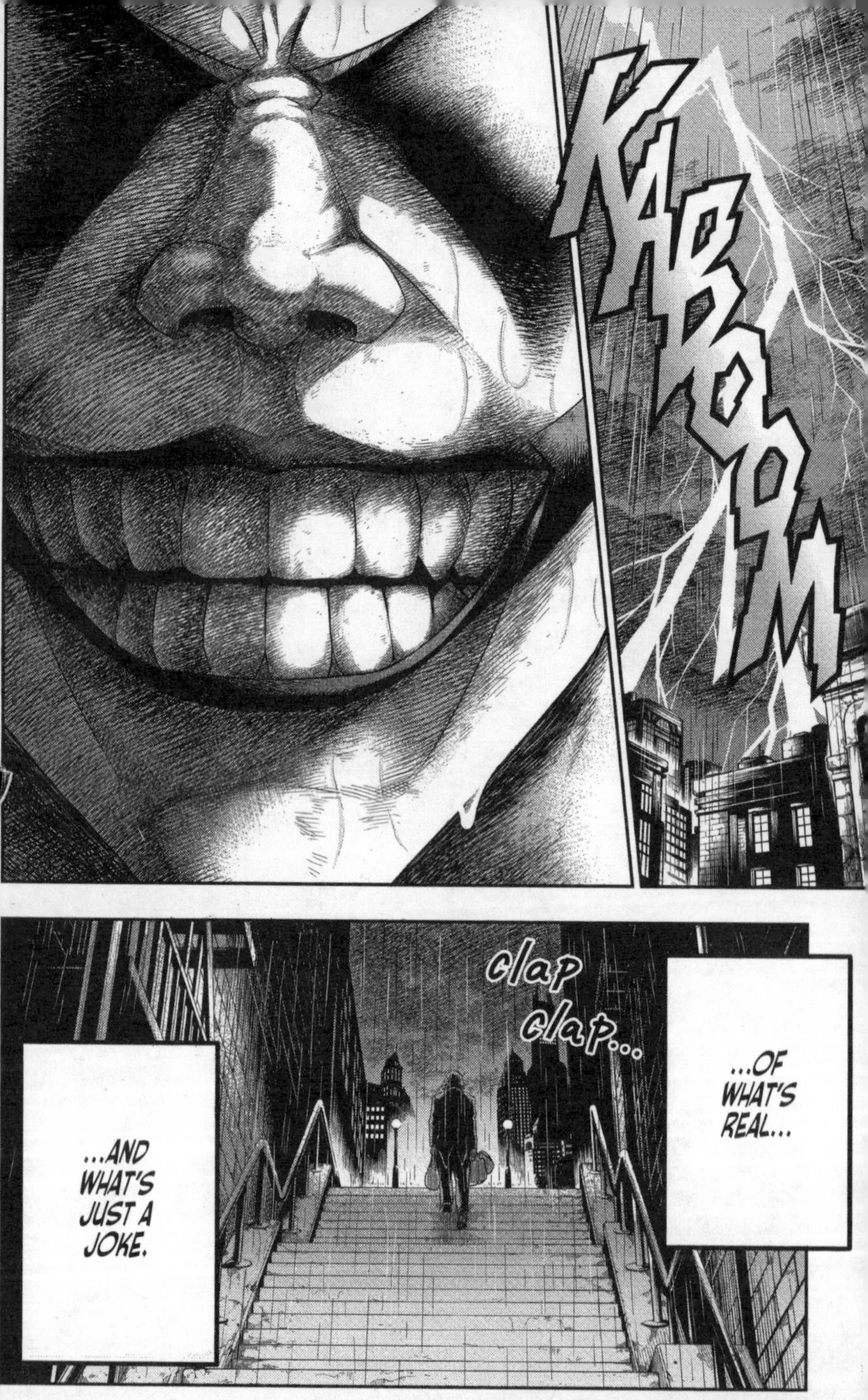
KABOOM
...OF WHAT'S REAL...
clap clap...
...AND WHAT'S JUST A JOKE.

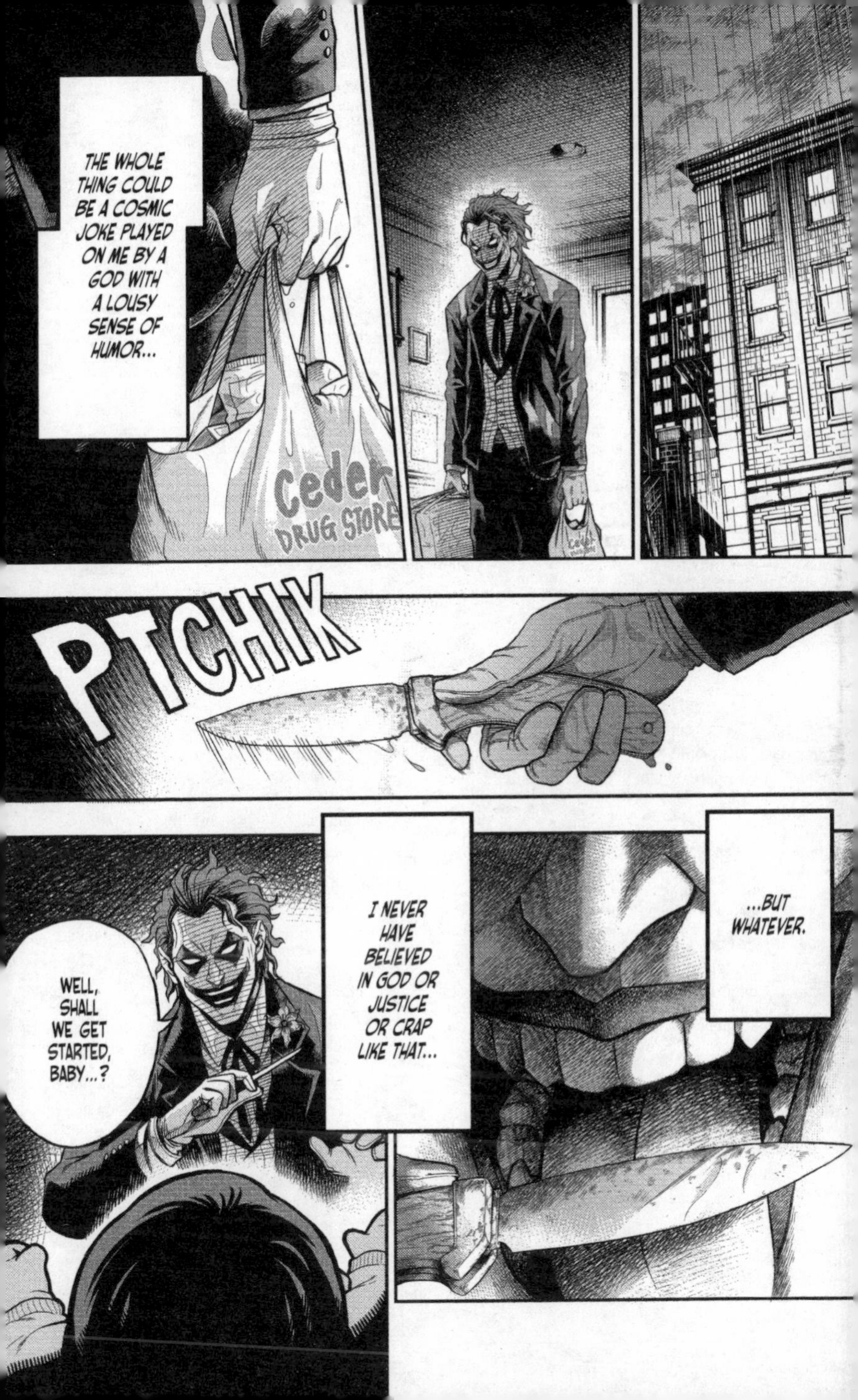

THE WHOLE THING COULD BE A COSMIC JOKE PLAYED ON ME BY A GOD WITH A LOUSY SENSE OF HUMOR...
Ceder DRUG STORE
PTCHIK
I NEVER HAVE BELIEVED IN GOD OR JUSTICE OR CRAP LIKE THAT...
...BUT WHATEVER.
WELL, SHALL WE GET STARTED, BABY...?

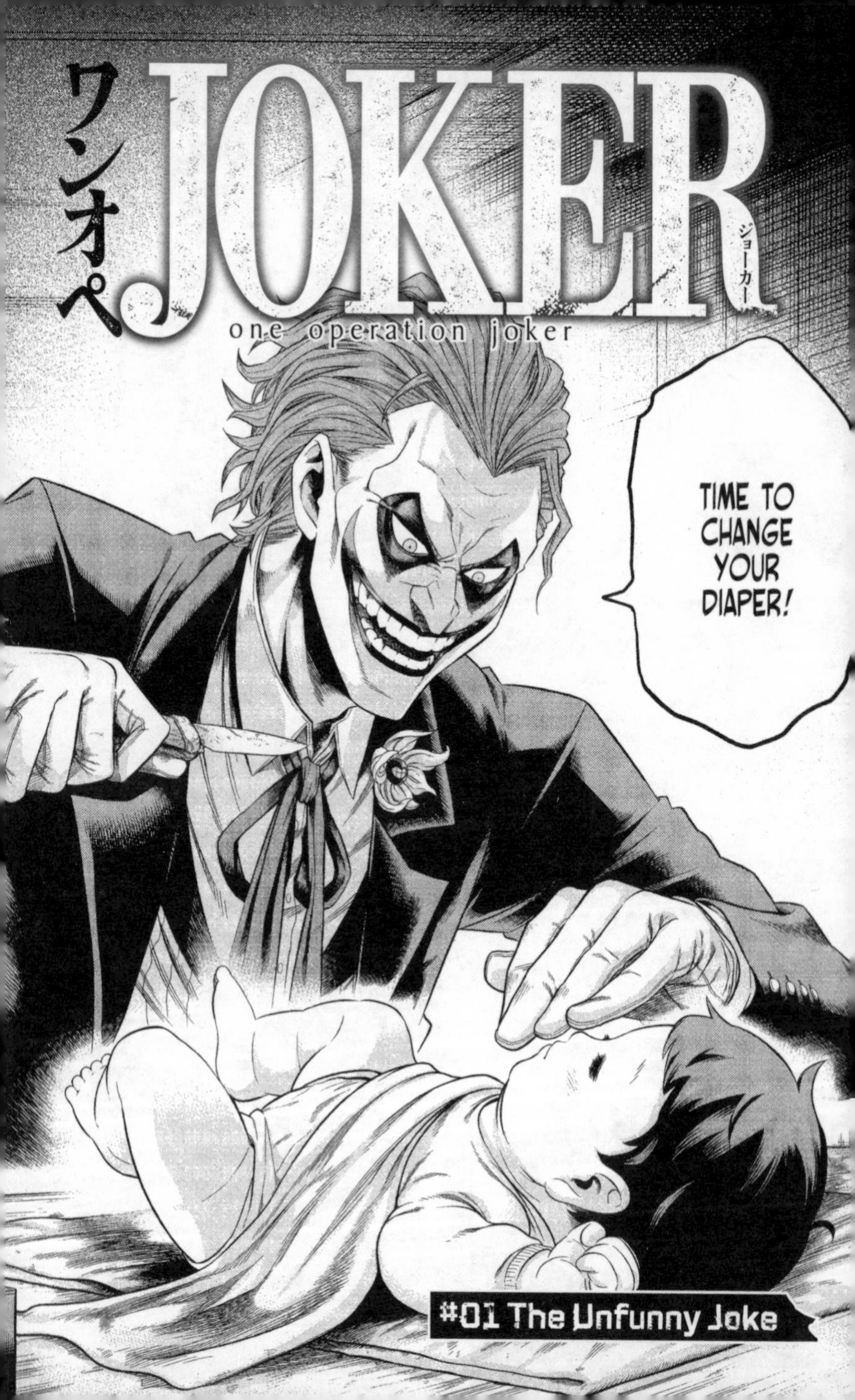
ワンオペ
JOKER
ジョーカー
one operation joker
TIME TO CHANGE YOUR DIAPER!
#01 The Unfunny Joke

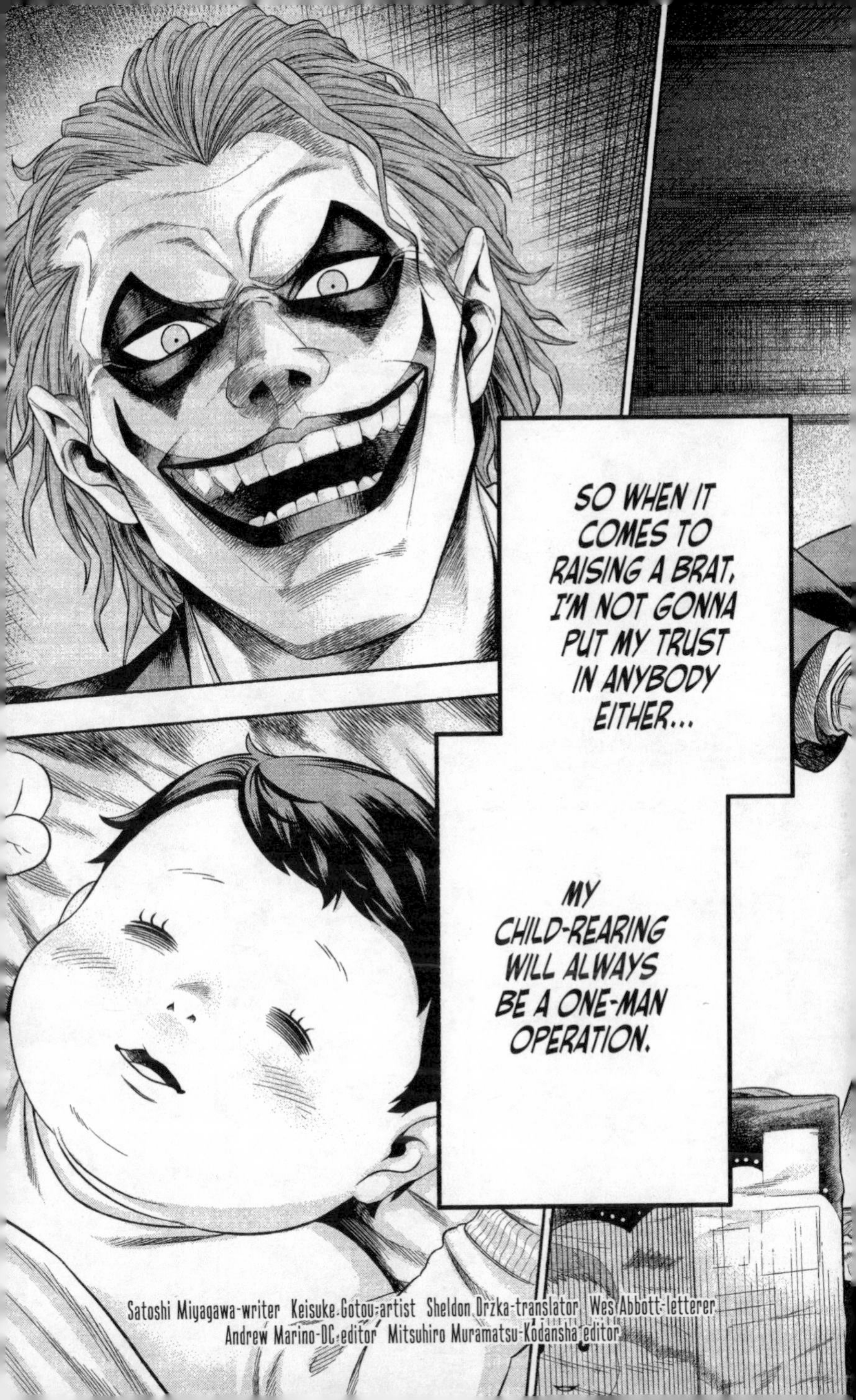
SO WHEN IT COMES TO RAISING A BRAT, I'M NOT GONNA PUT MY TRUST IN ANYBODY EITHER...
MY CHILD-REARING WILL ALWAYS BE A ONE-MAN OPERATION.

Satoshi Miyagawa-writer Keisuke Gotou-artist Sheldon Drzka-translator Wes Abbott-letterer
Andrew Marino-DC editor Mitsuhiro Muramatsu-Kodansha editor

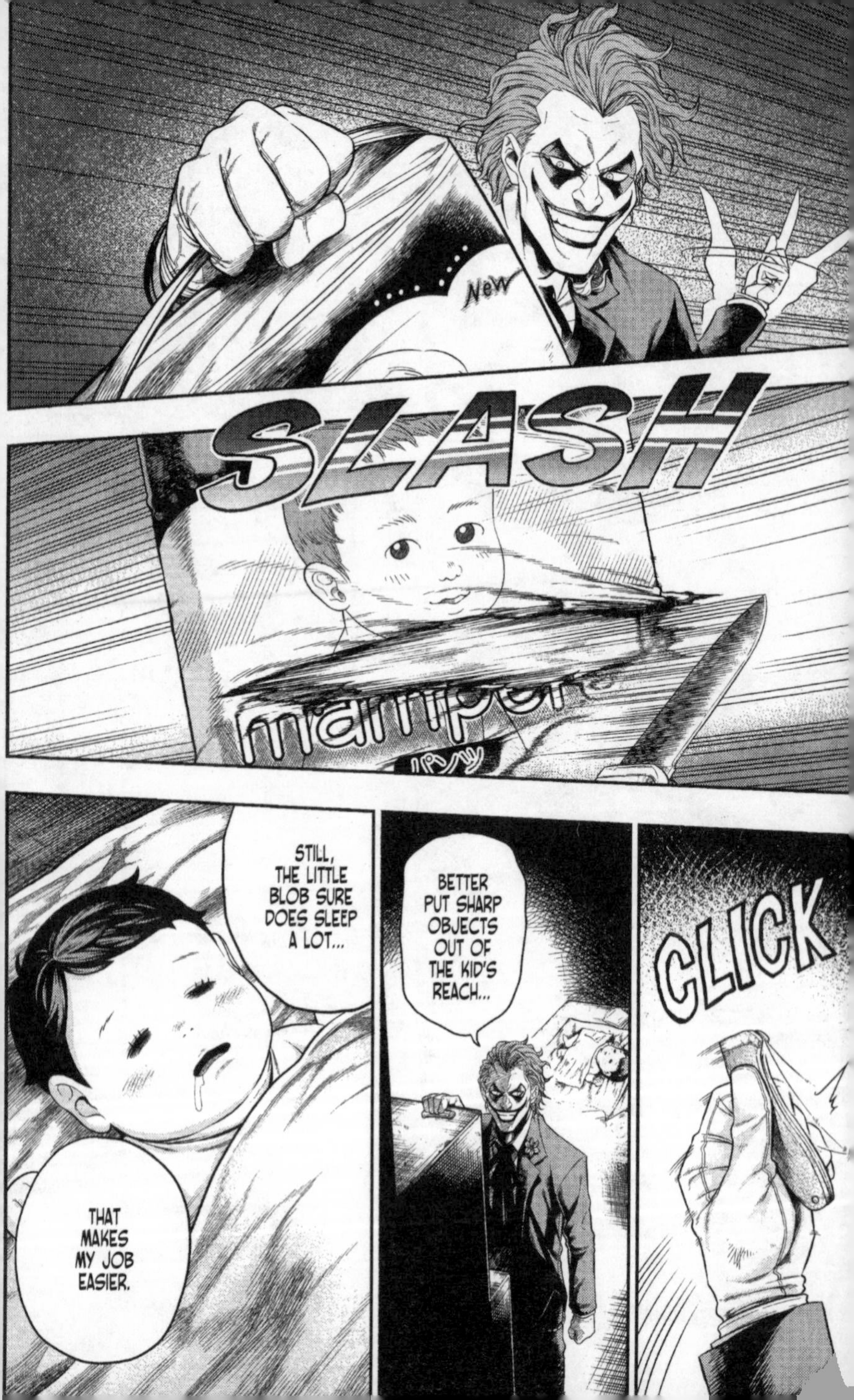
New
SLASH
CLICK
BETTER PUT SHARP OBJECTS OUT OF THE KID'S REACH...
STILL, THE LITTLE BLOB SURE DOES SLEEP A LOT...
THAT MAKES MY JOB EASIER.

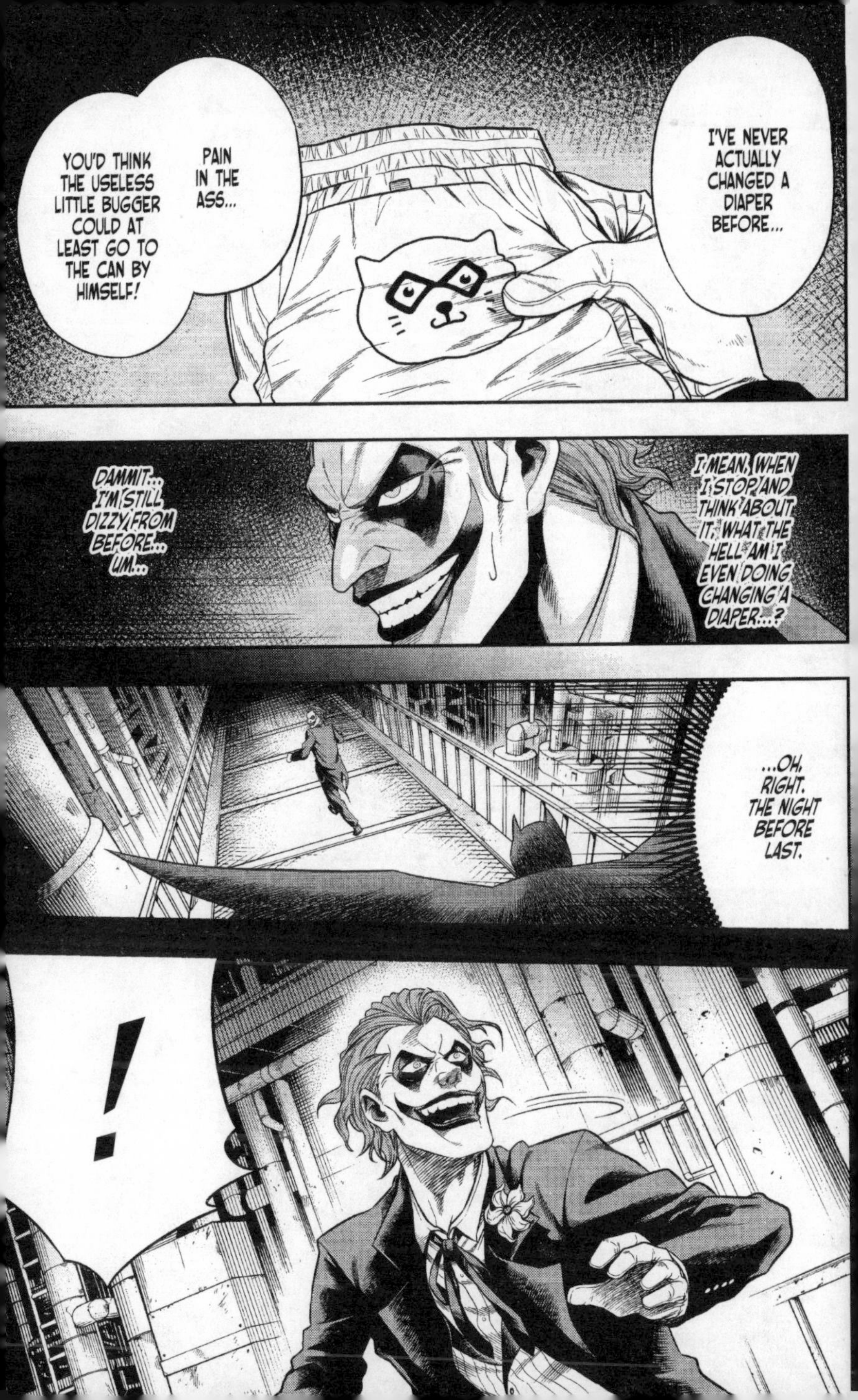
I'VE NEVER ACTUALLY CHANGED A DIAPER BEFORE...
PAIN IN THE ASS...
YOU'D THINK THE USELESS LITTLE BUGGER COULD AT LEAST GO TO THE CAN BY HIMSELF!
I MEAN, WHEN I STOP AND THINK ABOUT IT, WHAT THE HELL AM I EVEN DOING CHANGING A DIAPER...?
DAMMIT... I'M STILL DIZZY FROM BEFORE... UM...
...OH, RIGHT. THE NIGHT BEFORE LAST.
!

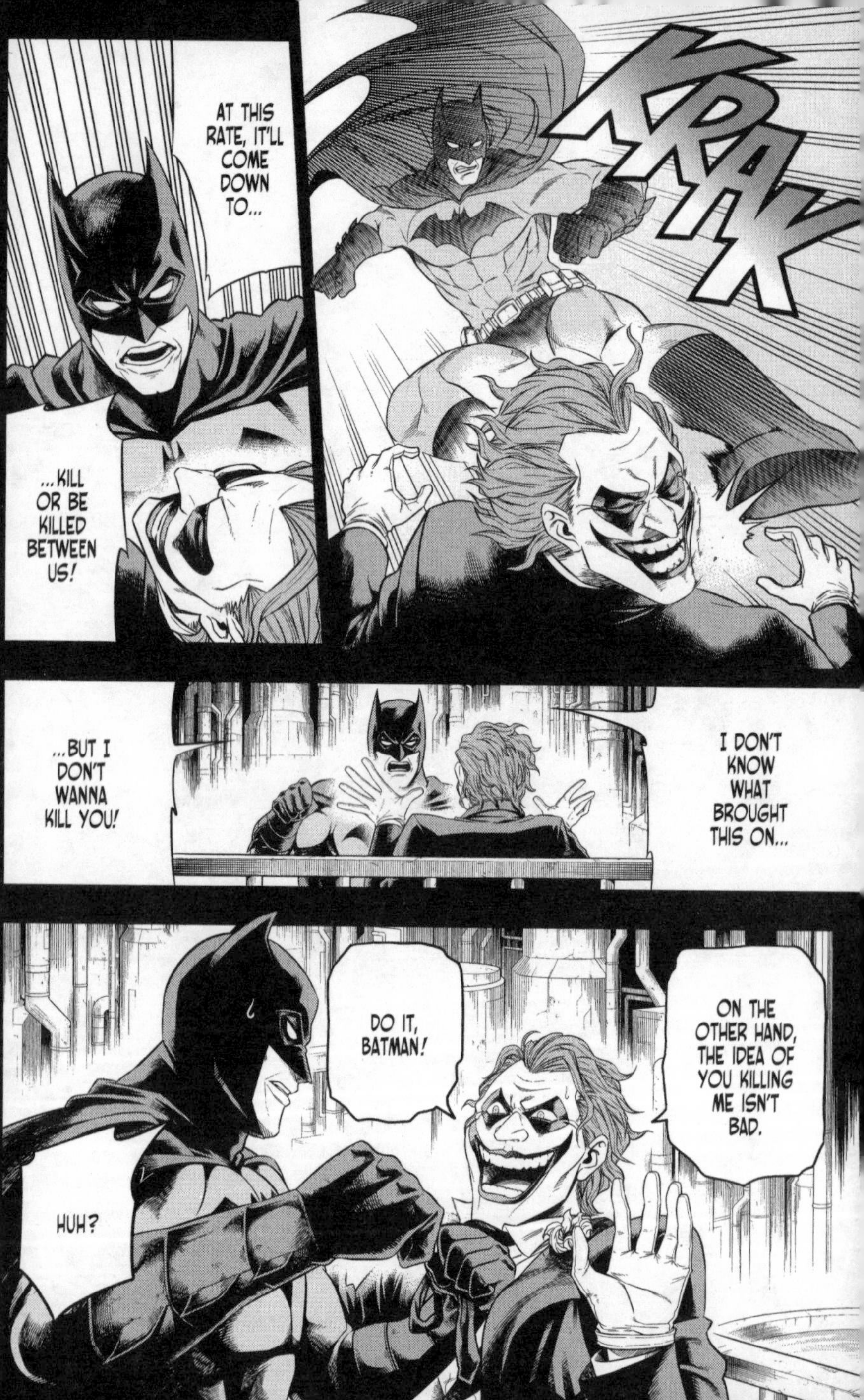
KRAK
AT THIS RATE, IT'LL COME DOWN TO...
...KILL OR BE KILLED BETWEEN US!
I DON'T KNOW WHAT BROUGHT THIS ON...
...BUT I DON'T WANNA KILL YOU!
ON THE OTHER HAND, THE IDEA OF YOU KILLING ME ISN'T BAD.
DO IT, BATMAN!
HUH?

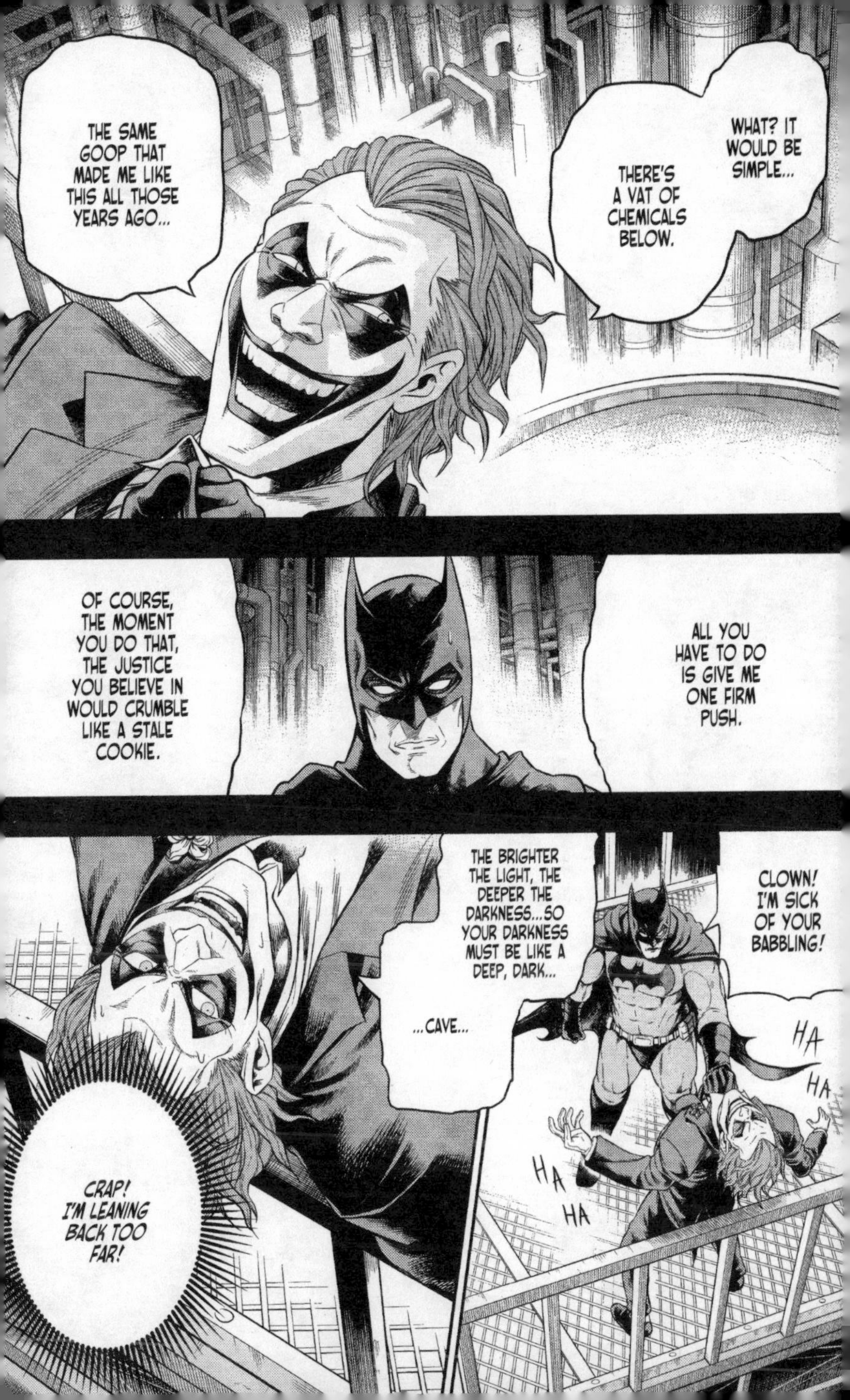
WHAT? IT WOULD BE SIMPLE...
THERE'S A VAT OF CHEMICALS BELOW.
THE SAME GOOP THAT MADE ME LIKE THIS ALL THOSE YEARS AGO...
ALL YOU HAVE TO DO IS GIVE ME ONE FIRM PUSH.
OF COURSE, THE MOMENT YOU DO THAT, THE JUSTICE YOU BELIEVE IN WOULD CRUMBLE LIKE A STALE COOKIE.
CLOWN! I'M SICK OF YOUR BABBLING!
THE BRIGHTER THE LIGHT, THE DEEPER THE DARKNESS...SO YOUR DARKNESS MUST BE LIKE A DEEP, DARK...
HA HA
HA HA
...CAVE...
CRAP! I'M LEANING BACK TOO FAR!

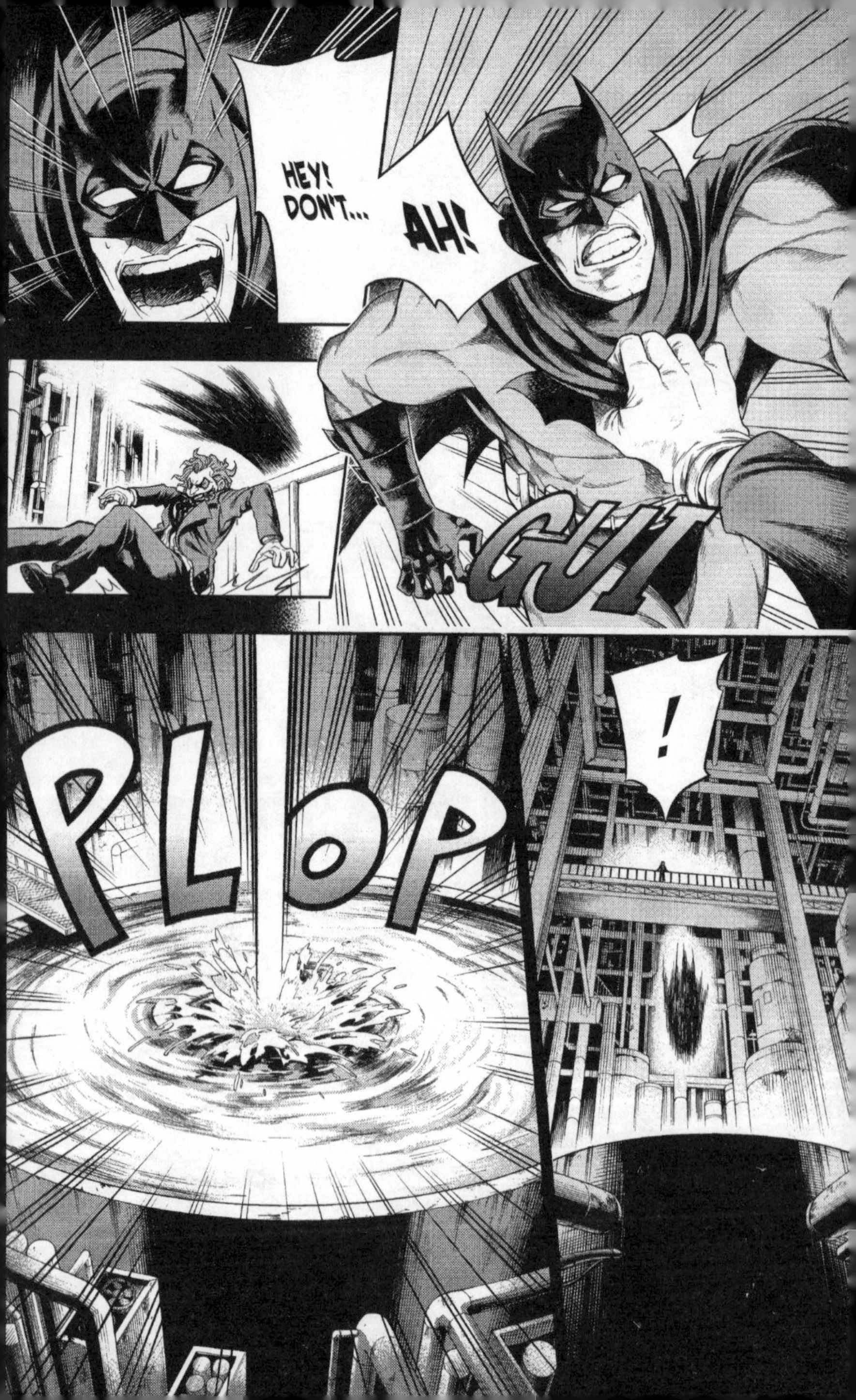
HEY! DON'T...
AH!
GUT
!
PLOP

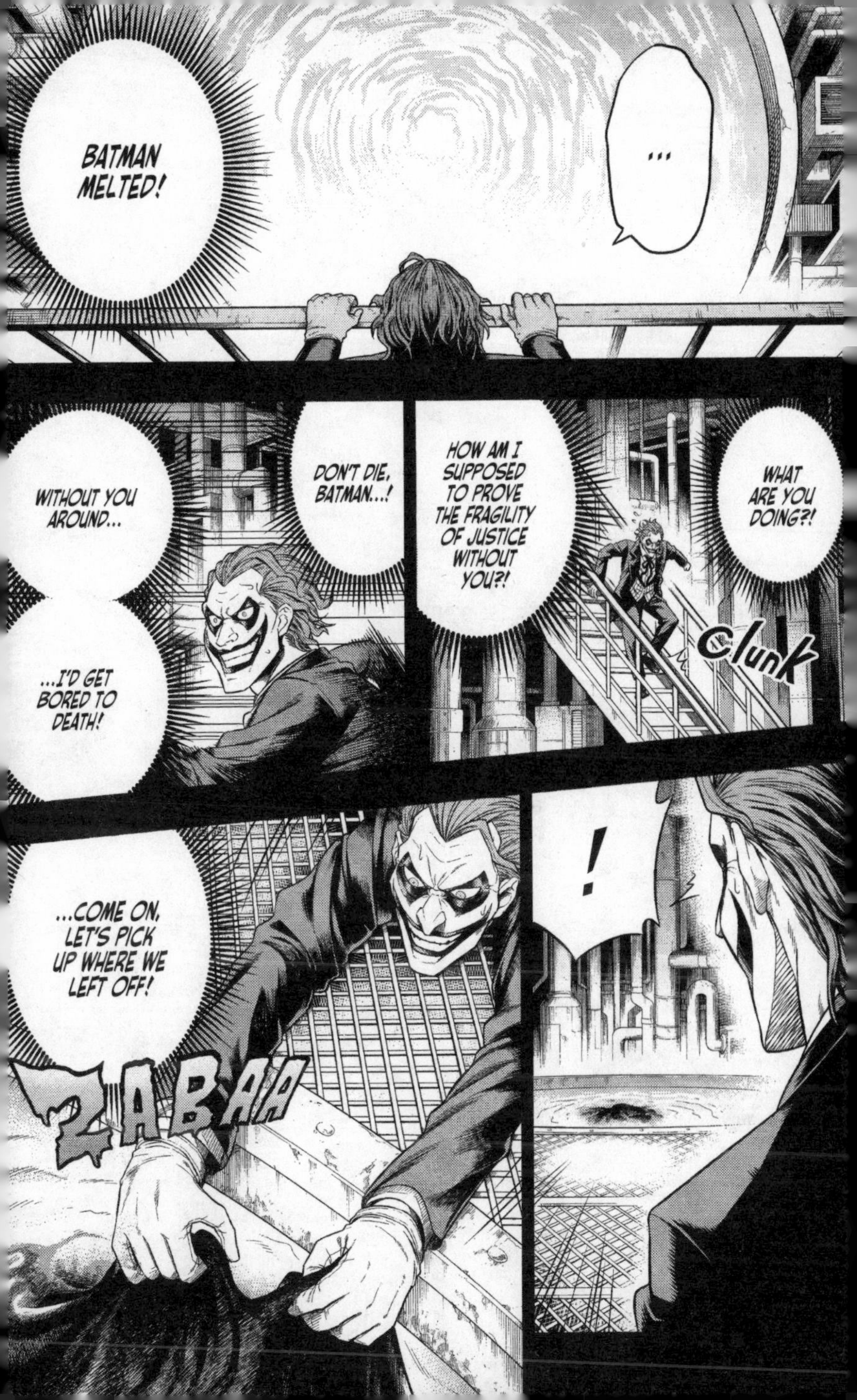
...
BATMAN MELTED!
WHAT ARE YOU DOING?!
HOW AM I SUPPOSED TO PROVE THE FRAGILITY OF JUSTICE WITHOUT YOU?!
Clunk
DON'T DIE, BATMAN...!
WITHOUT YOU AROUND...
...I'D GET BORED TO DEATH!
!
...COME ON, LET'S PICK UP WHERE WE LEFT OFF!
ZABAA

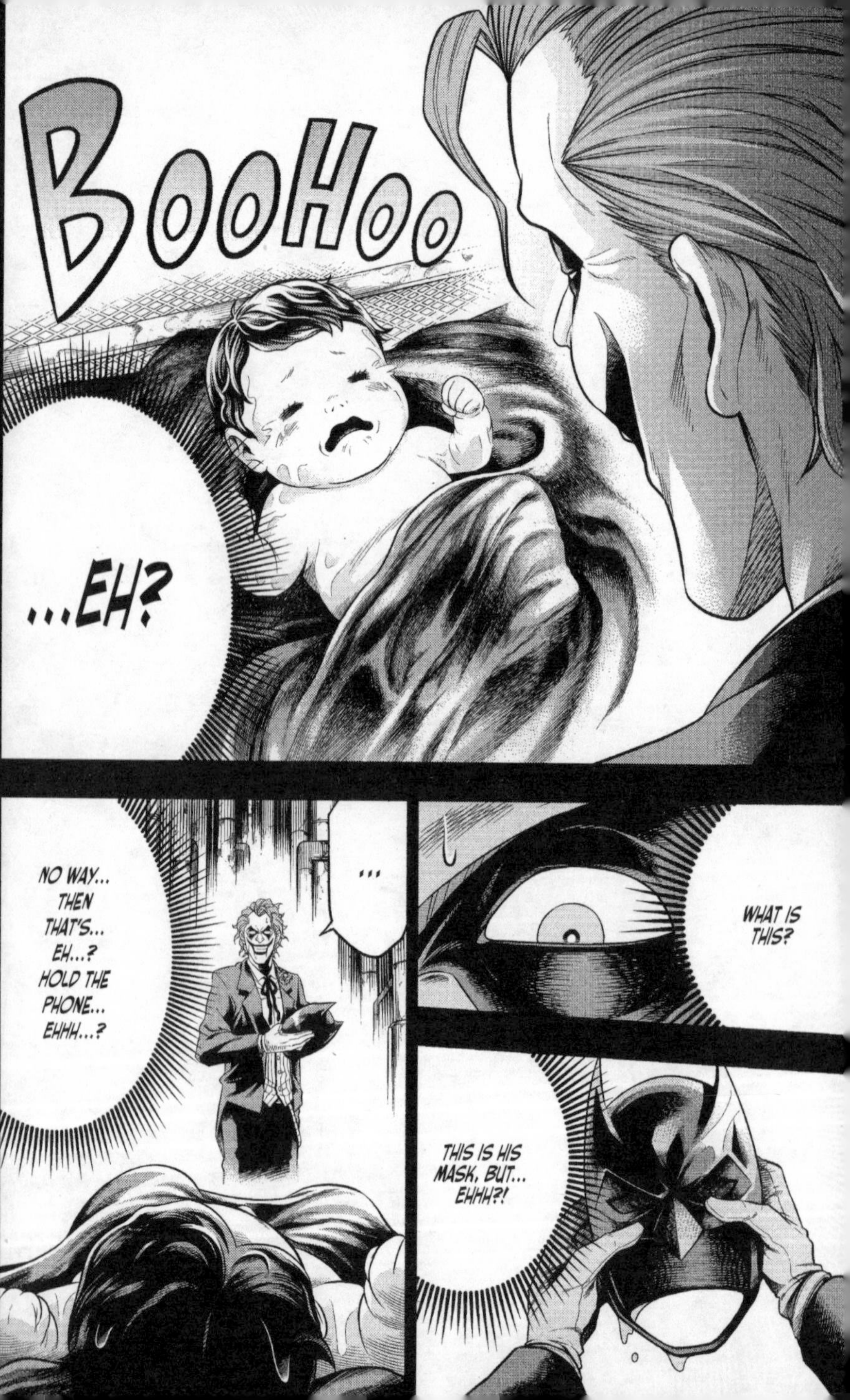
BOOHOO
...EH?
WHAT IS THIS?
THIS IS HIS MASK, BUT... EHHH?!
...
NO WAY... THEN THAT'S... EH...? HOLD THE PHONE... EHHH...?

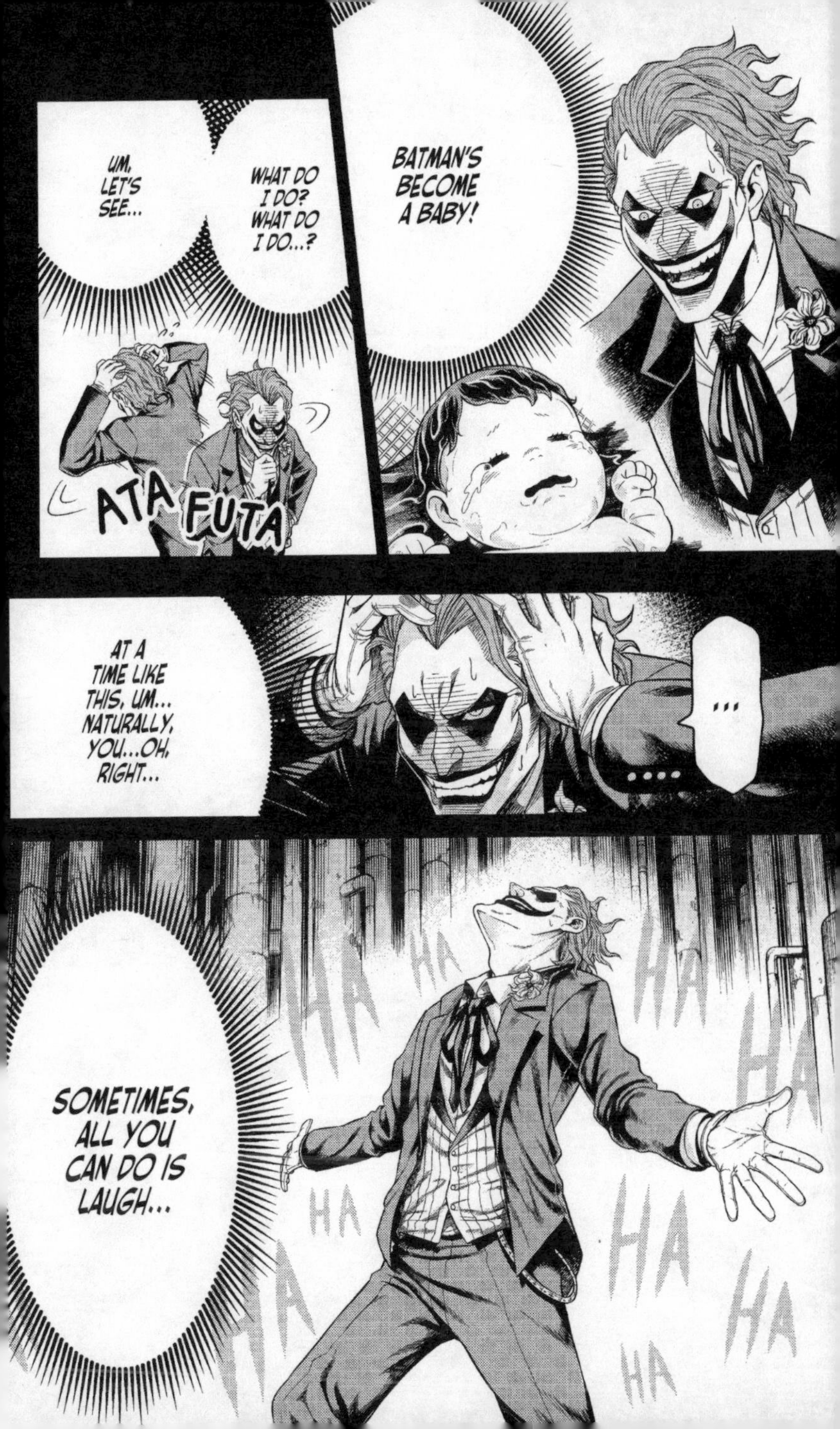

BATMAN'S BECOME A BABY!
WHAT DO I DO? WHAT DO I DO...?
UM, LET'S SEE...
ATA FUTA
...
AT A TIME LIKE THIS, UM... NATURALLY, YOU...OH, RIGHT...
HA HA HA HA HA HA HA HA HA HA HA HA
SOMETIMES, ALL YOU CAN DO IS LAUGH...

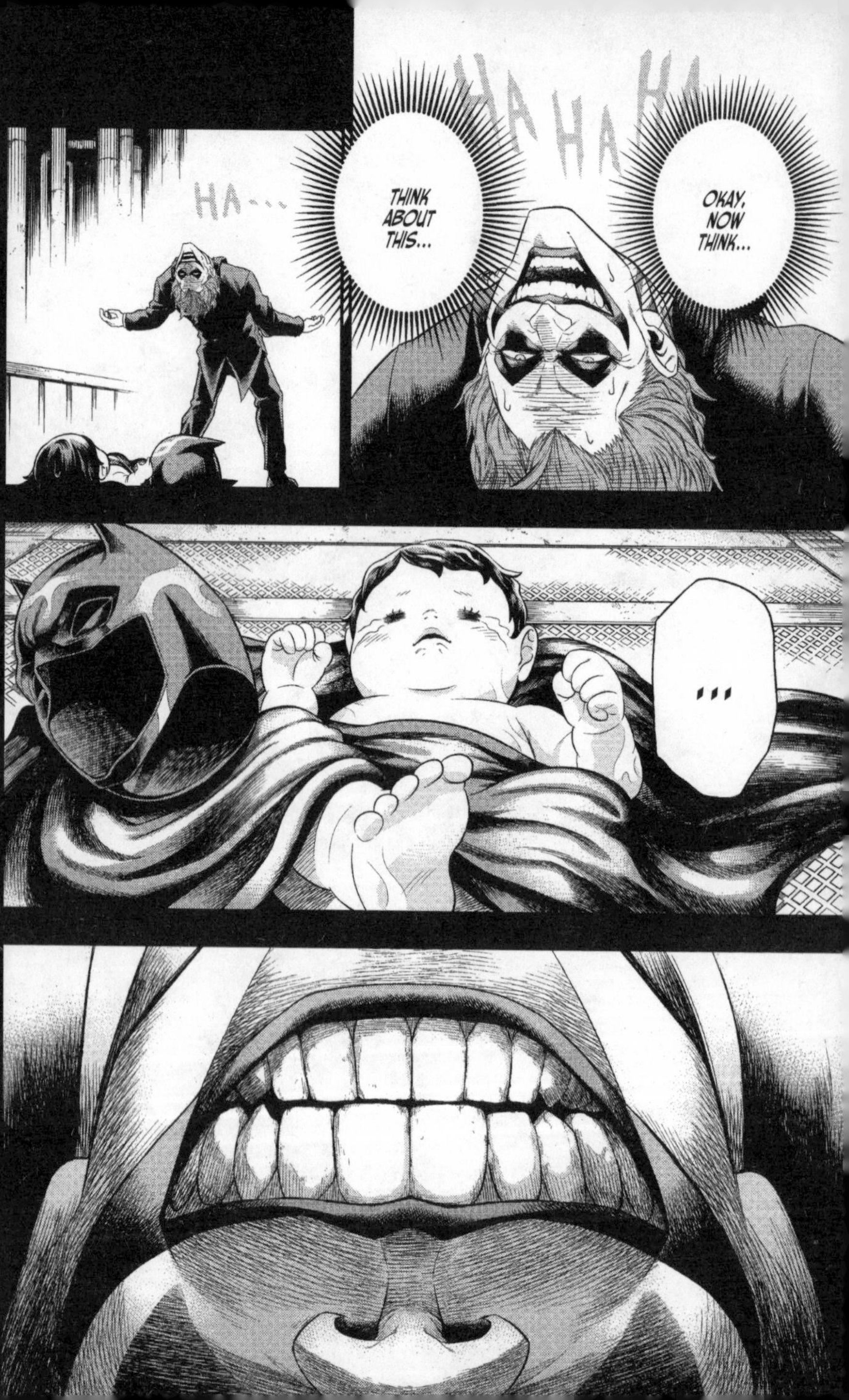
HA HA HA HA
OKAY, NOW THINK...
THINK ABOUT THIS...
HA...
...

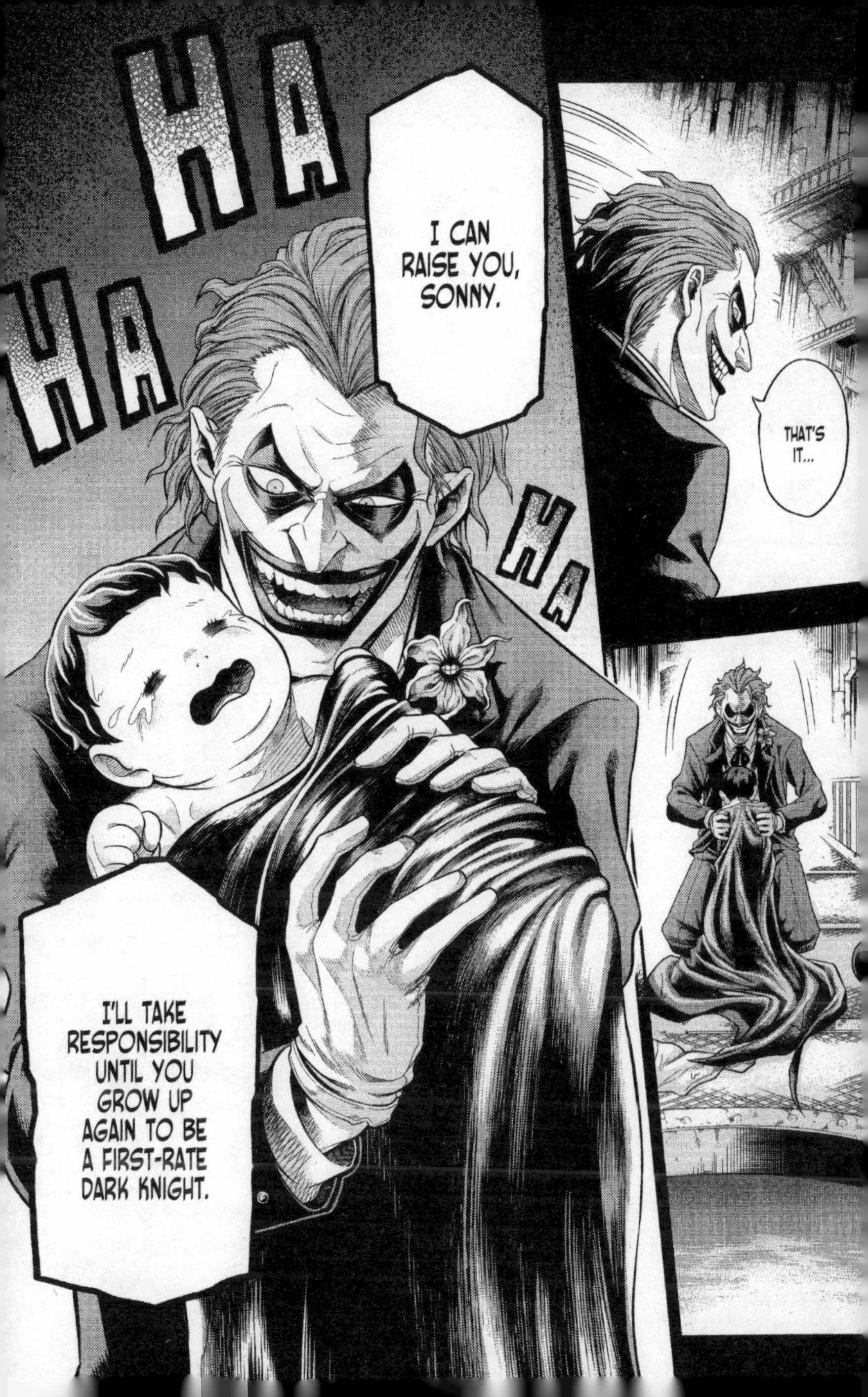
THAT'S IT...
I CAN RAISE YOU, SONNY.
HA HA
HA HA
HA HA
I'LL TAKE RESPONSIBILITY UNTIL YOU GROW UP AGAIN TO BE A FIRST-RATE DARK KNIGHT.

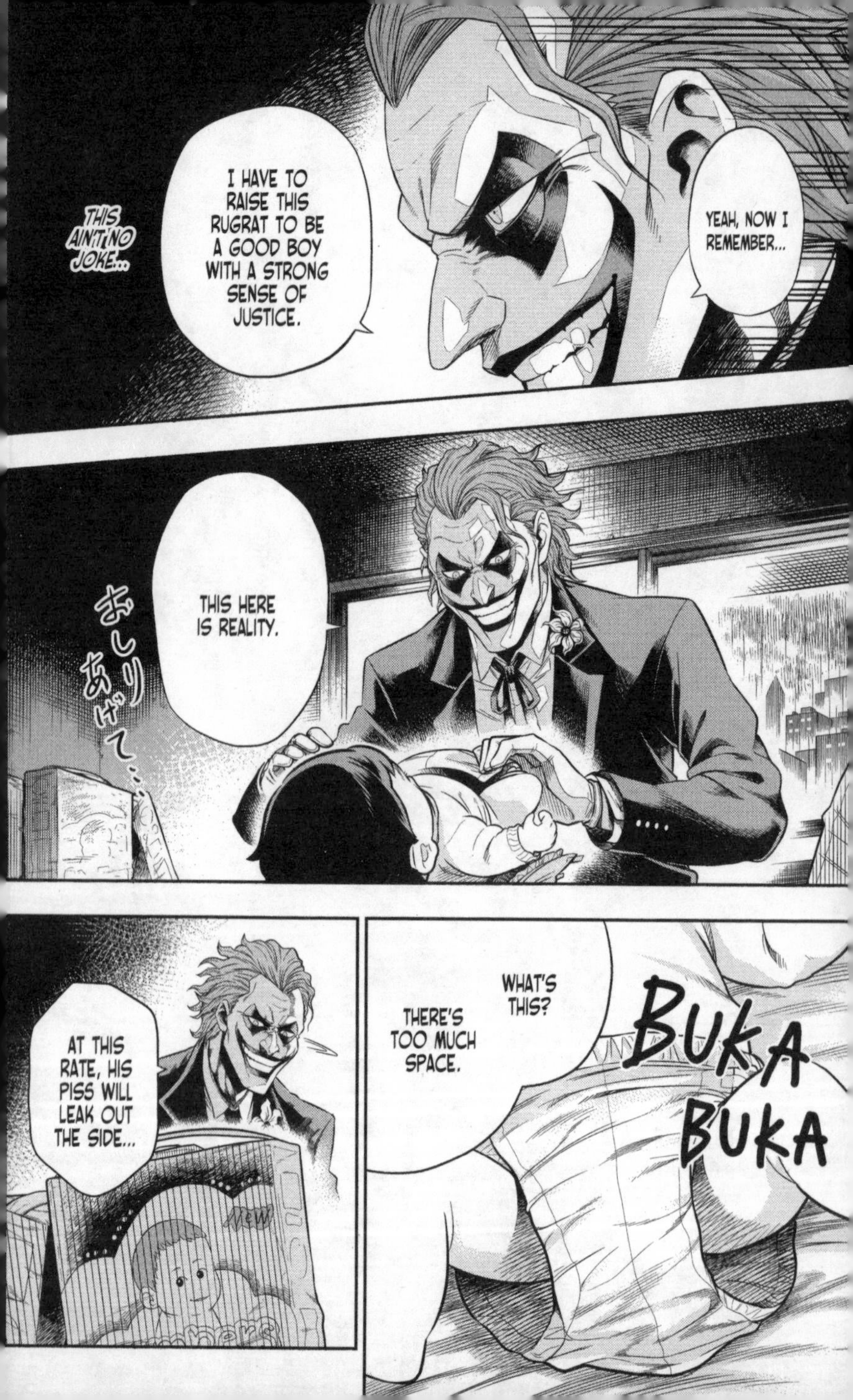

YEAH, NOW I REMEMBER...
I HAVE TO RAISE THIS RUGRAT TO BE A GOOD BOY WITH A STRONG SENSE OF JUSTICE.
THIS AIN'T NO JOKE...
THIS HERE IS REALITY.
おしりあげて…
WHAT'S THIS?
THERE'S TOO MUCH SPACE.
BUKA BUKA
AT THIS RATE, HIS PISS WILL LEAK OUT THE SIDE...
New

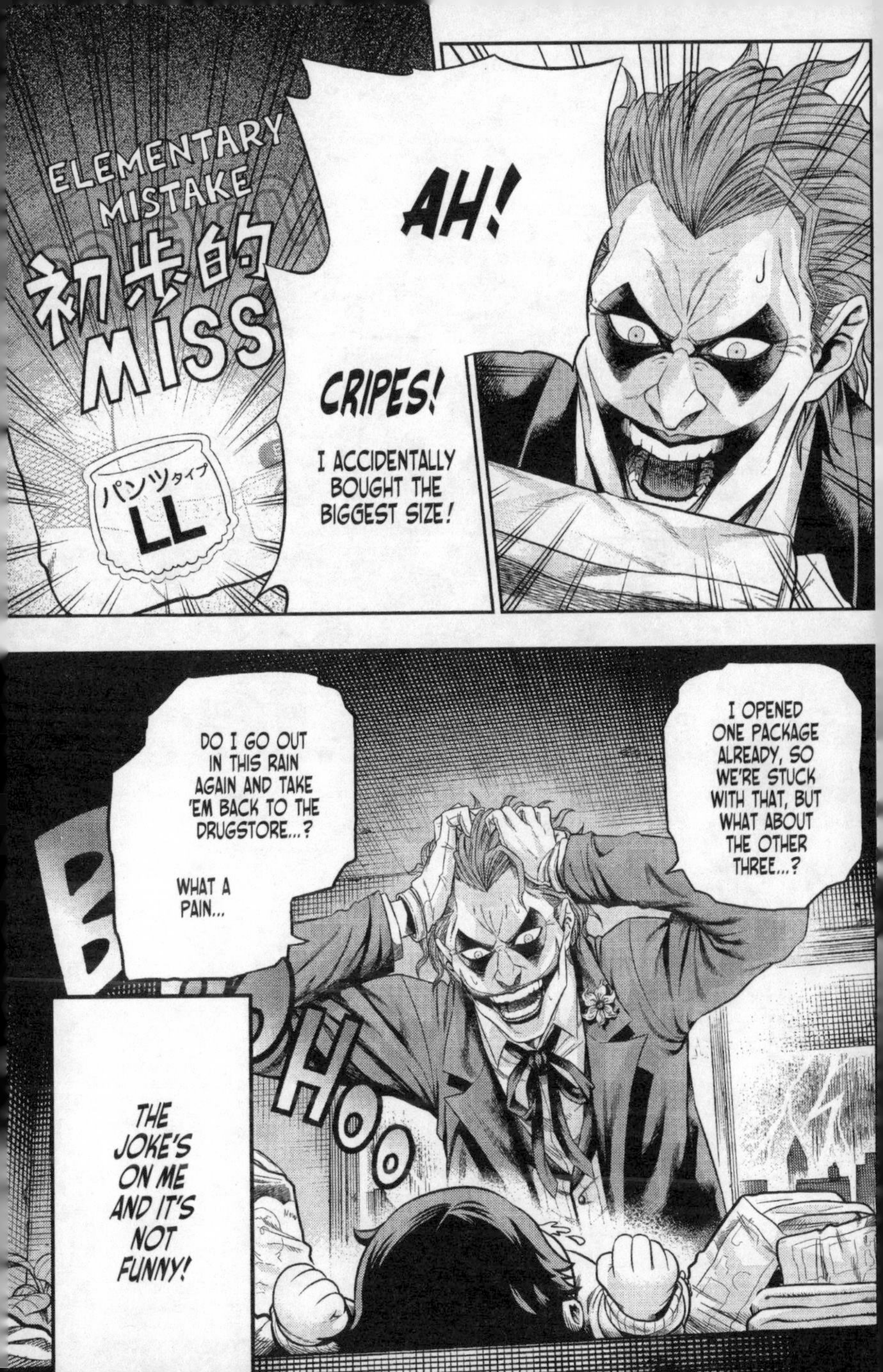
AH!
CRIPES!
I ACCIDENTALLY BOUGHT THE BIGGEST SIZE!
ELEMENTARY MISTAKE
初歩的 MISS
パンツタイプ
LL
I OPENED ONE PACKAGE ALREADY, SO WE'RE STUCK WITH THAT, BUT WHAT ABOUT THE OTHER THREE...?
DO I GO OUT IN THIS RAIN AGAIN AND TAKE 'EM BACK TO THE DRUGSTORE...?
WHAT A PAIN...
THE JOKE'S ON ME AND IT'S NOT FUNNY!

#01 The Unfunny Joke: The End

So, you're wondering what happened to the box of LL-size diapers I opened?

As you can see, I've taken responsibility in making sure they don't go to waste by wearing them myself...

...No, no, just kidding...I may wear a diaper in my senescence, but you know, it all depends... Hahahaha!

one operation joker

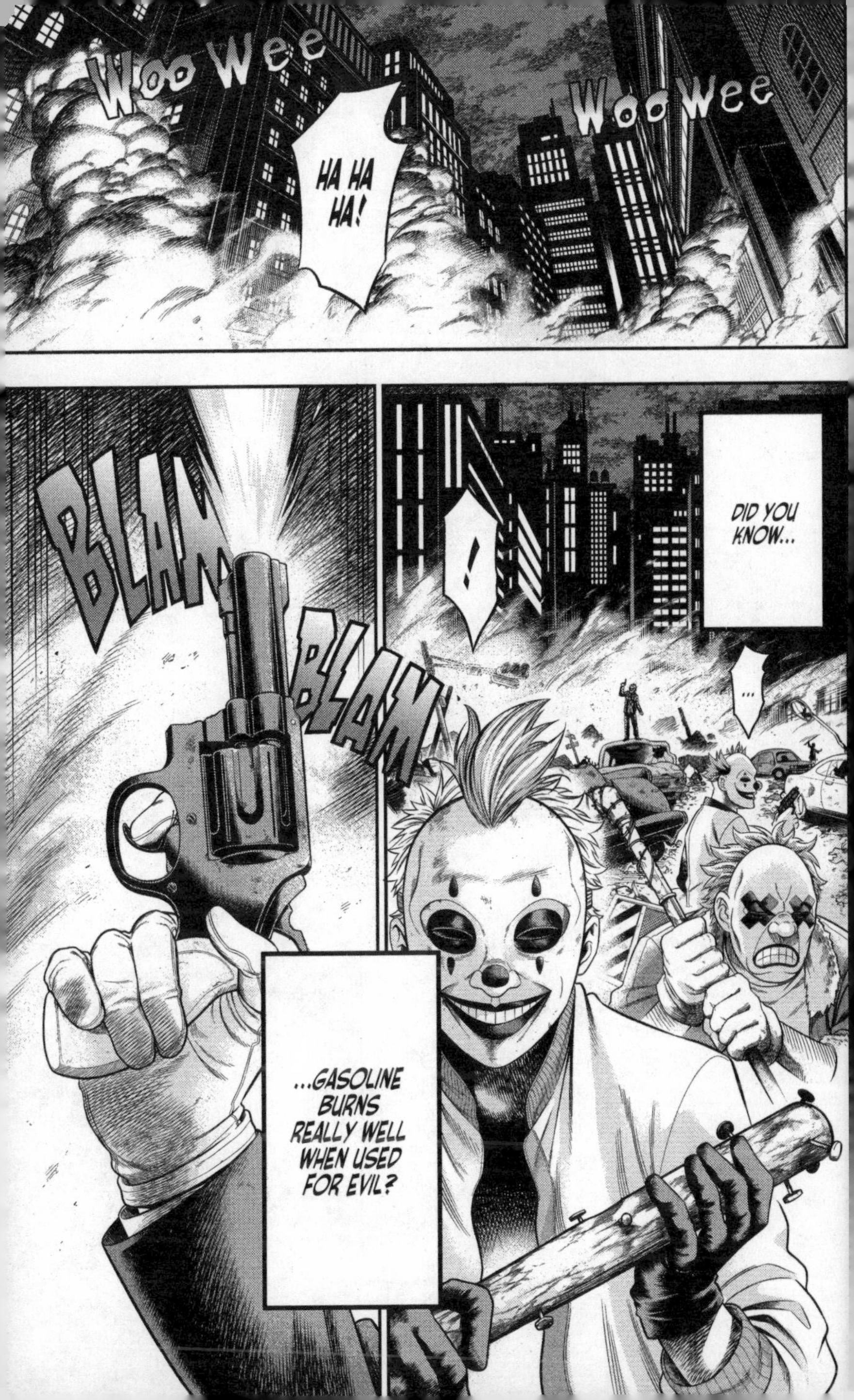
WOO WEE
HA HA HA!
WOO WEE
DID YOU KNOW...
!
...
...GASOLINE BURNS REALLY WELL WHEN USED FOR EVIL?
BLAM
BLAM

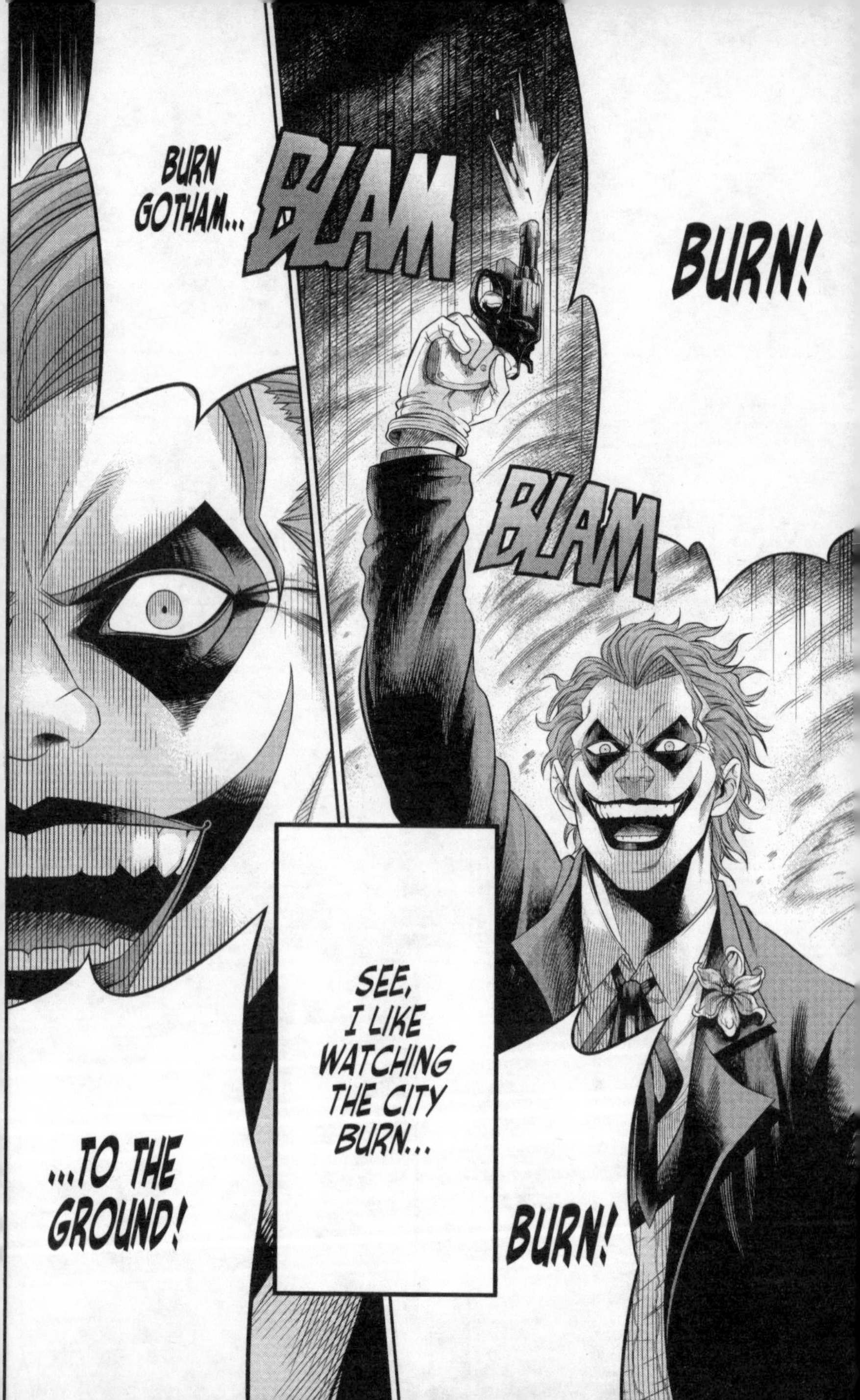
BURN!
BLAM
BLAM
SEE, I LIKE WATCHING THE CITY BURN...
BURN!
BURN GOTHAM...
...TO THE GROUND!

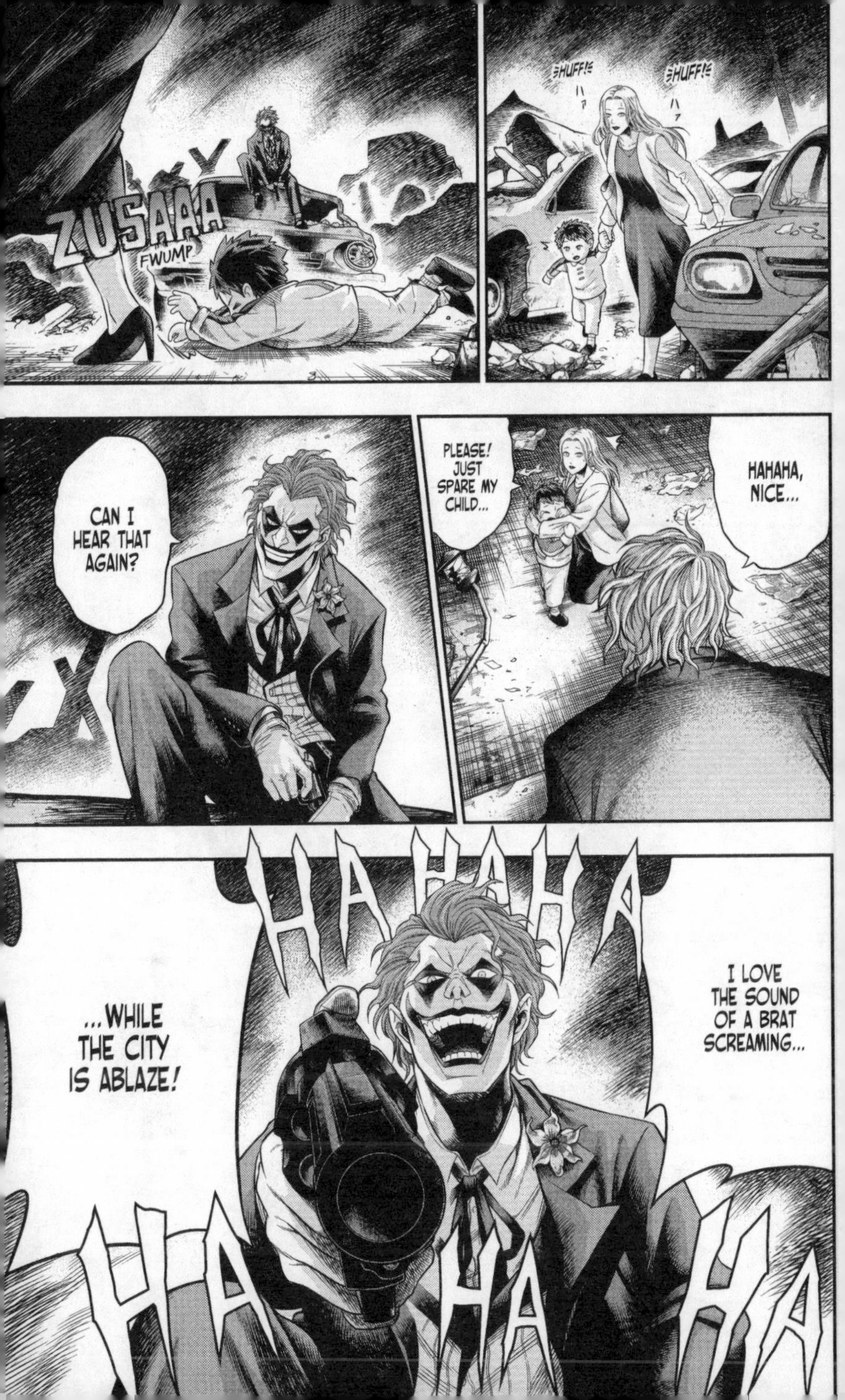
HUFF!
ハァ
HUFF!
ハァ
ZUSAAA
FWUMP
PLEASE! JUST SPARE MY CHILD...
HAHAHA, NICE...
CAN I HEAR THAT AGAIN?
HAHAHA
I LOVE THE SOUND OF A BRAT SCREAMING...
...WHILE THE CITY IS ABLAZE!
HA HA HA HA HA HA

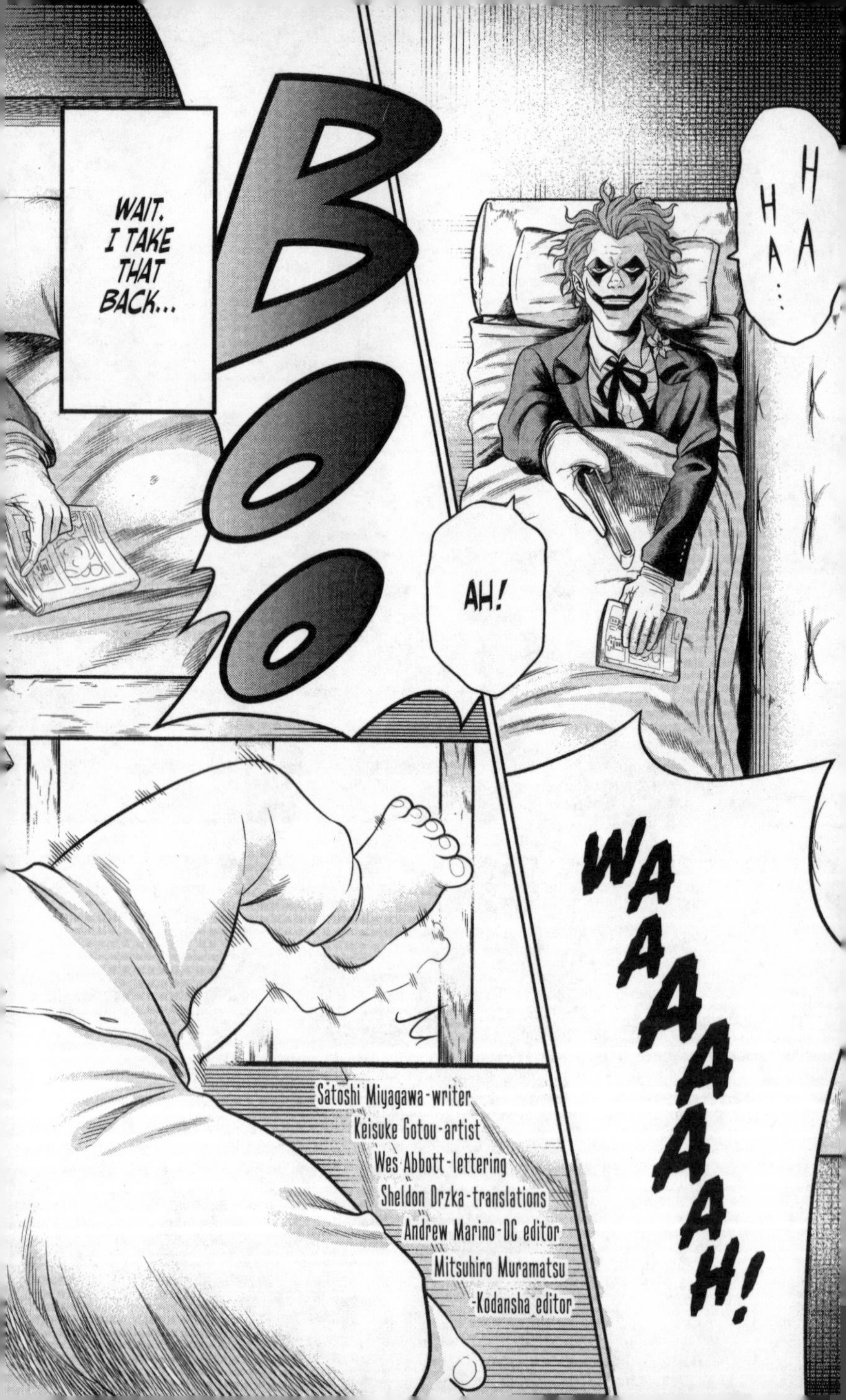
HA HA...
AH!
WAIT. I TAKE THAT BACK...
BOOO
WAAAAAAH!
Satoshi Miyagawa-writer
Keisuke Gotou-artist
Wes Abbott-lettering
Sheldon Drzka-translations
Andrew Marino-DC editor
Mitsuhiro Muramatsu
-Kodansha editor

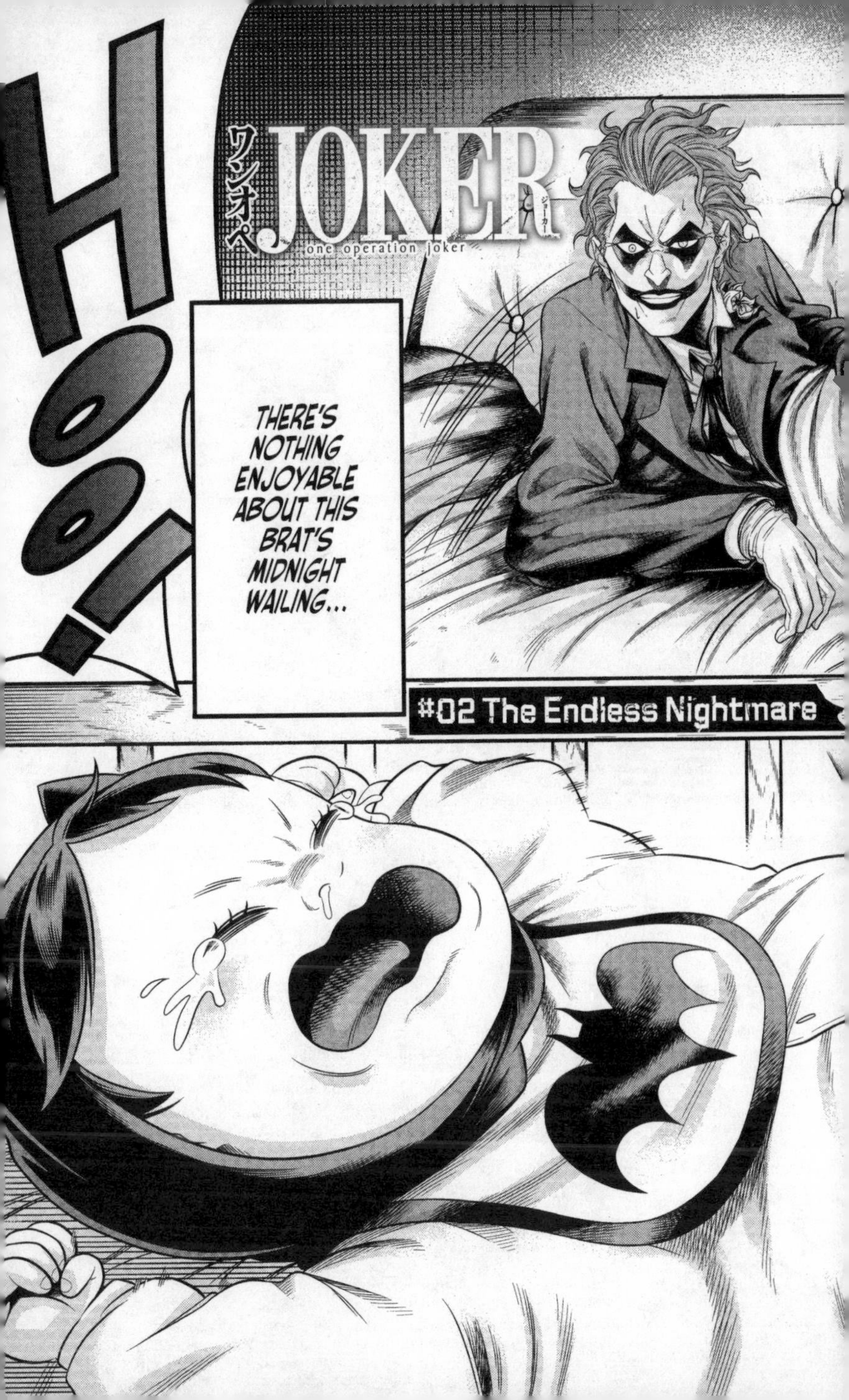

ワンオペ JOKER ジョーカー
one operation joker
#02 The Endless Nightmare
THERE'S NOTHING ENJOYABLE ABOUT THIS BRAT'S MIDNIGHT WAILING...
HOOO!

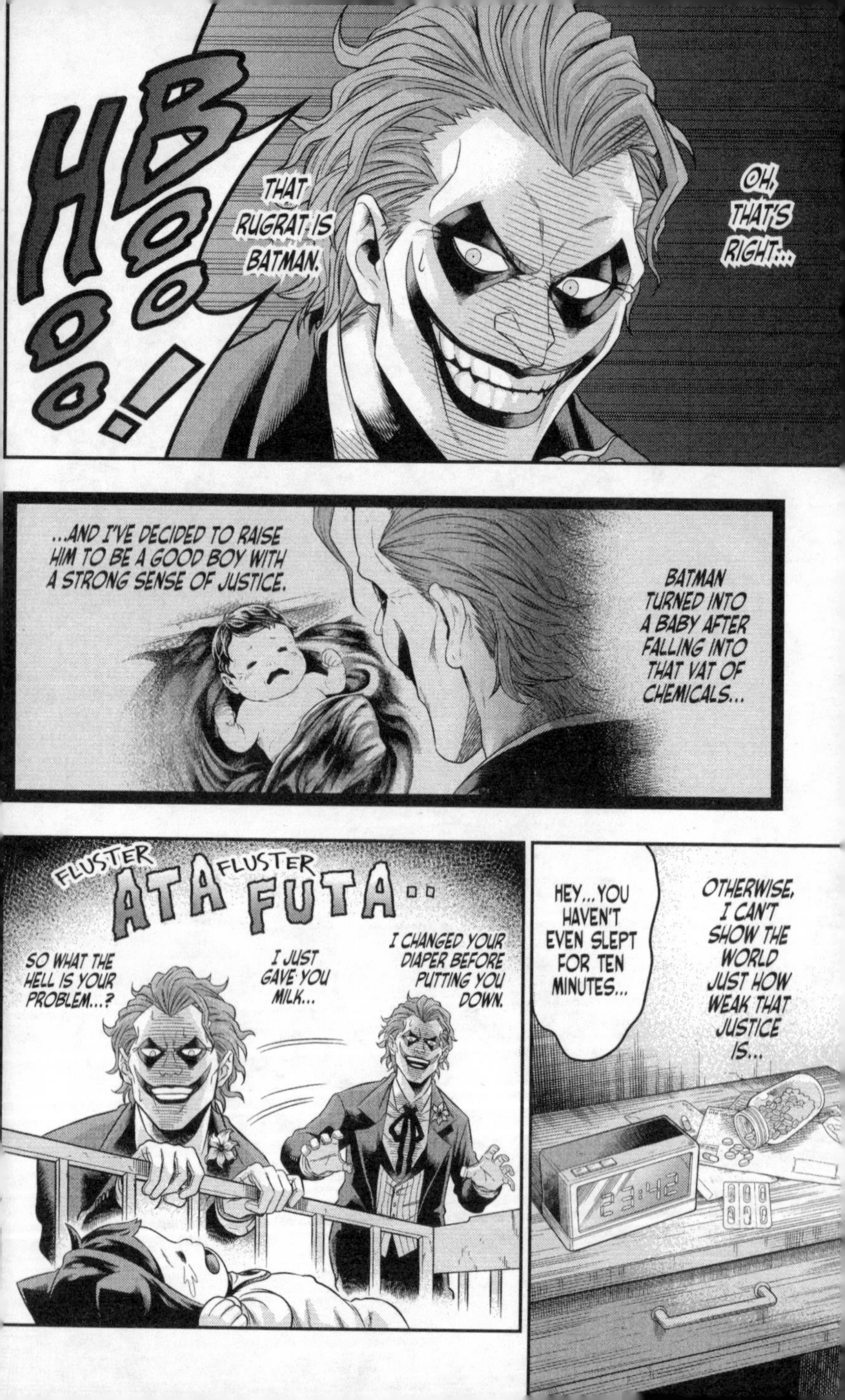

OH, THAT'S RIGHT...
THAT RUGRAT IS BATMAN.
HBOOOOO!
BATMAN TURNED INTO A BABY AFTER FALLING INTO THAT VAT OF CHEMICALS...
...AND I'VE DECIDED TO RAISE HIM TO BE A GOOD BOY WITH A STRONG SENSE OF JUSTICE.
OTHERWISE, I CAN'T SHOW THE WORLD JUST HOW WEAK THAT JUSTICE IS...
HEY...YOU HAVEN'T EVEN SLEPT FOR TEN MINUTES...
FLUSTER ATA FLUSTER FUTA..
I CHANGED YOUR DIAPER BEFORE PUTTING YOU DOWN.
I JUST GAVE YOU MILK...
SO WHAT THE HELL IS YOUR PROBLEM...?

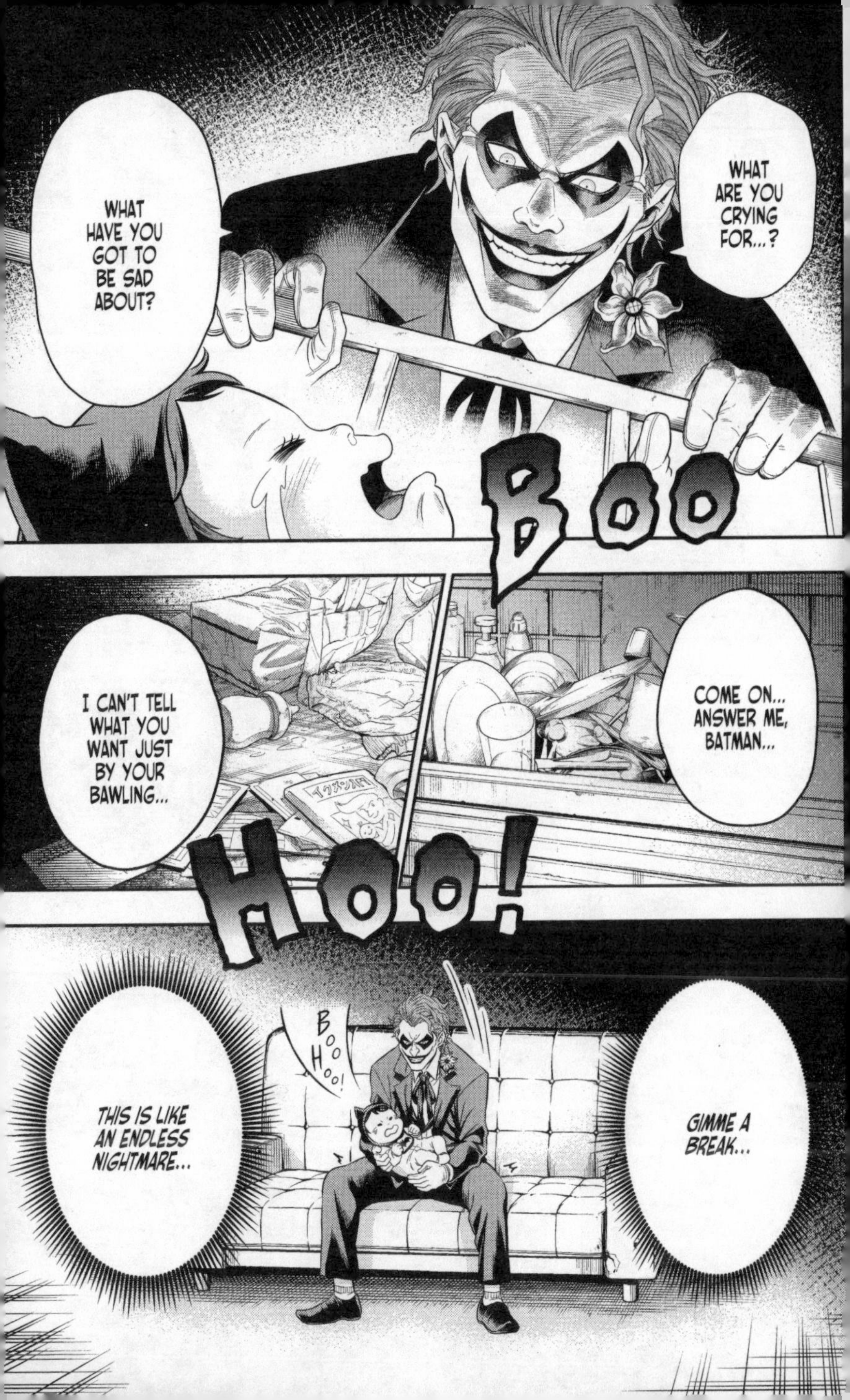
WHAT ARE YOU CRYING FOR...?
WHAT HAVE YOU GOT TO BE SAD ABOUT?
BOO
COME ON... ANSWER ME, BATMAN...
I CAN'T TELL WHAT YOU WANT JUST BY YOUR BAWLING...
HOO!
GIMME A BREAK...
BOO HOO!
THIS IS LIKE AN ENDLESS NIGHTMARE...

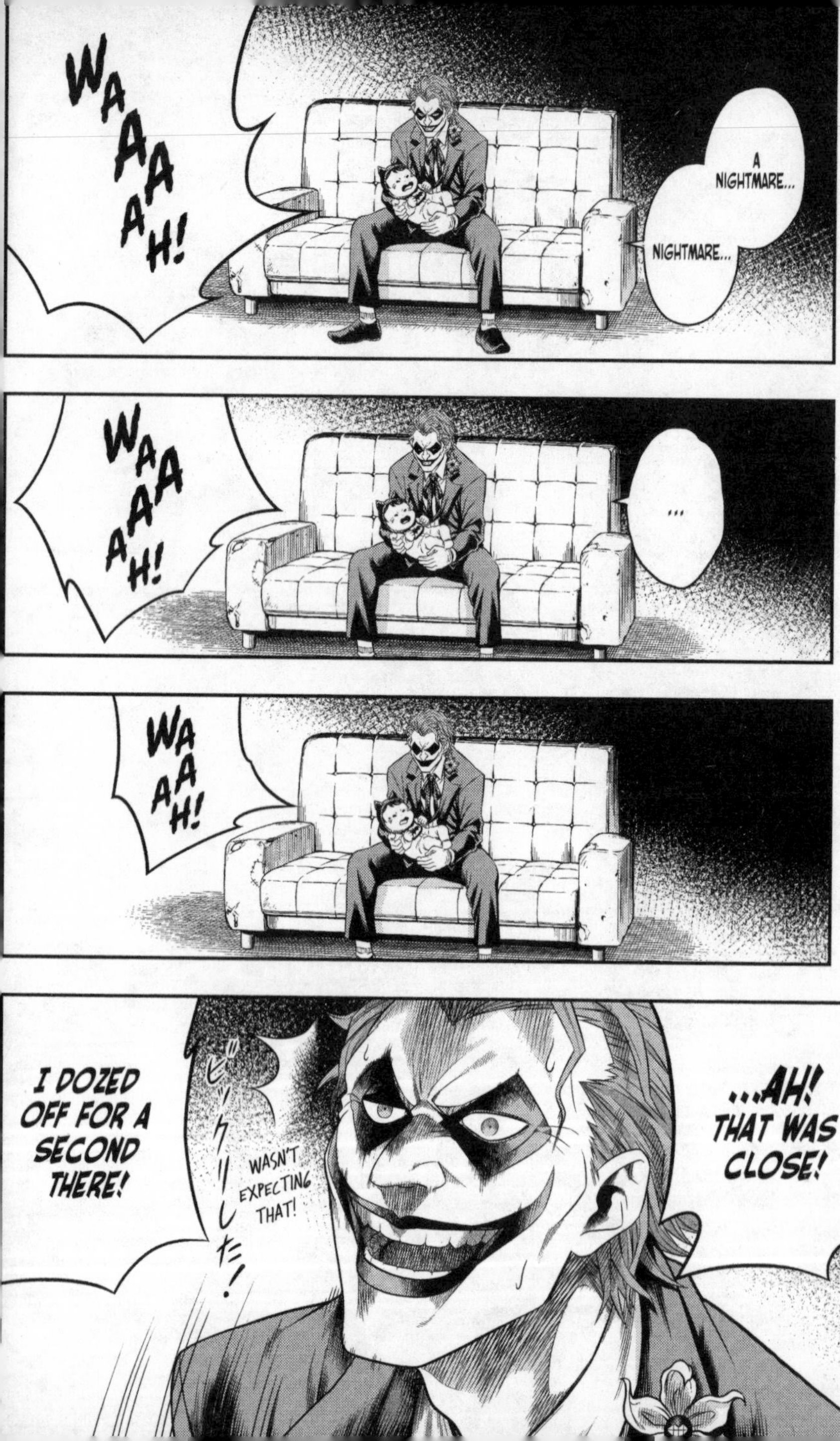
A NIGHTMARE...
NIGHTMARE...
WAAAAH!
...
WAAAAH!
WAAAH!
...AH! THAT WAS CLOSE!
WASN'T EXPECTING THAT!
ビックリした!
I DOZED OFF FOR A SECOND THERE!

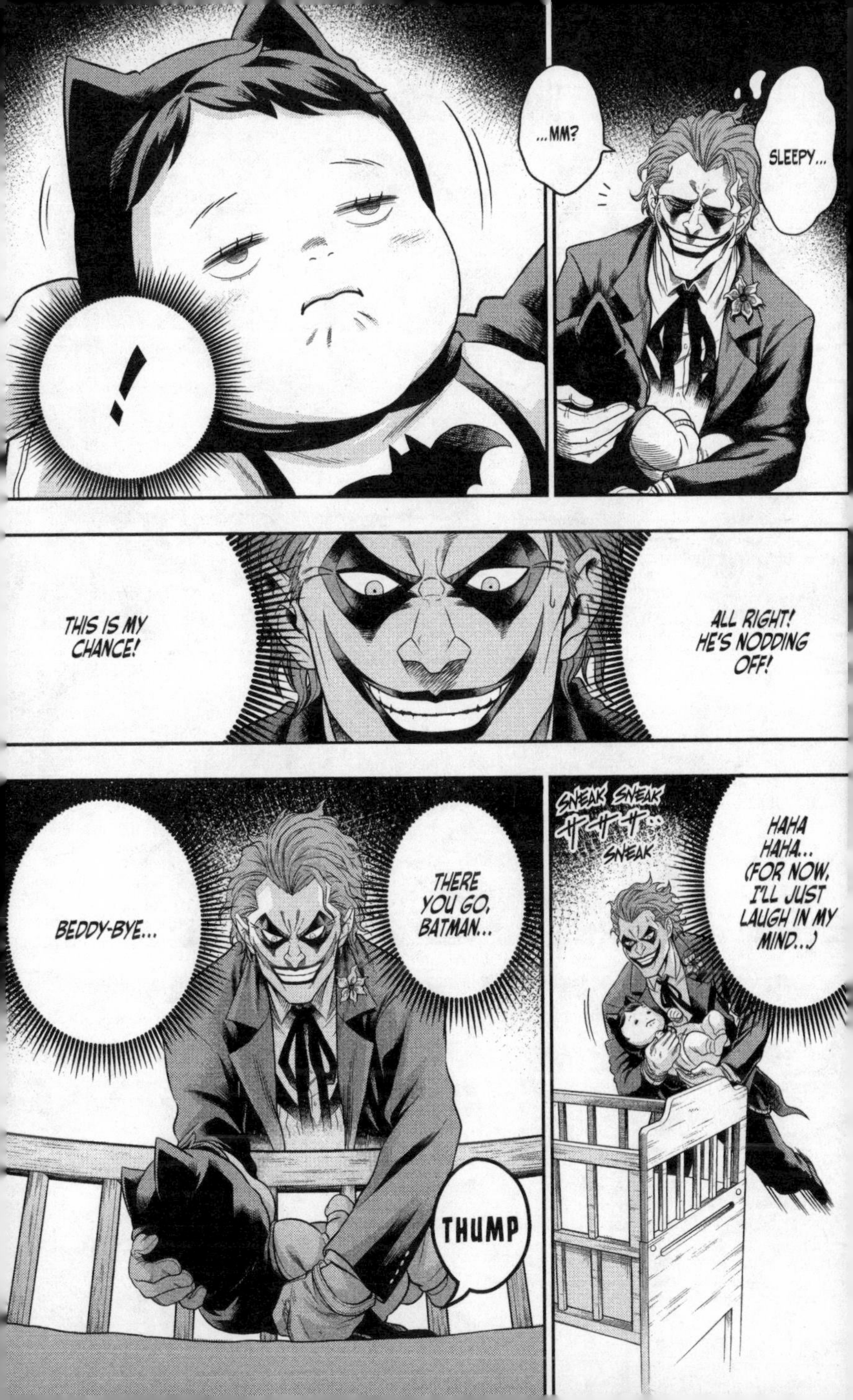
SLEEPY...
...MM?
!
ALL RIGHT! HE'S NODDING OFF!
THIS IS MY CHANCE!
HAHA HAHA... (FOR NOW, I'LL JUST LAUGH IN MY MIND...)
SNEAK SNEAK SNEAK
サササ
THERE YOU GO, BATMAN...
BEDDY-BYE...
THUMP

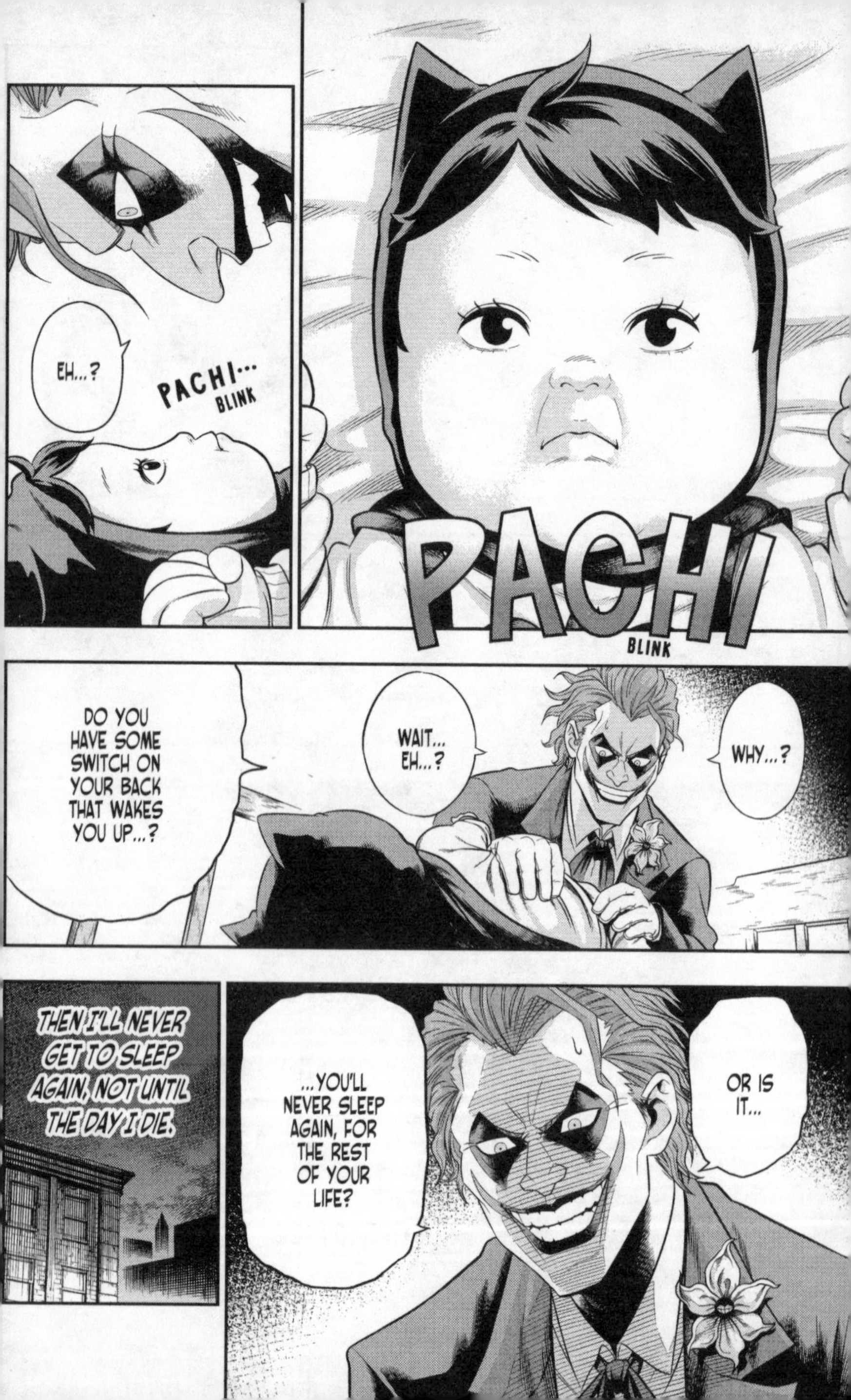
PACHI
BLINK
EH...?
PACHI...
BLINK
WHY...?
WAIT... EH...?
DO YOU HAVE SOME SWITCH ON YOUR BACK THAT WAKES YOU UP...?
OR IS IT...
...YOU'LL NEVER SLEEP AGAIN, FOR THE REST OF YOUR LIFE?
THEN I'LL NEVER GET TO SLEEP AGAIN, NOT UNTIL THE DAY I DIE.

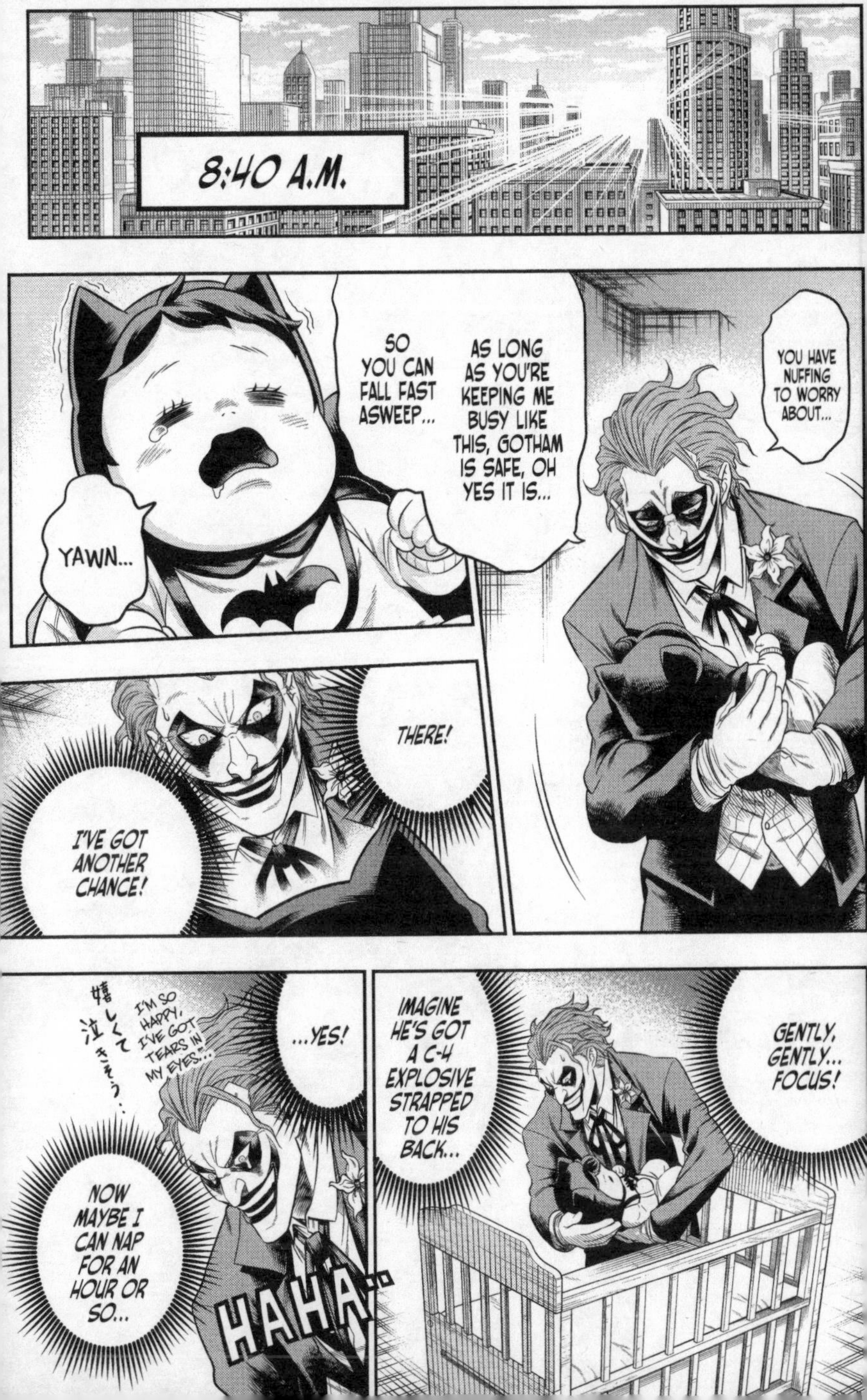
8:40 A.M.
YOU HAVE NUFFING TO WORRY ABOUT...
AS LONG AS YOU'RE KEEPING ME BUSY LIKE THIS, GOTHAM IS SAFE, OH YES IT IS...
SO YOU CAN FALL FAST ASWEEP...
YAWN...
THERE!
I'VE GOT ANOTHER CHANCE!
GENTLY, GENTLY... FOCUS!
IMAGINE HE'S GOT A C-4 EXPLOSIVE STRAPPED TO HIS BACK...
...YES!
嬉しくて泣きそう…
I'M SO HAPPY, I'VE GOT TEARS IN MY EYES...
NOW MAYBE I CAN NAP FOR AN HOUR OR SO...
HAHA...

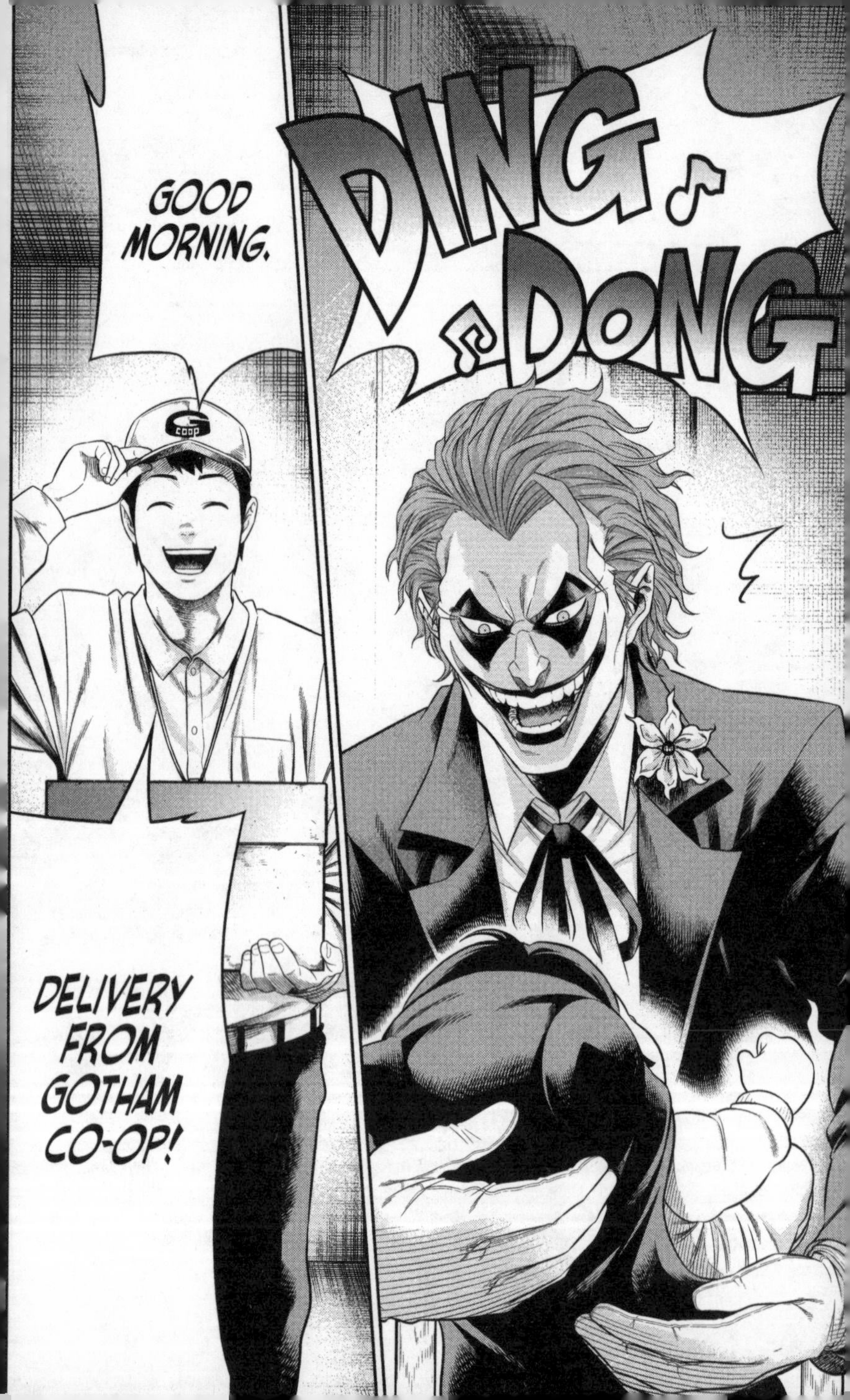
DING ♪ DONG ♪
GOOD MORNING.
DELIVERY FROM GOTHAM CO-OP!

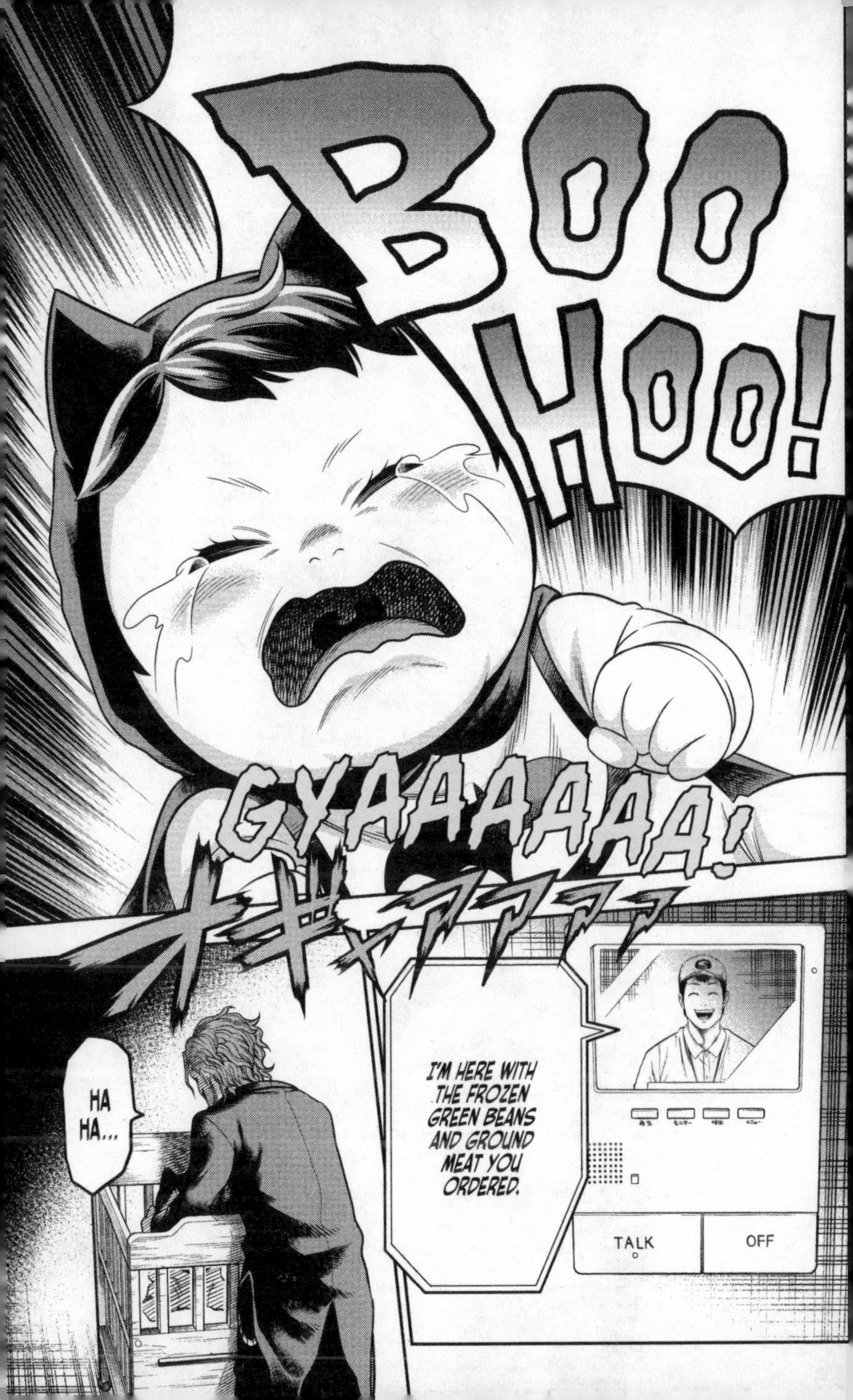
BOO HOO!
GYAAAAAA!
オギャアアア
I'M HERE WITH THE FROZEN GREEN BEANS AND GROUND MEAT YOU ORDERED.
TALK
OFF
HA HA...

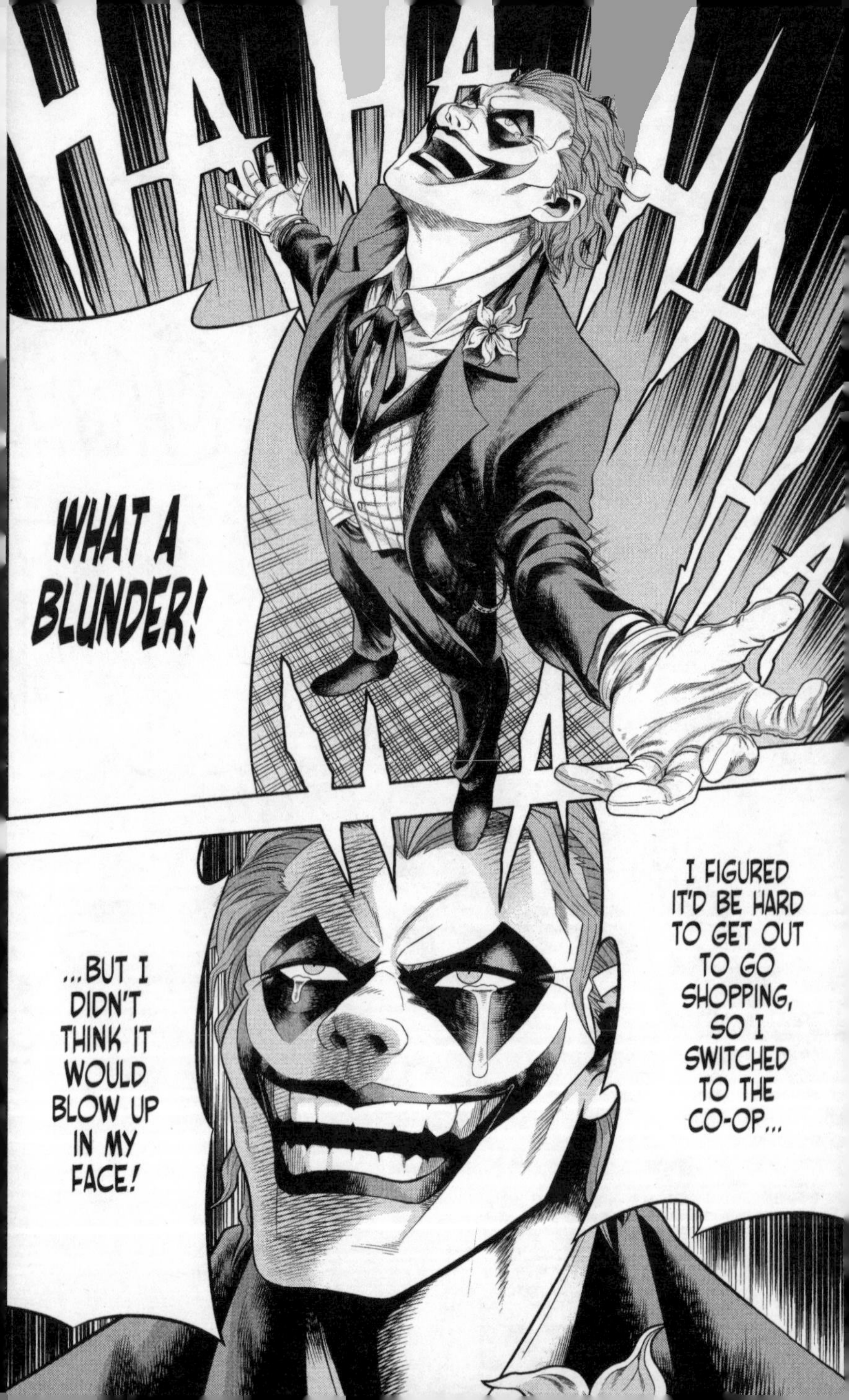
HAHAHA
WHAT A BLUNDER!
I FIGURED IT'D BE HARD TO GET OUT TO GO SHOPPING, SO I SWITCHED TO THE CO-OP...
...BUT I DIDN'T THINK IT WOULD BLOW UP IN MY FACE!

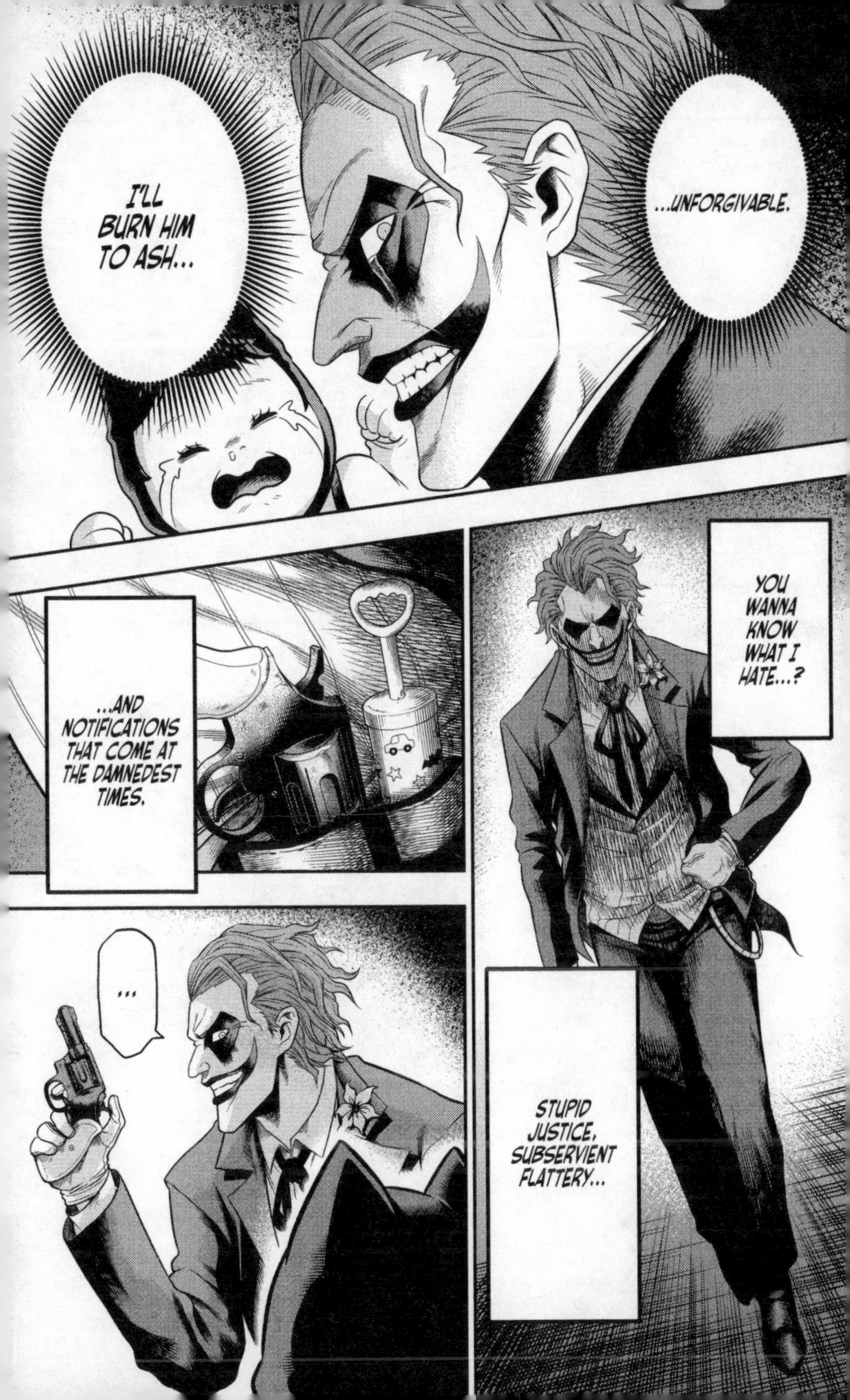
...UNFORGIVABLE.
I'LL BURN HIM TO ASH...
YOU WANNA KNOW WHAT I HATE...?
STUPID JUSTICE, SUBSERVIENT FLATTERY...
...AND NOTIFICATIONS THAT COME AT THE DAMNEDEST TIMES.
...

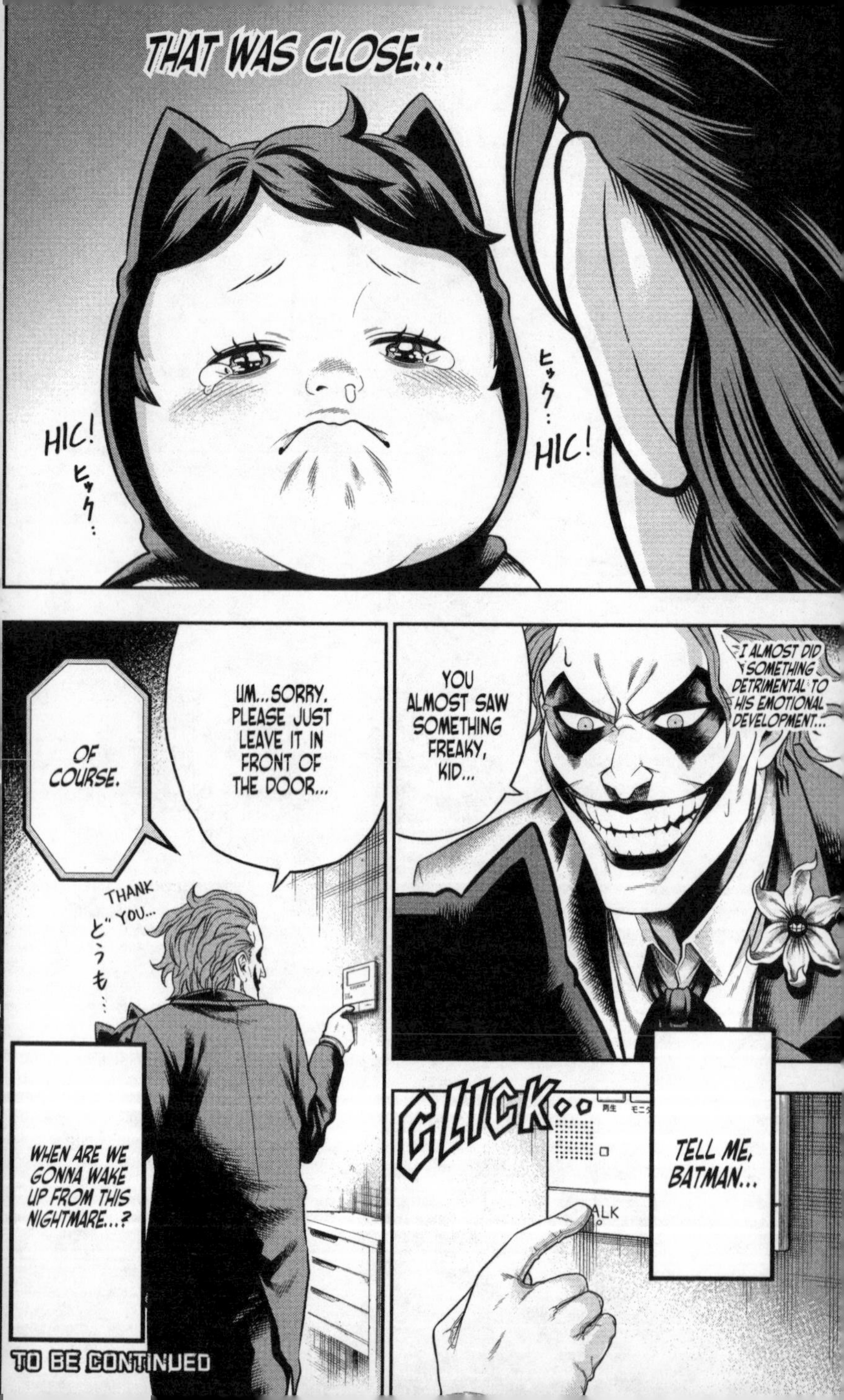
THAT WAS CLOSE...
ヒック…
HIC!
HIC!
ヒック…
I ALMOST DID SOMETHING DETRIMENTAL TO HIS EMOTIONAL DEVELOPMENT...
YOU ALMOST SAW SOMETHING FREAKY, KID...
CLICK
TELL ME, BATMAN...
UM...SORRY. PLEASE JUST LEAVE IT IN FRONT OF THE DOOR...
OF COURSE.
THANK YOU...
どうも…
WHEN ARE WE GONNA WAKE UP FROM THIS NIGHTMARE...?
TO BE CONTINUED

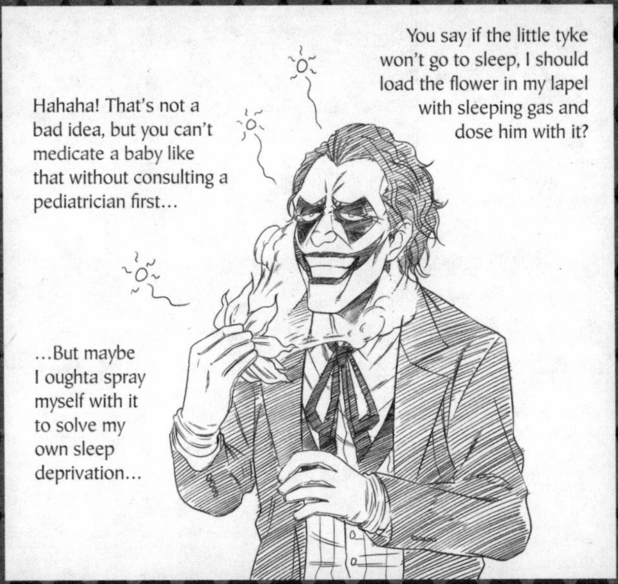
You say if the little tyke won't go to sleep, I should load the flower in my lapel with sleeping gas and dose him with it?
Hahaha! That's not a bad idea, but you can't medicate a baby like that without consulting a pediatrician first...
...But maybe I oughta spray myself with it to solve my own sleep deprivation...

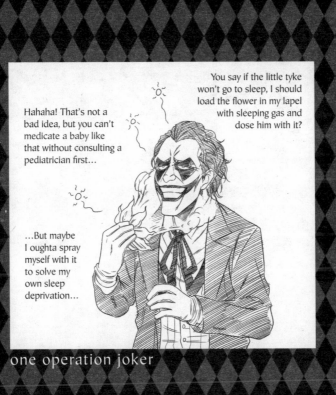

one operation joker

JOKER
ワンオペ
one operation joker　　vol. 1

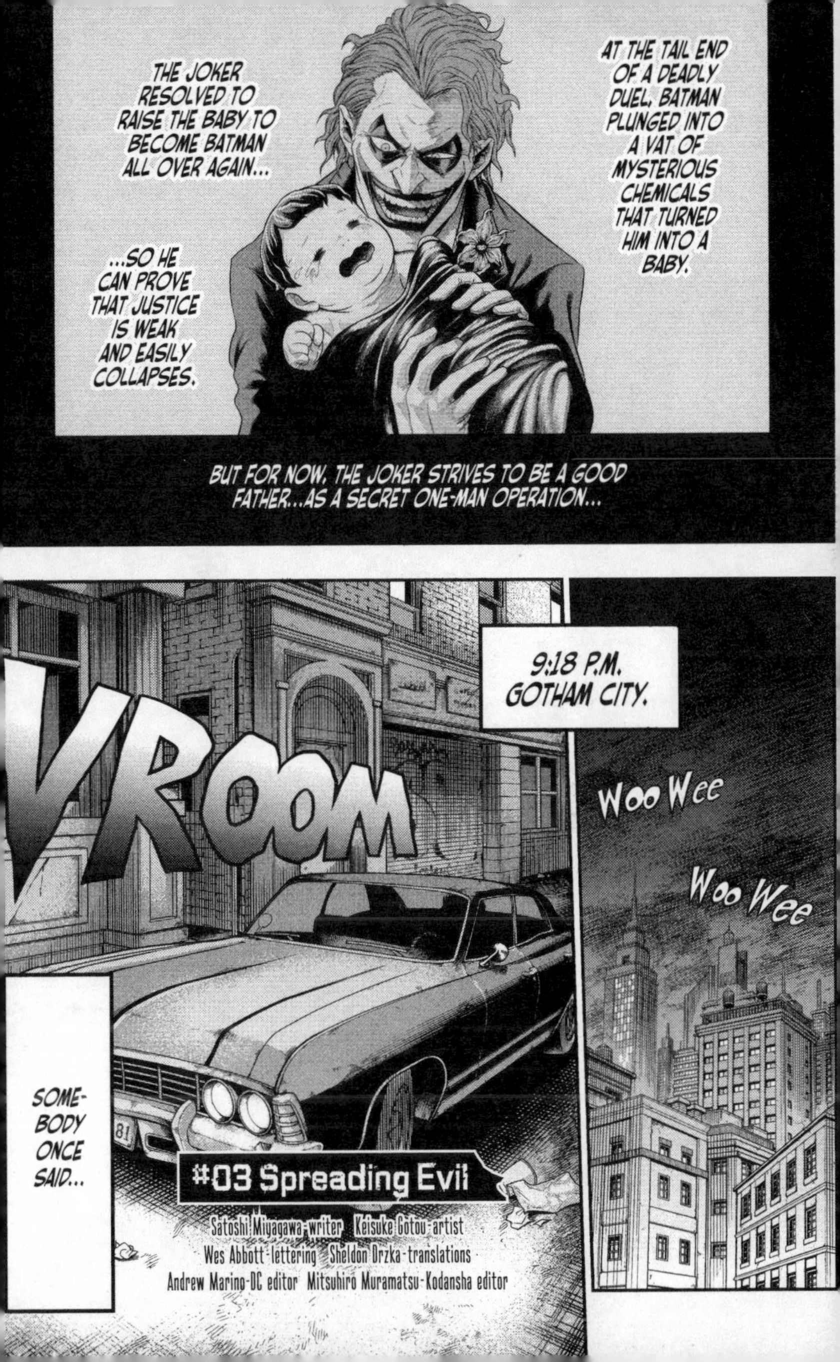
AT THE TAIL END OF A DEADLY DUEL, BATMAN PLUNGED INTO A VAT OF MYSTERIOUS CHEMICALS THAT TURNED HIM INTO A BABY.
THE JOKER RESOLVED TO RAISE THE BABY TO BECOME BATMAN ALL OVER AGAIN...
...SO HE CAN PROVE THAT JUSTICE IS WEAK AND EASILY COLLAPSES.
BUT FOR NOW, THE JOKER STRIVES TO BE A GOOD FATHER...AS A SECRET ONE-MAN OPERATION...
9:18 P.M. GOTHAM CITY.
Woo Wee
Woo Wee
VROOM
SOME-BODY ONCE SAID...
#03 Spreading Evil
Satoshi Miyagawa-writer Keisuke Gotou-artist
Wes Abbott-lettering Sheldon Drzka-translations
Andrew Marino-DC editor Mitsuhiro Muramatsu-Kodansha editor

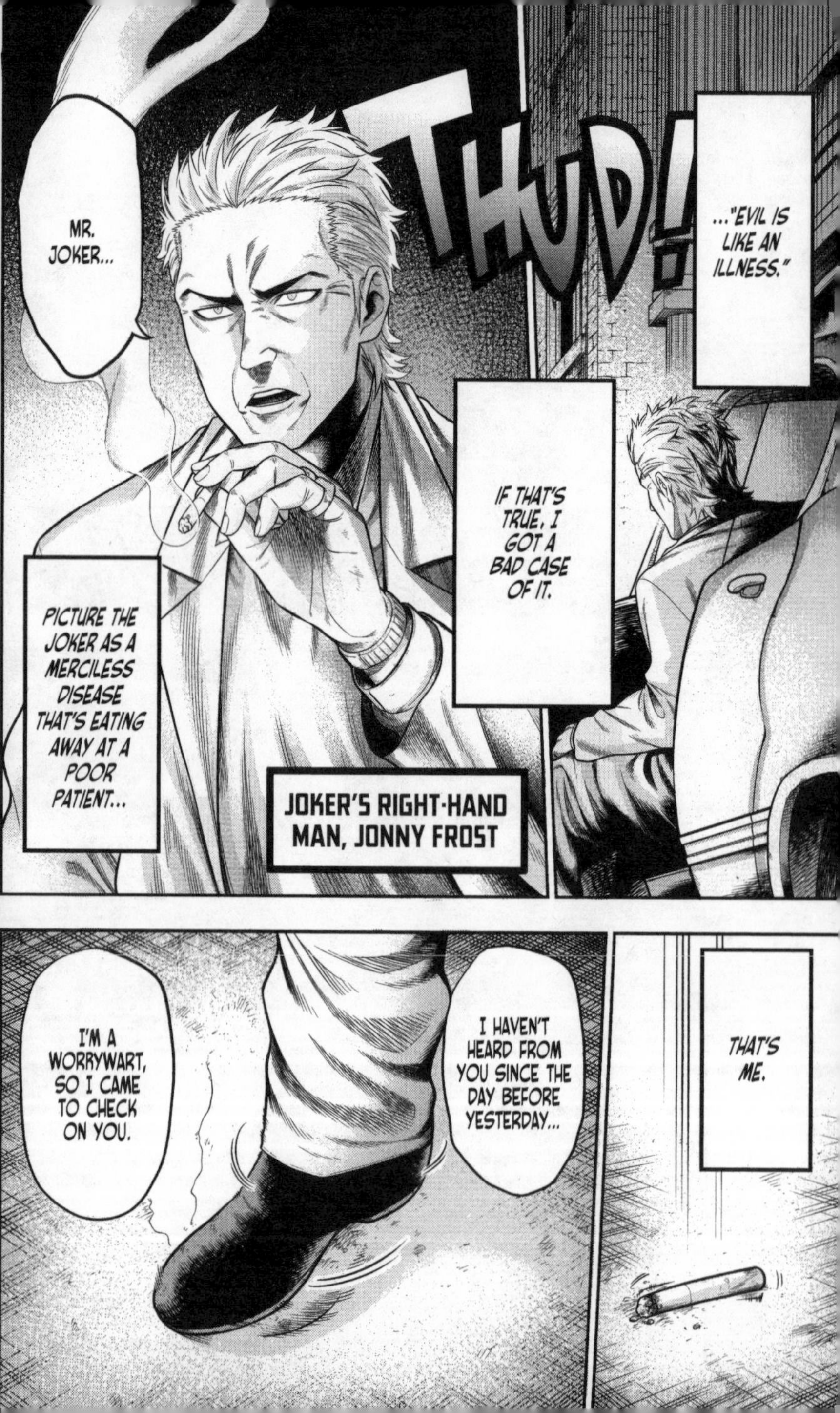
..."EVIL IS LIKE AN ILLNESS."
IF THAT'S TRUE, I GOT A BAD CASE OF IT.
THUD!
MR. JOKER...
PICTURE THE JOKER AS A MERCILESS DISEASE THAT'S EATING AWAY AT A POOR PATIENT...
JOKER'S RIGHT-HAND MAN, JONNY FROST
THAT'S ME.
I HAVEN'T HEARD FROM YOU SINCE THE DAY BEFORE YESTERDAY...
I'M A WORRYWART, SO I CAME TO CHECK ON YOU.

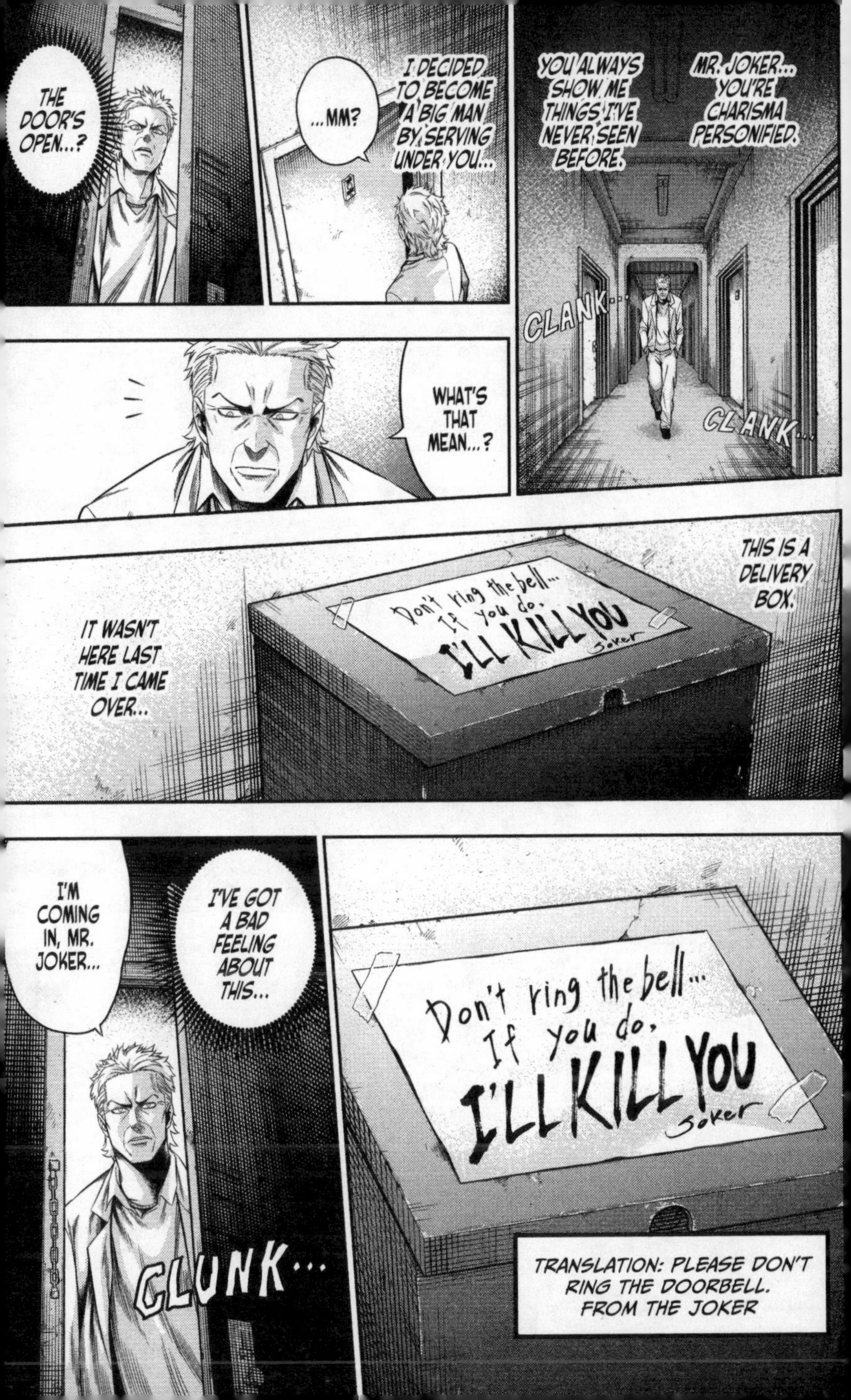
MR. JOKER... YOU'RE CHARISMA PERSONIFIED.
YOU ALWAYS SHOW ME THINGS I'VE NEVER SEEN BEFORE.
CLANK...
CLANK...
I DECIDED TO BECOME A BIG MAN BY SERVING UNDER YOU...
...MM?
THE DOOR'S OPEN...?
WHAT'S THAT MEAN...?
THIS IS A DELIVERY BOX.
Don't ring the bell... If you do, I'LL KILL YOU Joker
IT WASN'T HERE LAST TIME I CAME OVER...
Don't ring the bell... If you do, I'LL KILL YOU Joker
TRANSLATION: PLEASE DON'T RING THE DOORBELL. FROM THE JOKER
I'VE GOT A BAD FEELING ABOUT THIS...
I'M COMING IN, MR. JOKER...
CLUNK...

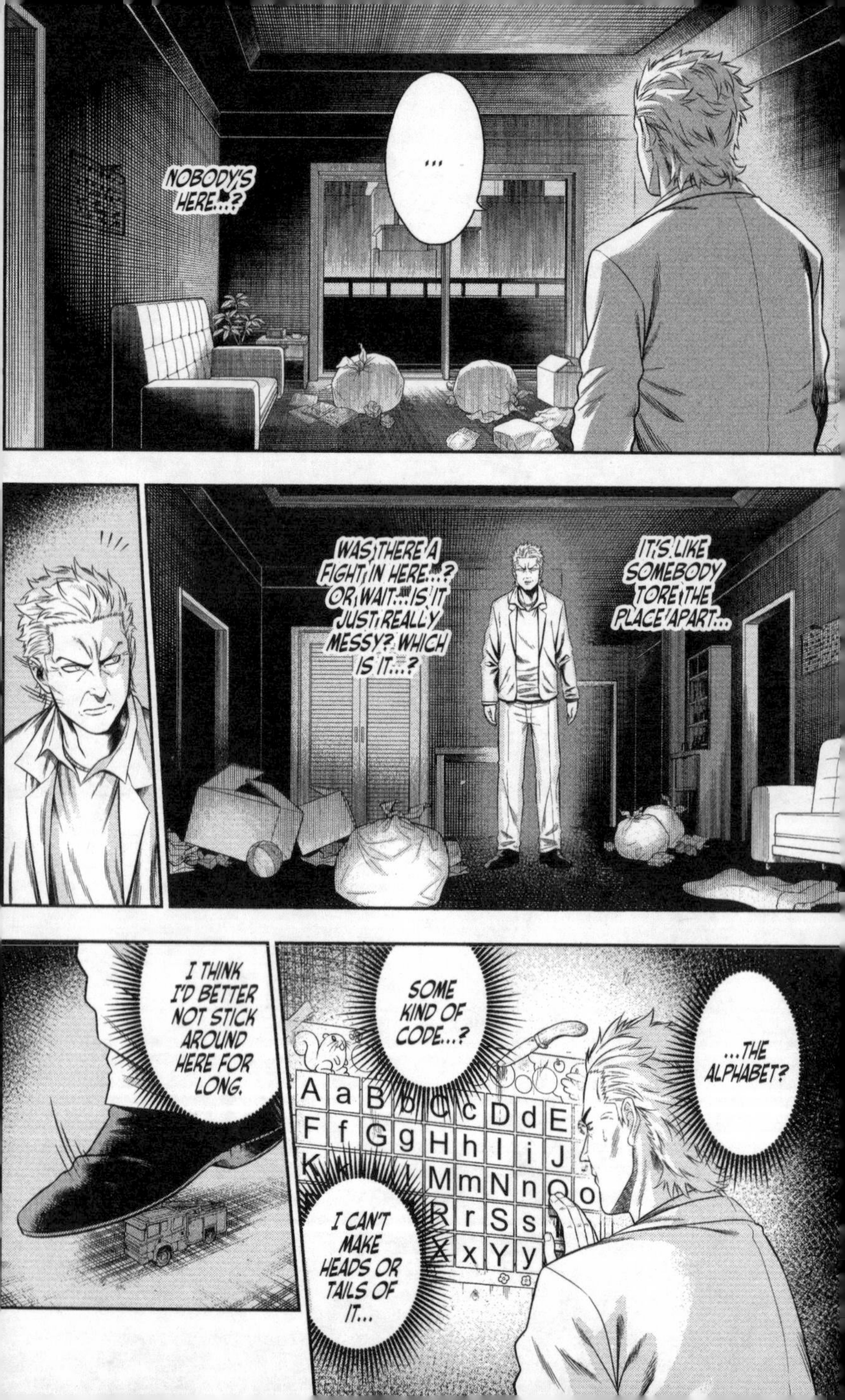
...
NOBODY'S HERE...?
IT'S LIKE SOMEBODY TORE THE PLACE APART...
WAS THERE A FIGHT IN HERE...? OR WAIT... IS IT JUST REALLY MESSY? WHICH IS IT...?
...THE ALPHABET?
SOME KIND OF CODE...?
A a B b C c D d E
F f G g H h I i J
M m N n O o
R r S s
X x Y y
I CAN'T MAKE HEADS OR TAILS OF IT...
I THINK I'D BETTER NOT STICK AROUND HERE FOR LONG.

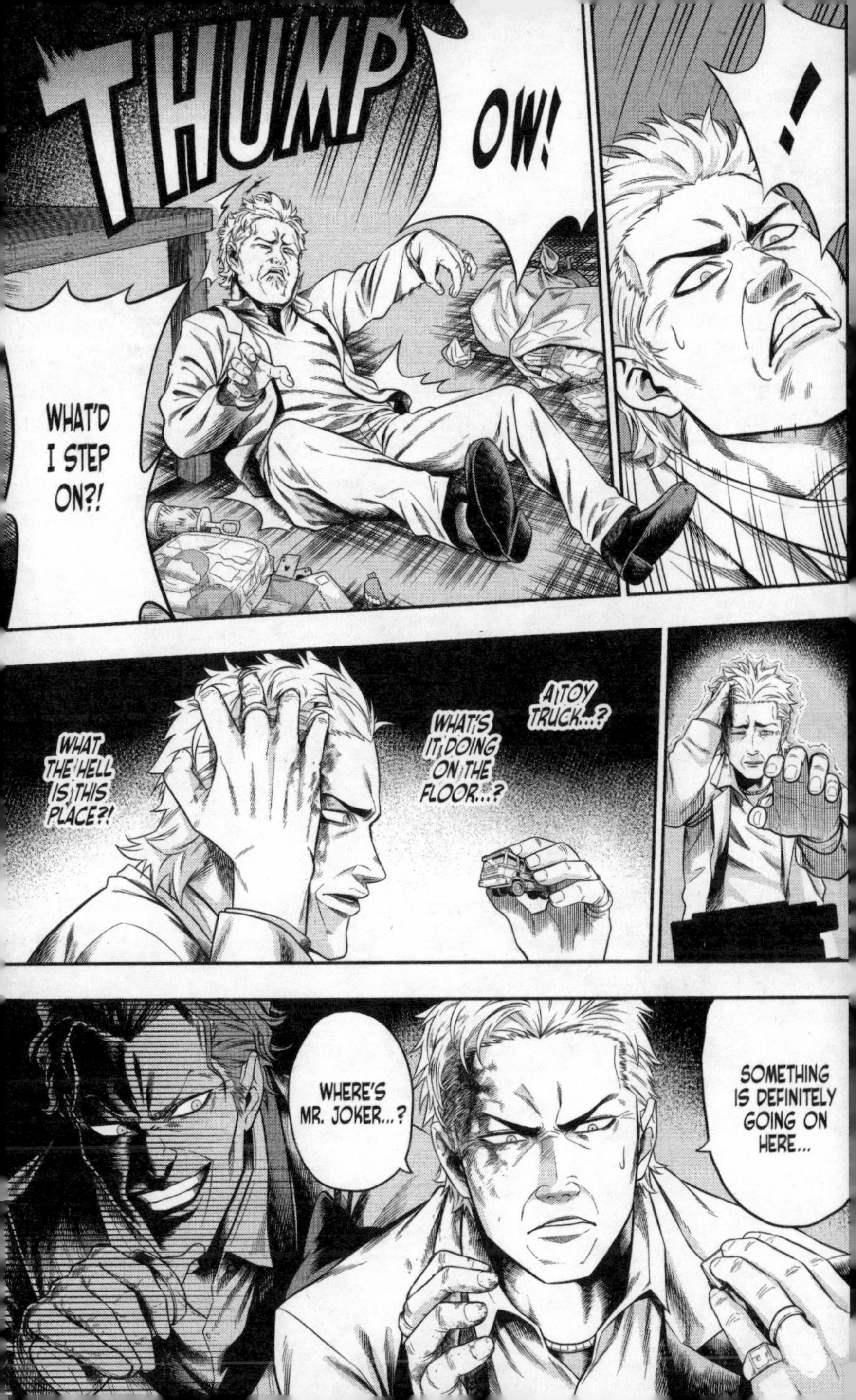
!
THUMP
OW!
WHAT'D I STEP ON?!
A TOY TRUCK...?
WHAT'S IT DOING ON THE FLOOR...?
WHAT THE HELL IS THIS PLACE?!
SOMETHING IS DEFINITELY GOING ON HERE...
WHERE'S MR. JOKER...?

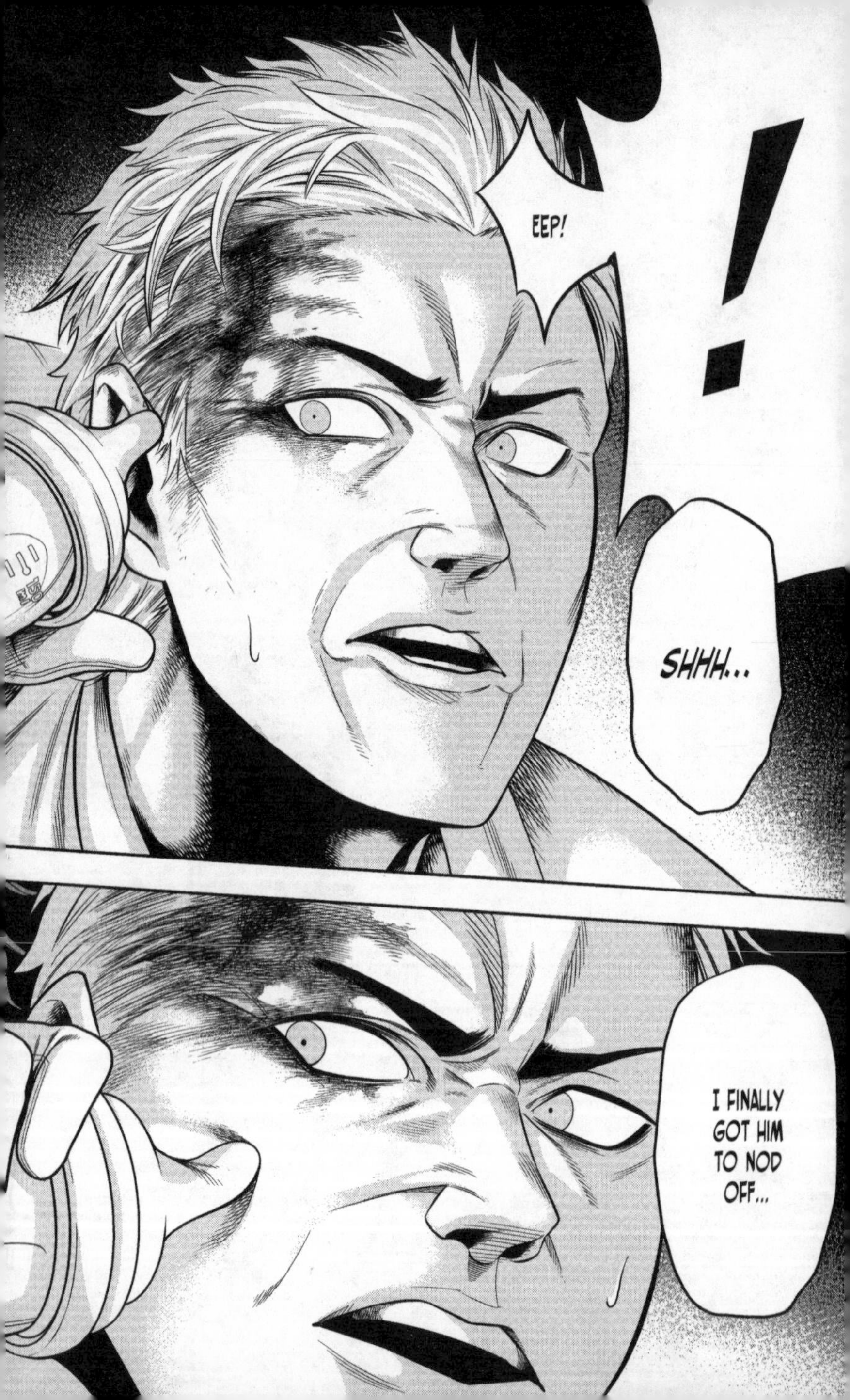
!
EEP!
SHHH...
I FINALLY GOT HIM TO NOD OFF...

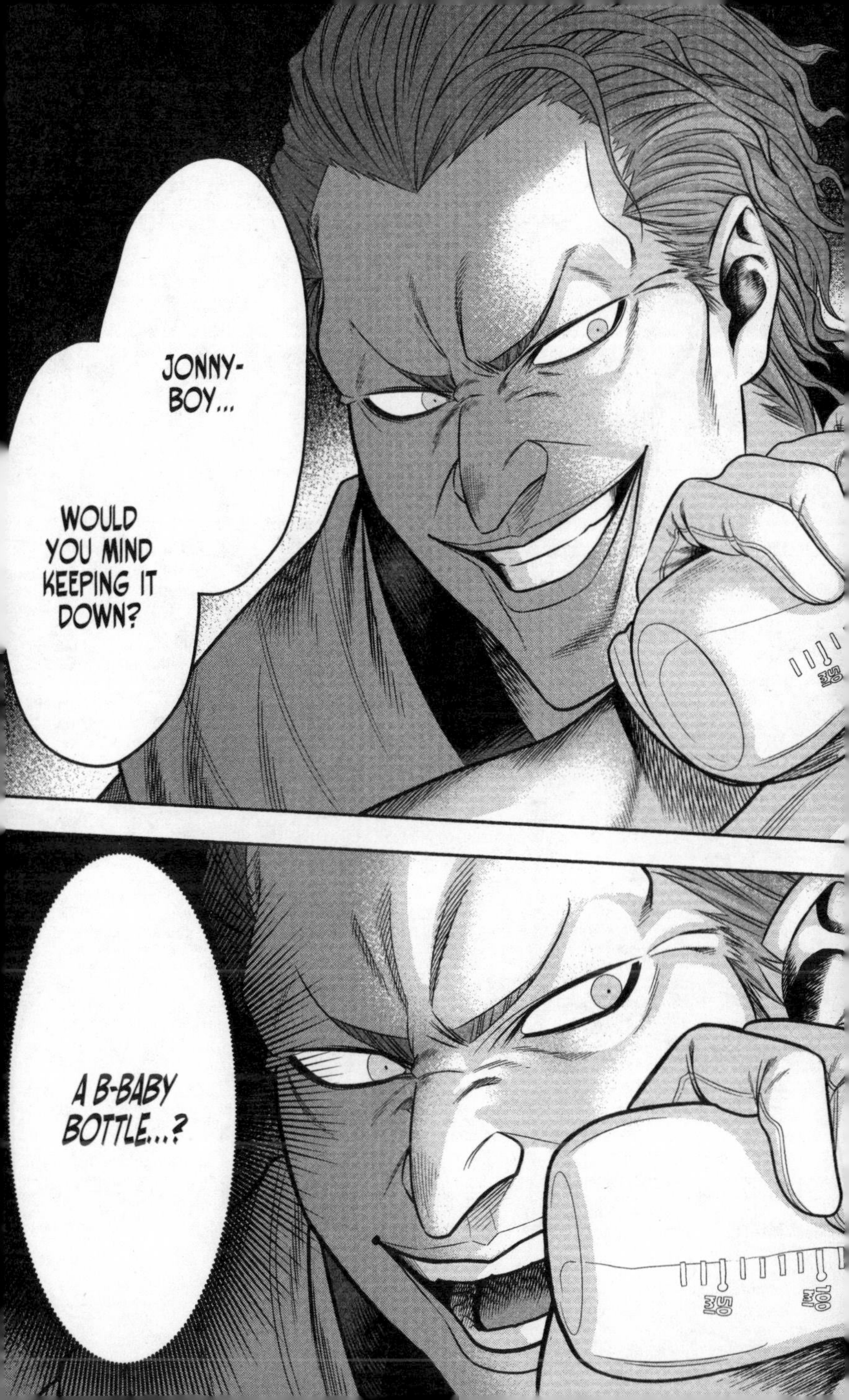
JONNY-BOY...
WOULD YOU MIND KEEPING IT DOWN?
50 ml
A B-BABY BOTTLE...?
50 ml
100 ml

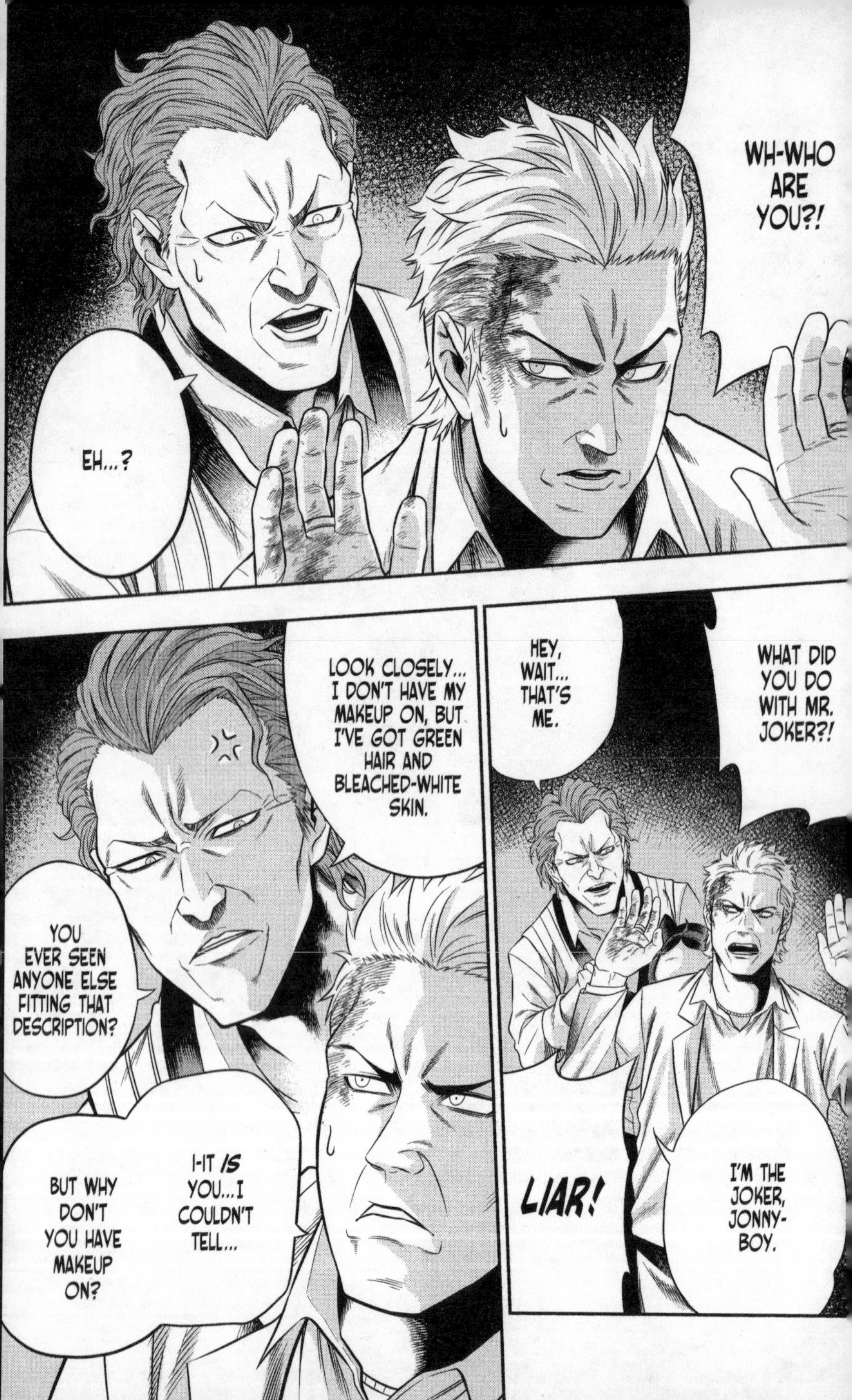
WH-WHO ARE YOU?!
EH...?
WHAT DID YOU DO WITH MR. JOKER?!
HEY, WAIT... THAT'S ME.
I'M THE JOKER, JONNY-BOY.
LIAR!
LOOK CLOSELY... I DON'T HAVE MY MAKEUP ON, BUT I'VE GOT GREEN HAIR AND BLEACHED-WHITE SKIN.
YOU EVER SEEN ANYONE ELSE FITTING THAT DESCRIPTION?
I-IT *IS* YOU...I COULDN'T TELL...
BUT WHY DON'T YOU HAVE MAKEUP ON?

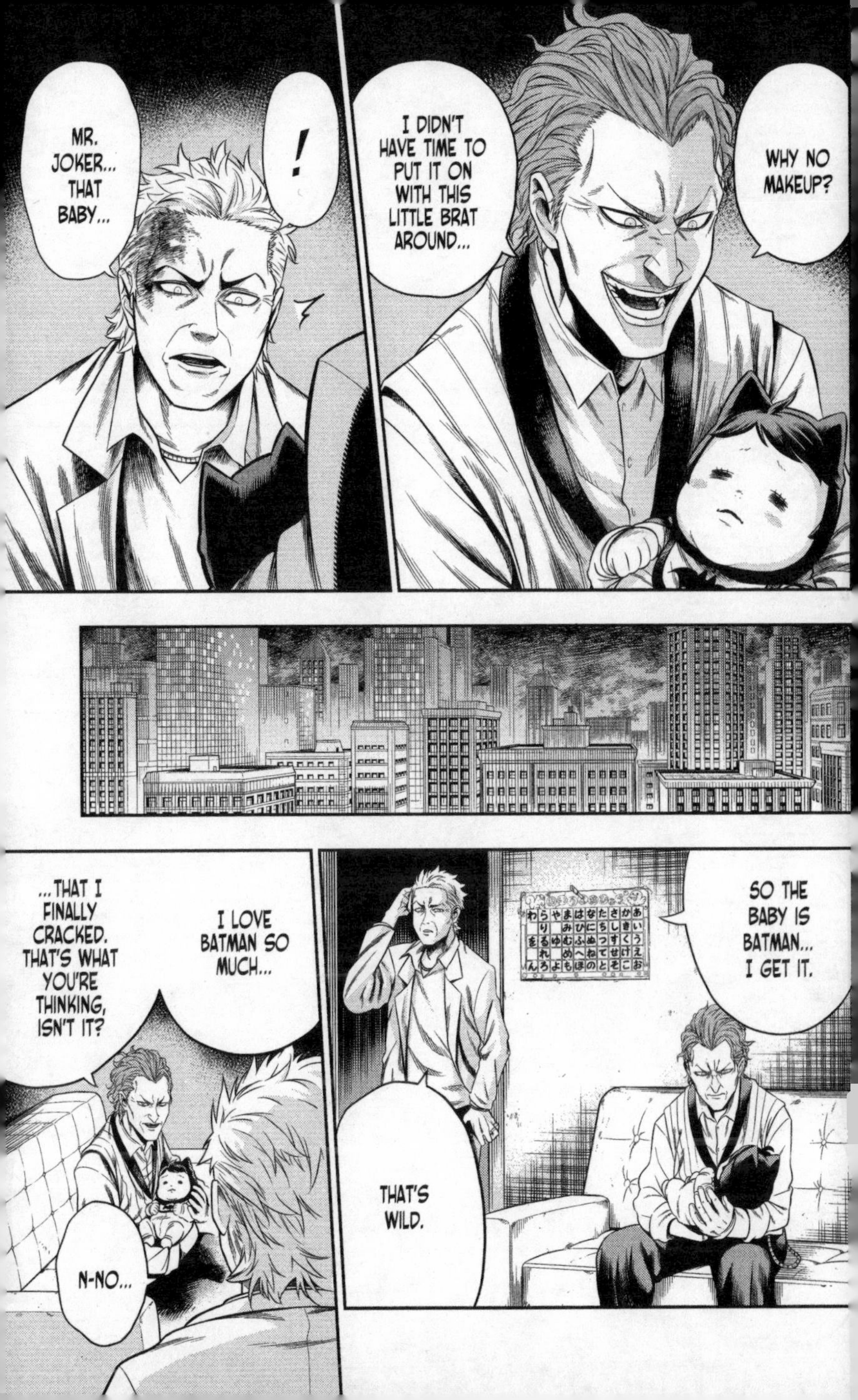
WHY NO MAKEUP?
I DIDN'T HAVE TIME TO PUT IT ON WITH THIS LITTLE BRAT AROUND...
!
MR. JOKER... THAT BABY...
SO THE BABY IS BATMAN... I GET IT.
THAT'S WILD.
I LOVE BATMAN SO MUCH...
...THAT I FINALLY CRACKED. THAT'S WHAT YOU'RE THINKING, ISN'T IT?
N-NO...

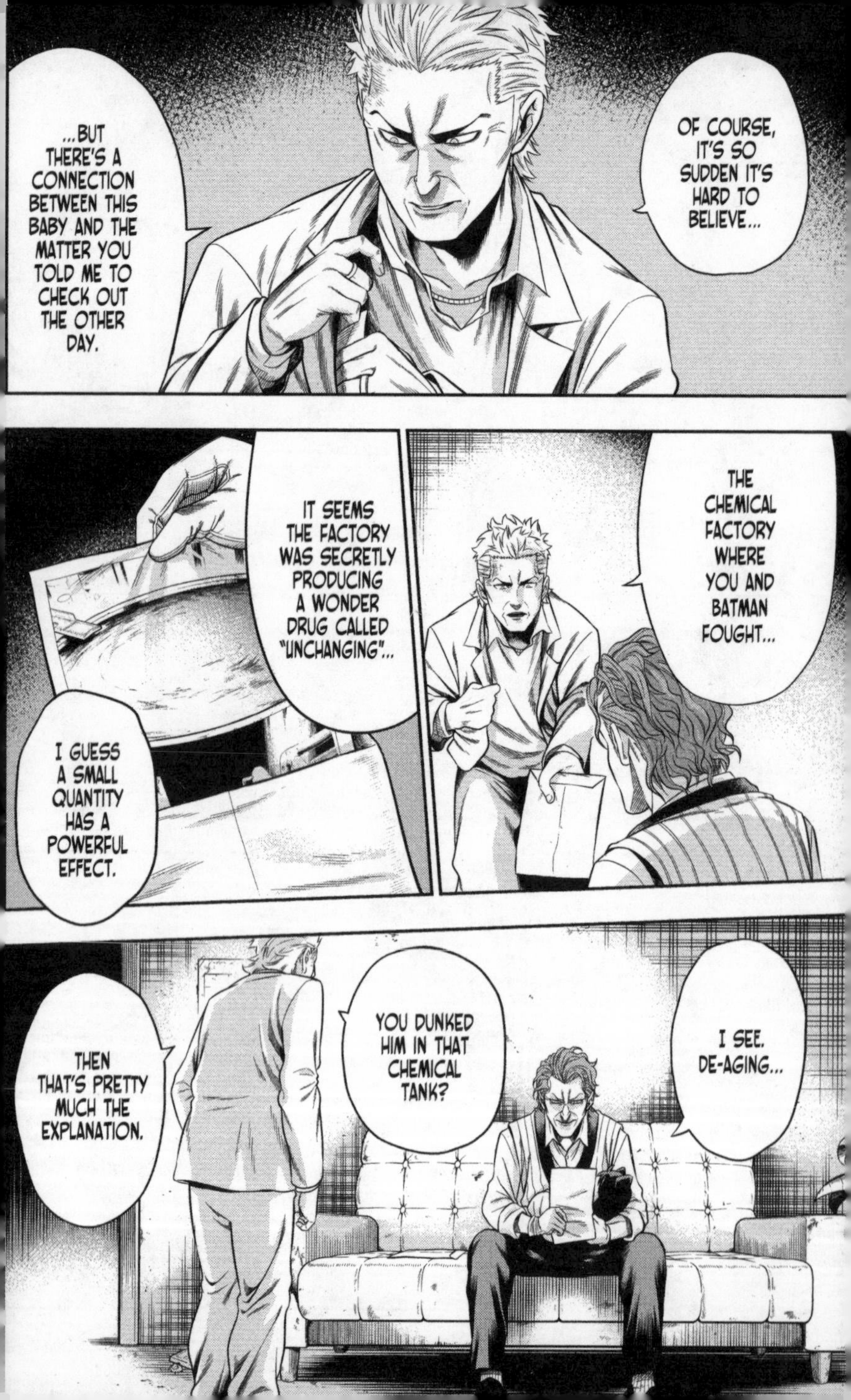
OF COURSE, IT'S SO SUDDEN IT'S HARD TO BELIEVE...
...BUT THERE'S A CONNECTION BETWEEN THIS BABY AND THE MATTER YOU TOLD ME TO CHECK OUT THE OTHER DAY.
THE CHEMICAL FACTORY WHERE YOU AND BATMAN FOUGHT...
IT SEEMS THE FACTORY WAS SECRETLY PRODUCING A WONDER DRUG CALLED "UNCHANGING"...
I GUESS A SMALL QUANTITY HAS A POWERFUL EFFECT.
I SEE. DE-AGING...
YOU DUNKED HIM IN THAT CHEMICAL TANK?
THEN THAT'S PRETTY MUCH THE EXPLANATION.

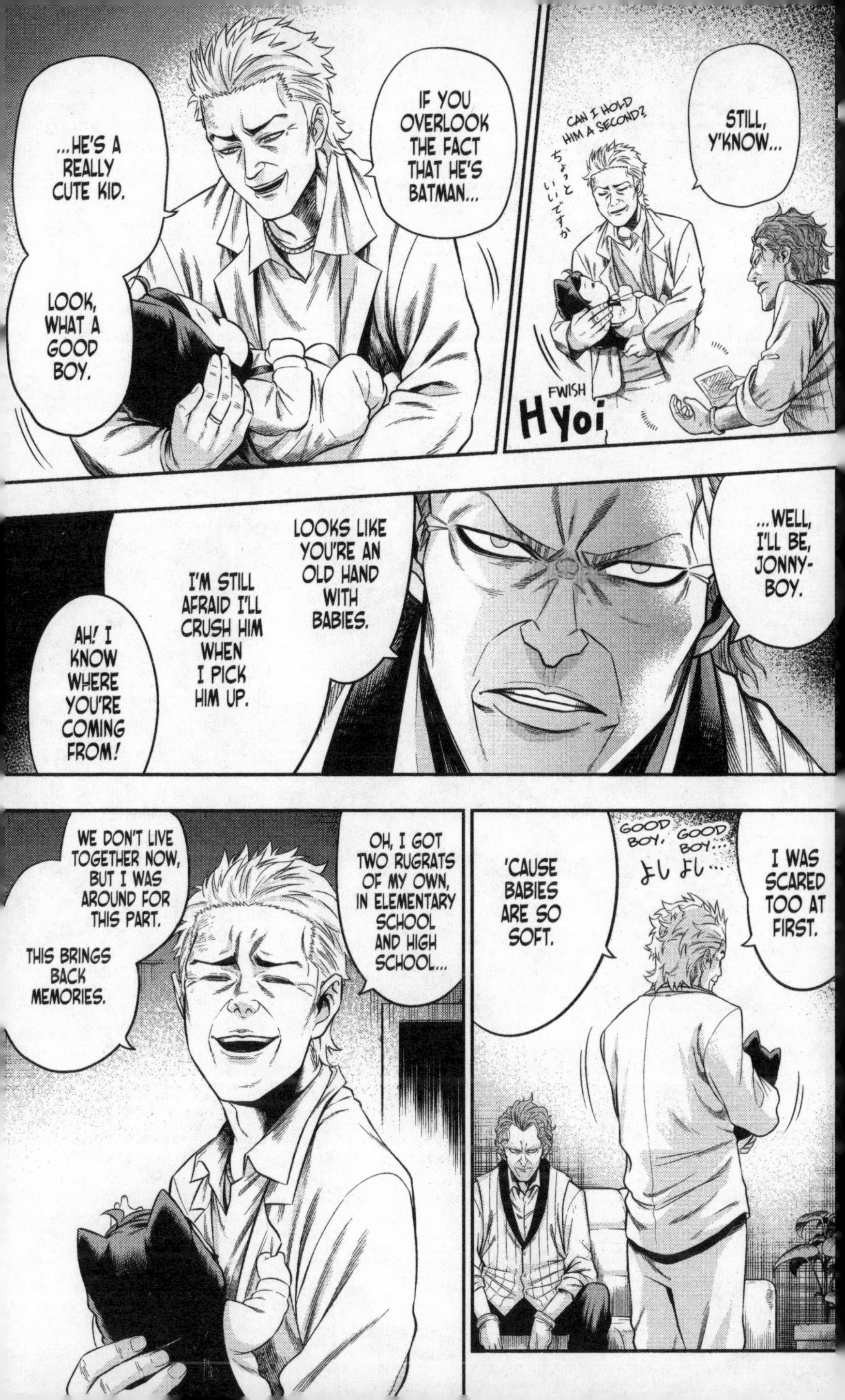
STILL, Y'KNOW...
CAN I HOLD HIM A SECOND?
ちょっといいですか
FWISH
Hyoi
IF YOU OVERLOOK THE FACT THAT HE'S BATMAN...
...HE'S A REALLY CUTE KID.
LOOK, WHAT A GOOD BOY.
...WELL, I'LL BE, JONNY-BOY.
LOOKS LIKE YOU'RE AN OLD HAND WITH BABIES.
I'M STILL AFRAID I'LL CRUSH HIM WHEN I PICK HIM UP.
AH! I KNOW WHERE YOU'RE COMING FROM!
I WAS SCARED TOO AT FIRST.
GOOD BOY, GOOD BOY...
よしよし…
'CAUSE BABIES ARE SO SOFT.
OH, I GOT TWO RUGRATS OF MY OWN, IN ELEMENTARY SCHOOL AND HIGH SCHOOL...
WE DON'T LIVE TOGETHER NOW, BUT I WAS AROUND FOR THIS PART.
THIS BRINGS BACK MEMORIES.

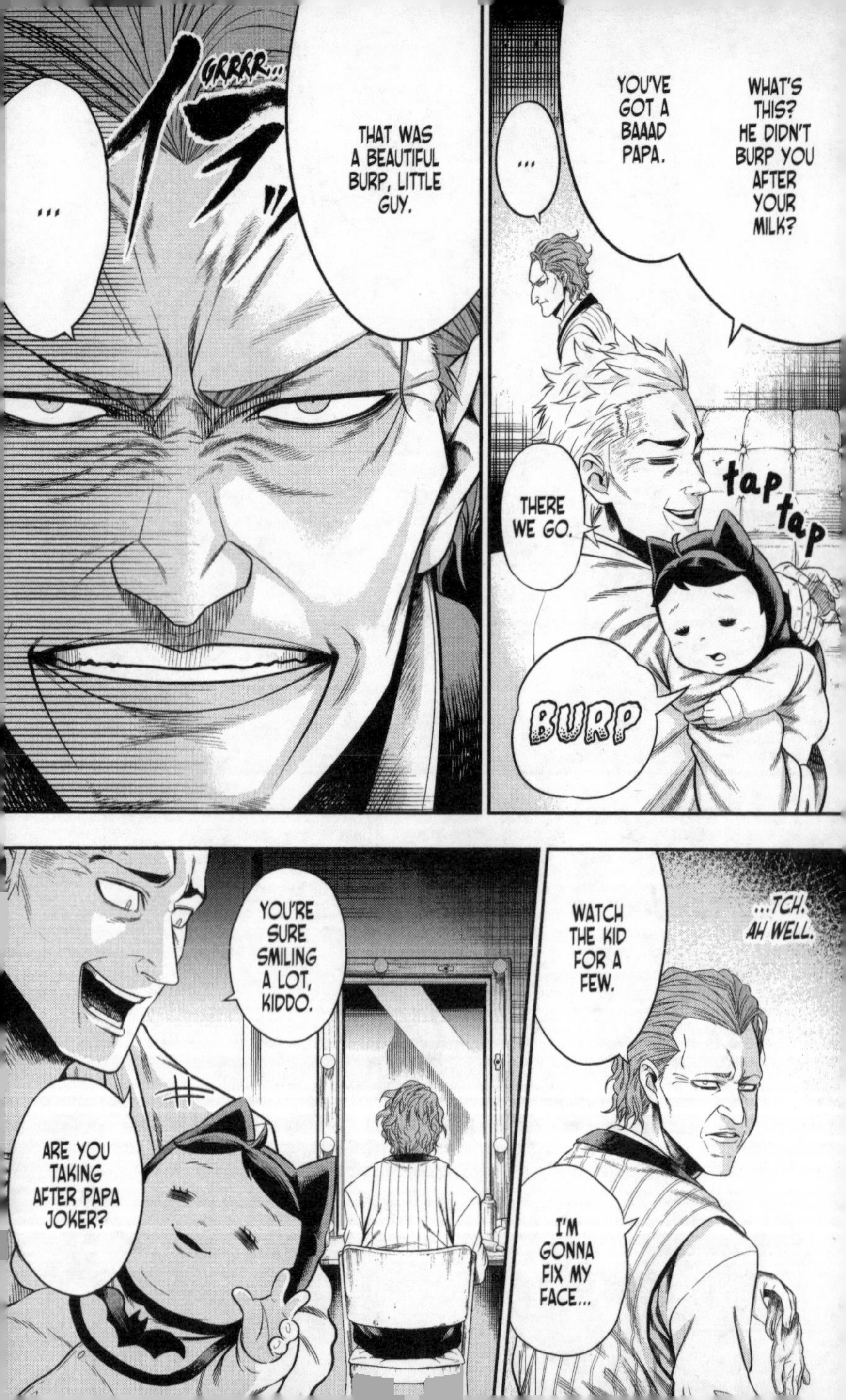
WHAT'S THIS? HE DIDN'T BURP YOU AFTER YOUR MILK?
YOU'VE GOT A BAAAD PAPA.
...
tap tap
THERE WE GO.
BURP
THAT WAS A BEAUTIFUL BURP, LITTLE GUY.
GRRRR...
...
...TCH. AH WELL.
WATCH THE KID FOR A FEW.
I'M GONNA FIX MY FACE...
YOU'RE SURE SMILING A LOT, KIDDO.
ARE YOU TAKING AFTER PAPA JOKER?

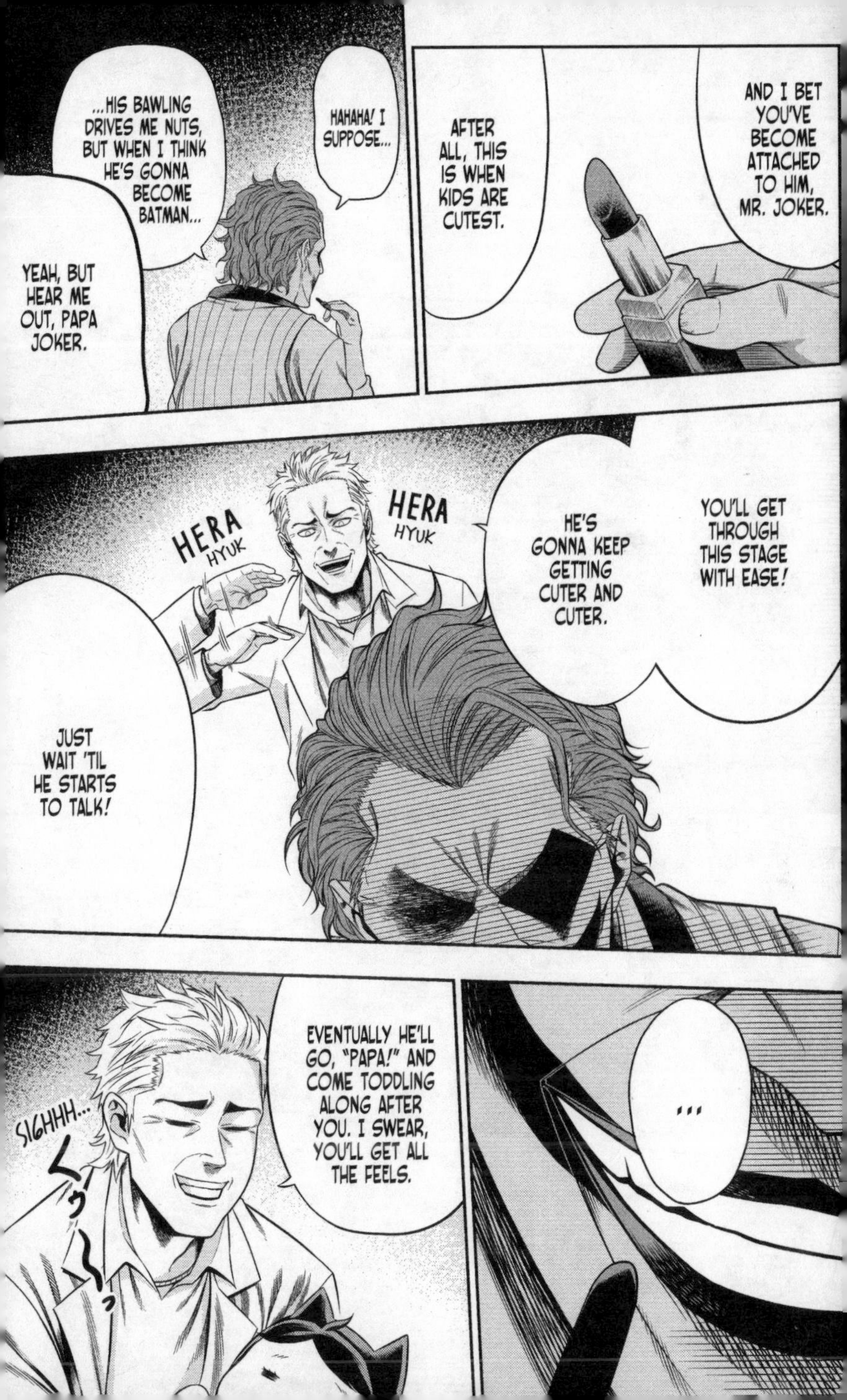
AND I BET YOU'VE BECOME ATTACHED TO HIM, MR. JOKER.
AFTER ALL, THIS IS WHEN KIDS ARE CUTEST.
HAHAHA! I SUPPOSE...
...HIS BAWLING DRIVES ME NUTS, BUT WHEN I THINK HE'S GONNA BECOME BATMAN...
YEAH, BUT HEAR ME OUT, PAPA JOKER.
YOU'LL GET THROUGH THIS STAGE WITH EASE!
HE'S GONNA KEEP GETTING CUTER AND CUTER.
HERA HYUK
HERA HYUK
JUST WAIT 'TIL HE STARTS TO TALK!
...
EVENTUALLY HE'LL GO, "PAPA!" AND COME TODDLING ALONG AFTER YOU. I SWEAR, YOU'LL GET ALL THE FEELS.
SIGHHH...

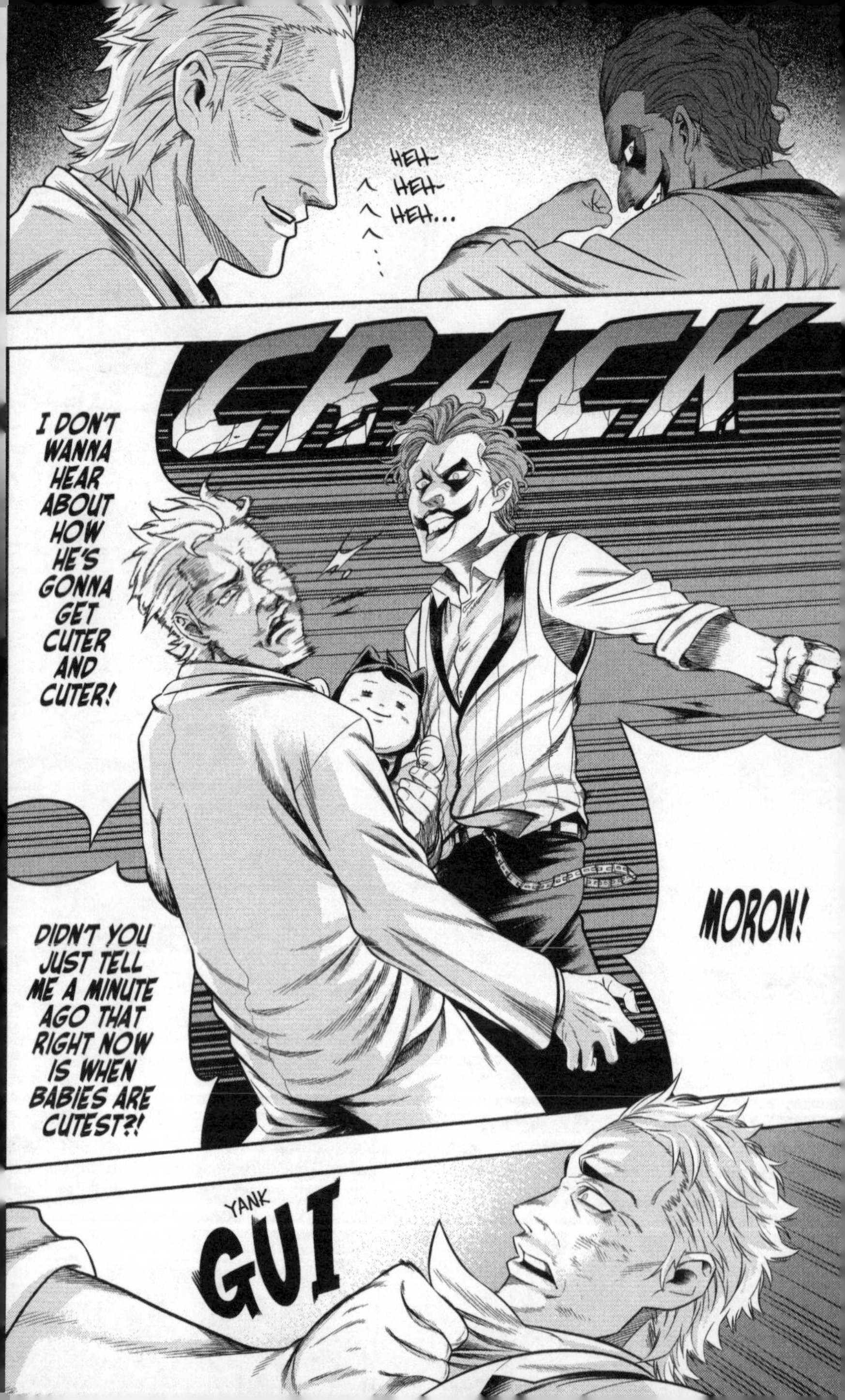
HEH-
HEH-
HEH...
CRACK
I DON'T WANNA HEAR ABOUT HOW HE'S GONNA GET CUTER AND CUTER!
MORON!
DIDN'T YOU JUST TELL ME A MINUTE AGO THAT RIGHT NOW IS WHEN BABIES ARE CUTEST?!
YANK
GUI

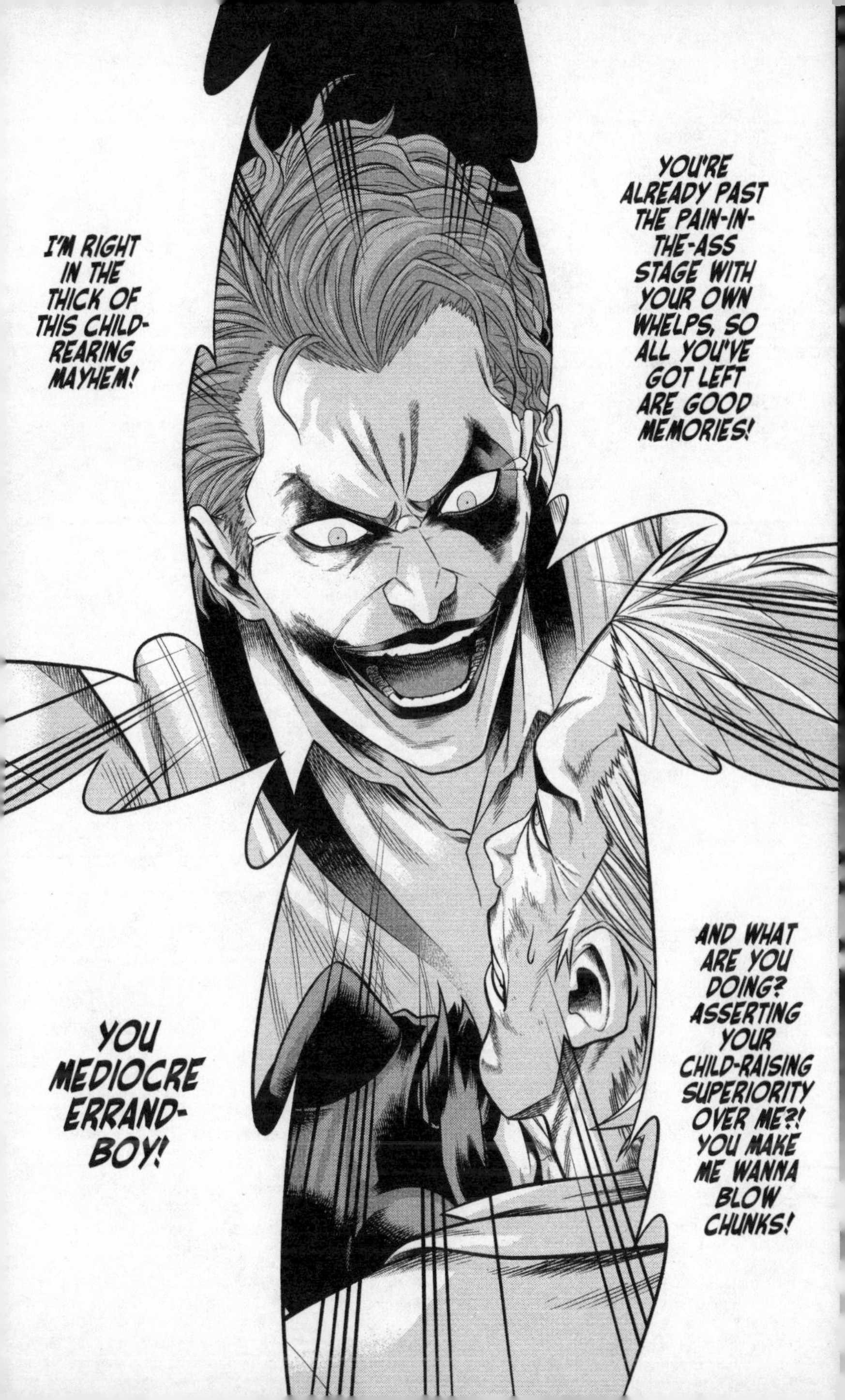
YOU'RE ALREADY PAST THE PAIN-IN-THE-ASS STAGE WITH YOUR OWN WHELPS, SO ALL YOU'VE GOT LEFT ARE GOOD MEMORIES!
I'M RIGHT IN THE THICK OF THIS CHILD-REARING MAYHEM!
AND WHAT ARE YOU DOING? ASSERTING YOUR CHILD-RAISING SUPERIORITY OVER ME?! YOU MAKE ME WANNA BLOW CHUNKS!
YOU MEDIOCRE ERRAND-BOY!

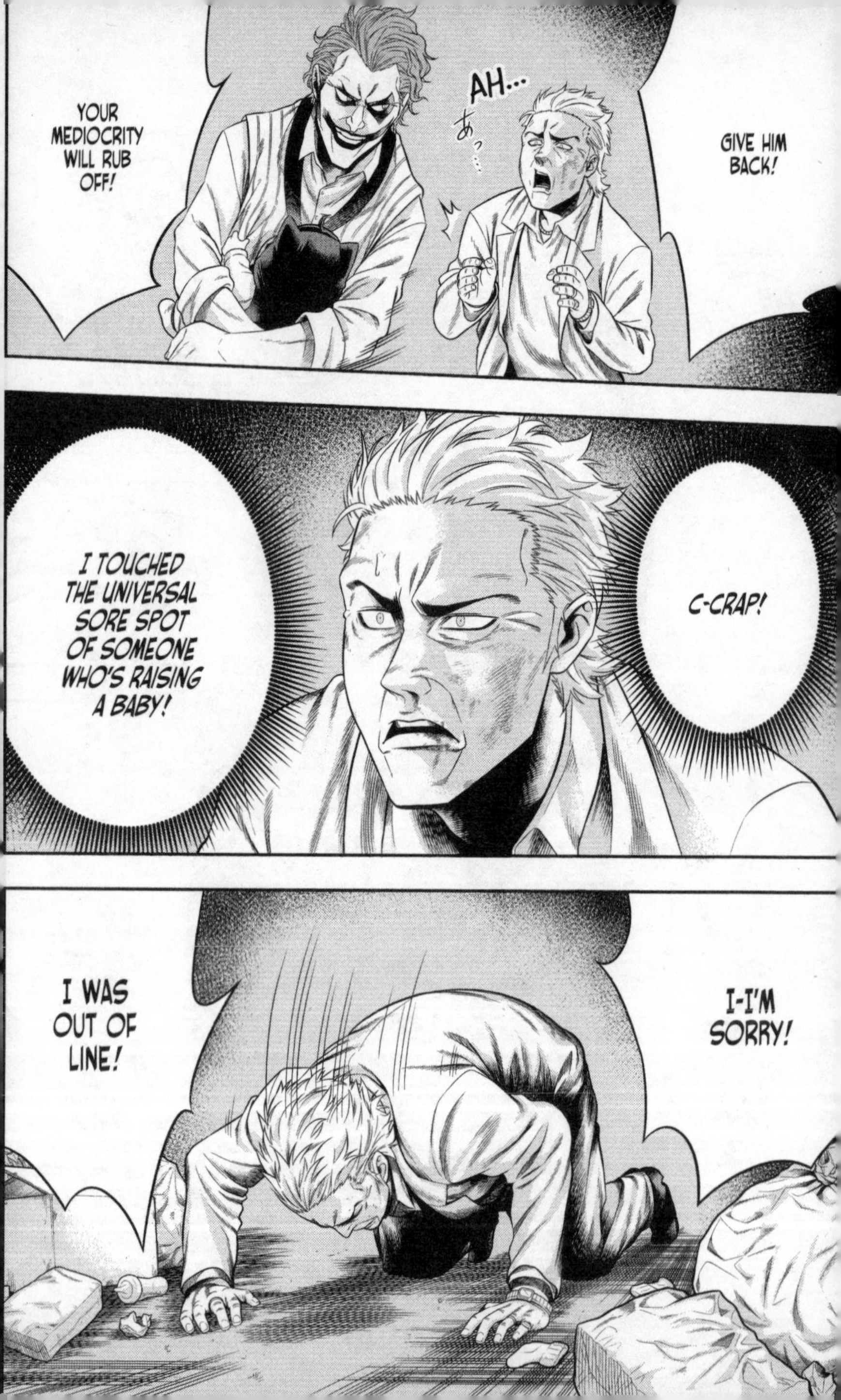
GIVE HIM BACK!
AH...
あっ…
YOUR MEDIOCRITY WILL RUB OFF!
C-CRAP!
I TOUCHED THE UNIVERSAL SORE SPOT OF SOMEONE WHO'S RAISING A BABY!
I-I'M SORRY!
I WAS OUT OF LINE!

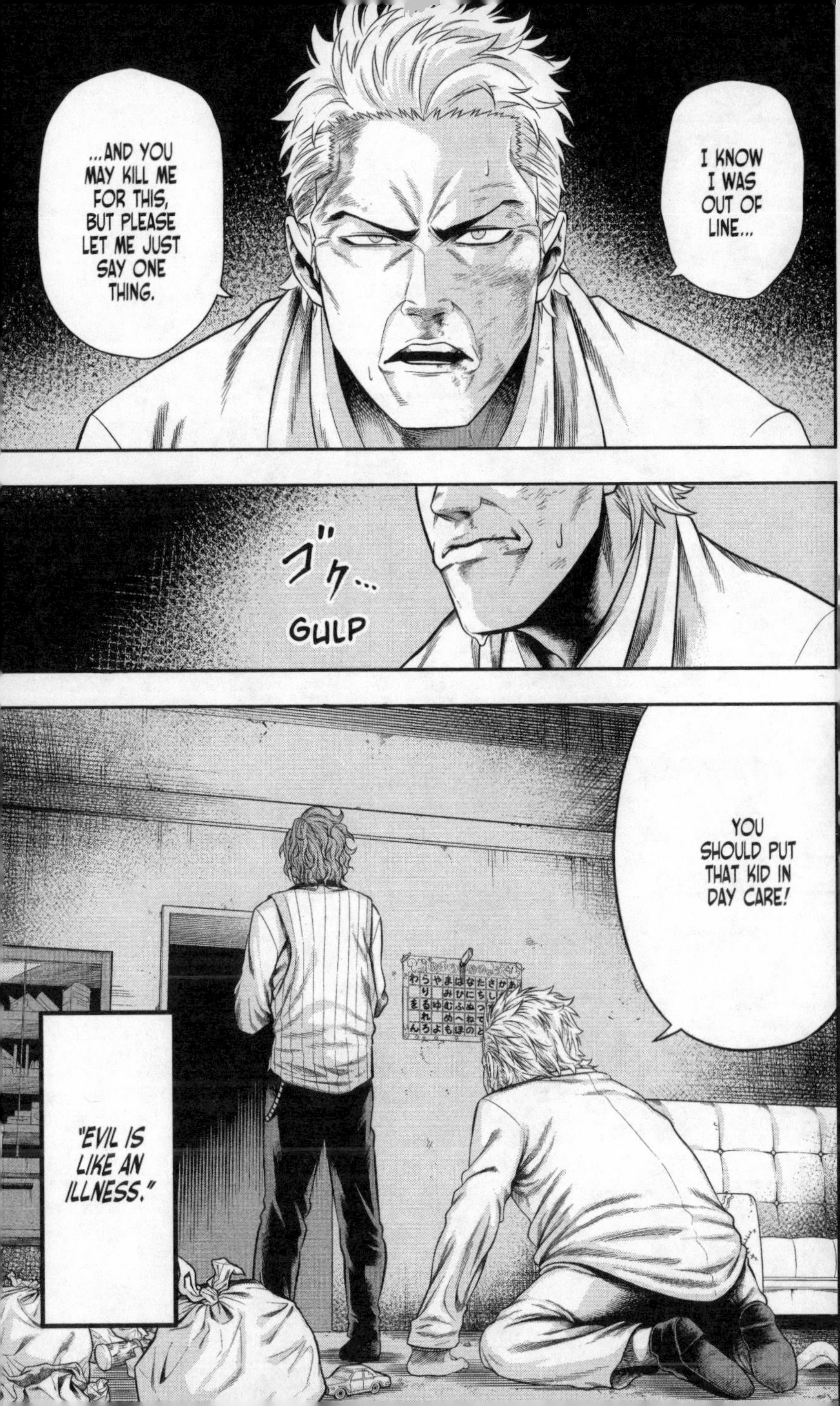
I KNOW I WAS OUT OF LINE...
...AND YOU MAY KILL ME FOR THIS, BUT PLEASE LET ME JUST SAY ONE THING.
ゴク...
GULP
YOU SHOULD PUT THAT KID IN DAY CARE!
"EVIL IS LIKE AN ILLNESS."

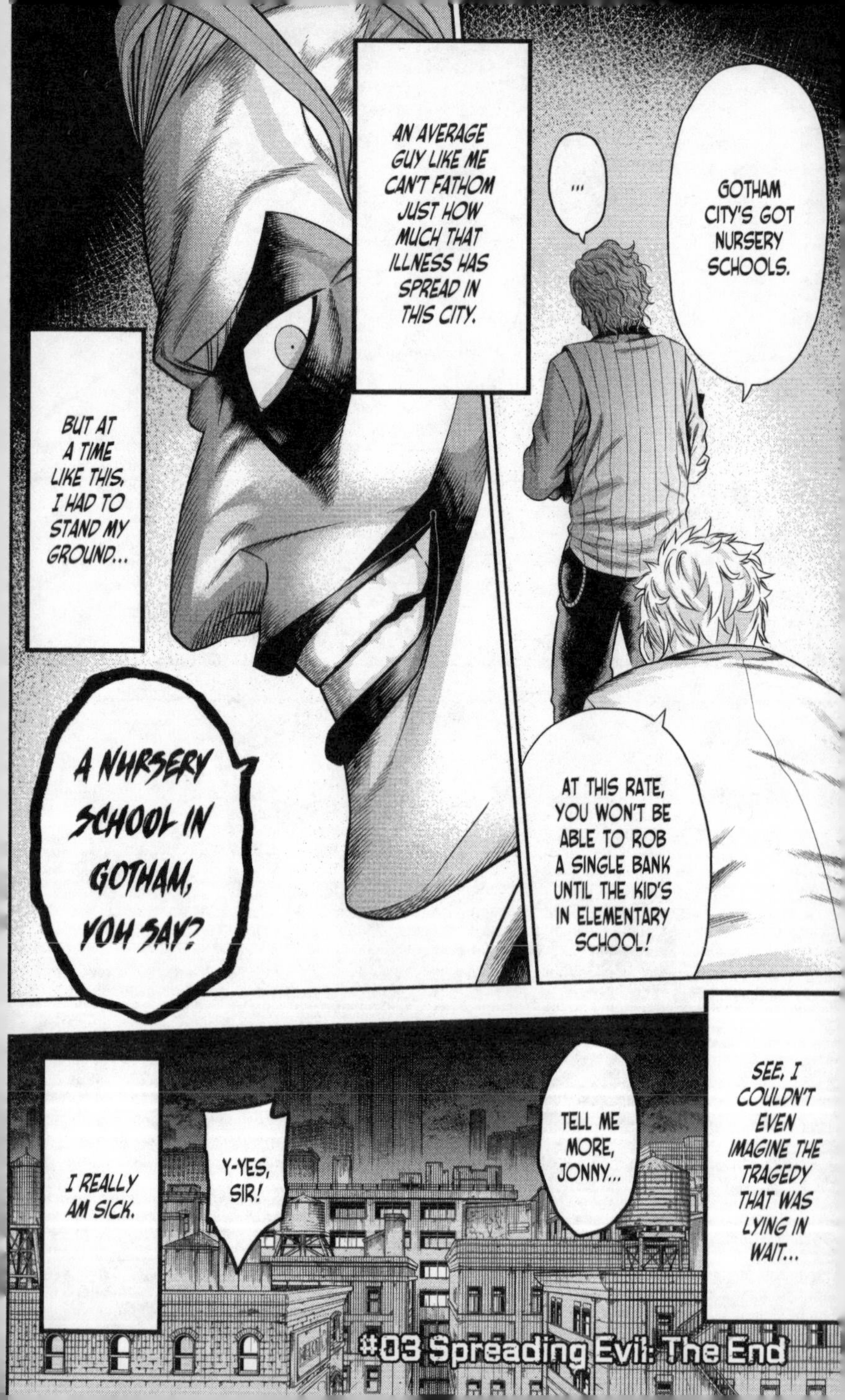
GOTHAM CITY'S GOT NURSERY SCHOOLS.
...
AT THIS RATE, YOU WON'T BE ABLE TO ROB A SINGLE BANK UNTIL THE KID'S IN ELEMENTARY SCHOOL!
AN AVERAGE GUY LIKE ME CAN'T FATHOM JUST HOW MUCH THAT ILLNESS HAS SPREAD IN THIS CITY.
BUT AT A TIME LIKE THIS, I HAD TO STAND MY GROUND...
A NURSERY SCHOOL IN GOTHAM, YOU SAY?
SEE, I COULDN'T EVEN IMAGINE THE TRAGEDY THAT WAS LYING IN WAIT...
TELL ME MORE, JONNY...
Y-YES, SIR!
I REALLY AM SICK.
#03 Spreading Evil: The End

You looked all over for the Batbaby clothes he wears this chapter, but couldn't find 'em?

Well, I'll tell ya, I had to order them special from the net…

…the international distributor and shipping cost me an arm and a leg! Hahahaha!

one operation joker

ワンオペ JOKER

one operation joker vol. 1

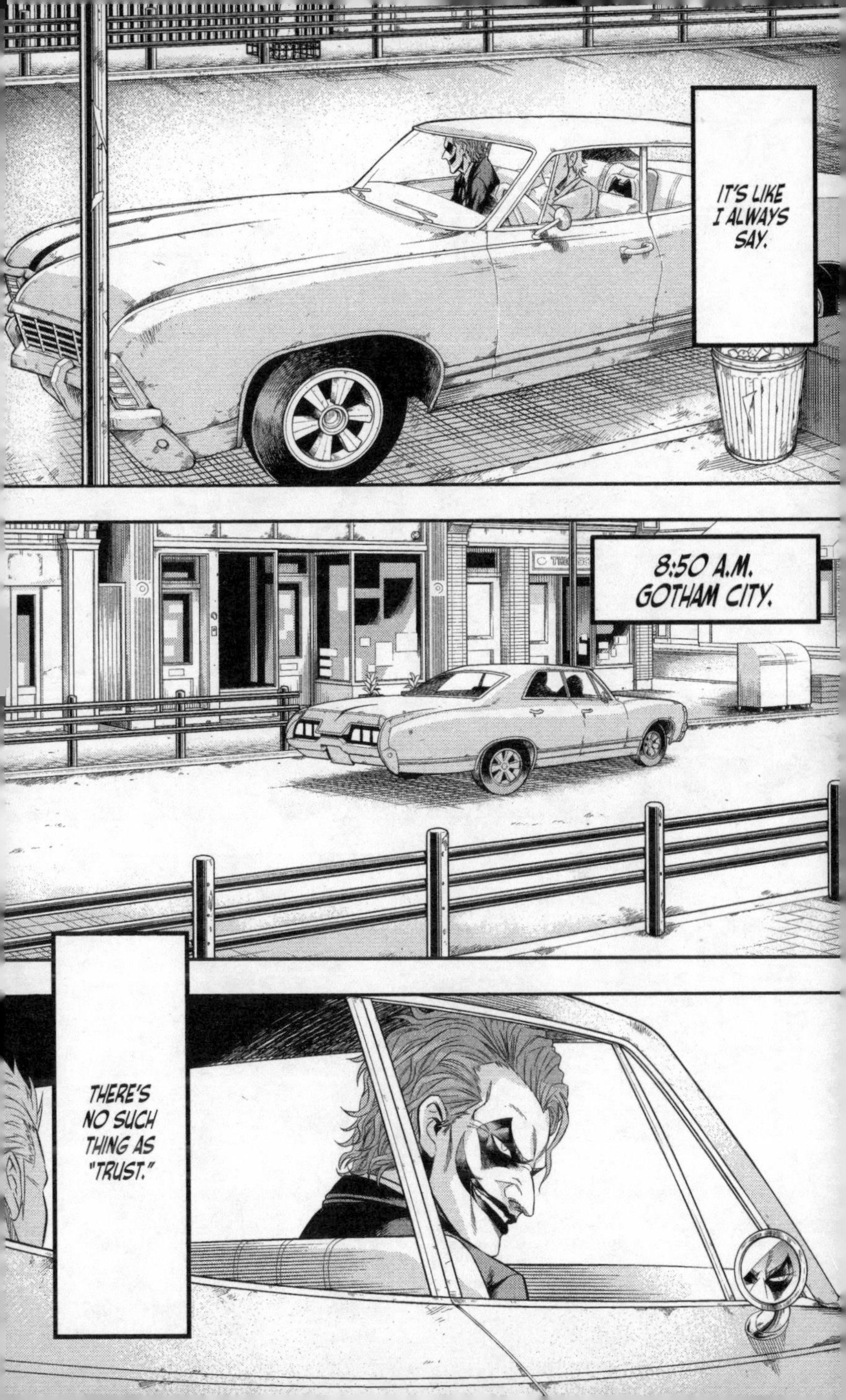
IT'S LIKE I ALWAYS SAY.
8:50 A.M. GOTHAM CITY.
THERE'S NO SUCH THING AS "TRUST."

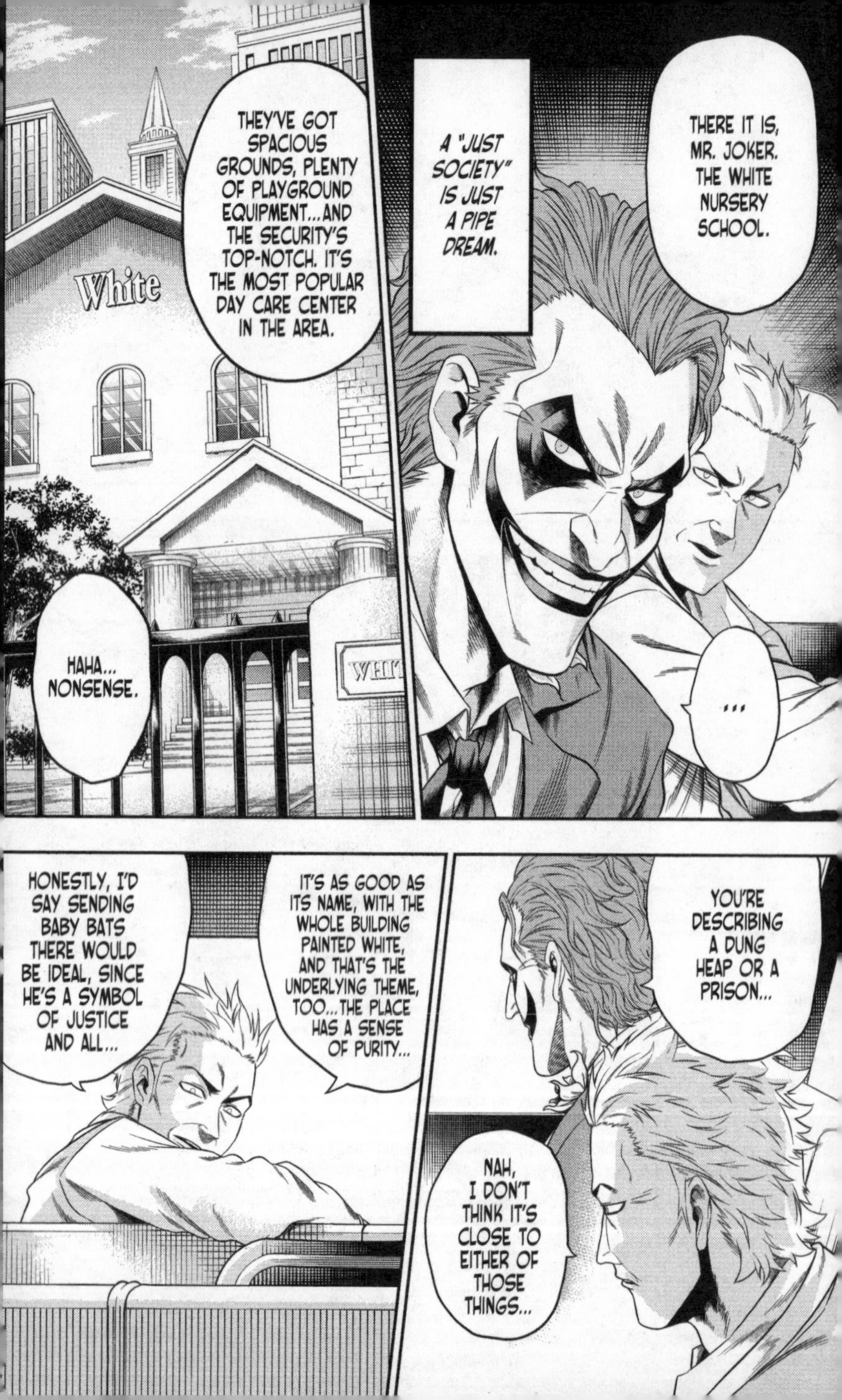
THERE IT IS, MR. JOKER. THE WHITE NURSERY SCHOOL.
A "JUST SOCIETY" IS JUST A PIPE DREAM.
...
THEY'VE GOT SPACIOUS GROUNDS, PLENTY OF PLAYGROUND EQUIPMENT...AND THE SECURITY'S TOP-NOTCH. IT'S THE MOST POPULAR DAY CARE CENTER IN THE AREA.
White
HAHA... NONSENSE.
YOU'RE DESCRIBING A DUNG HEAP OR A PRISON...
NAH, I DON'T THINK IT'S CLOSE TO EITHER OF THOSE THINGS...
IT'S AS GOOD AS ITS NAME, WITH THE WHOLE BUILDING PAINTED WHITE, AND THAT'S THE UNDERLYING THEME, TOO...THE PLACE HAS A SENSE OF PURITY...
HONESTLY, I'D SAY SENDING BABY BATS THERE WOULD BE IDEAL, SINCE HE'S A SYMBOL OF JUSTICE AND ALL...

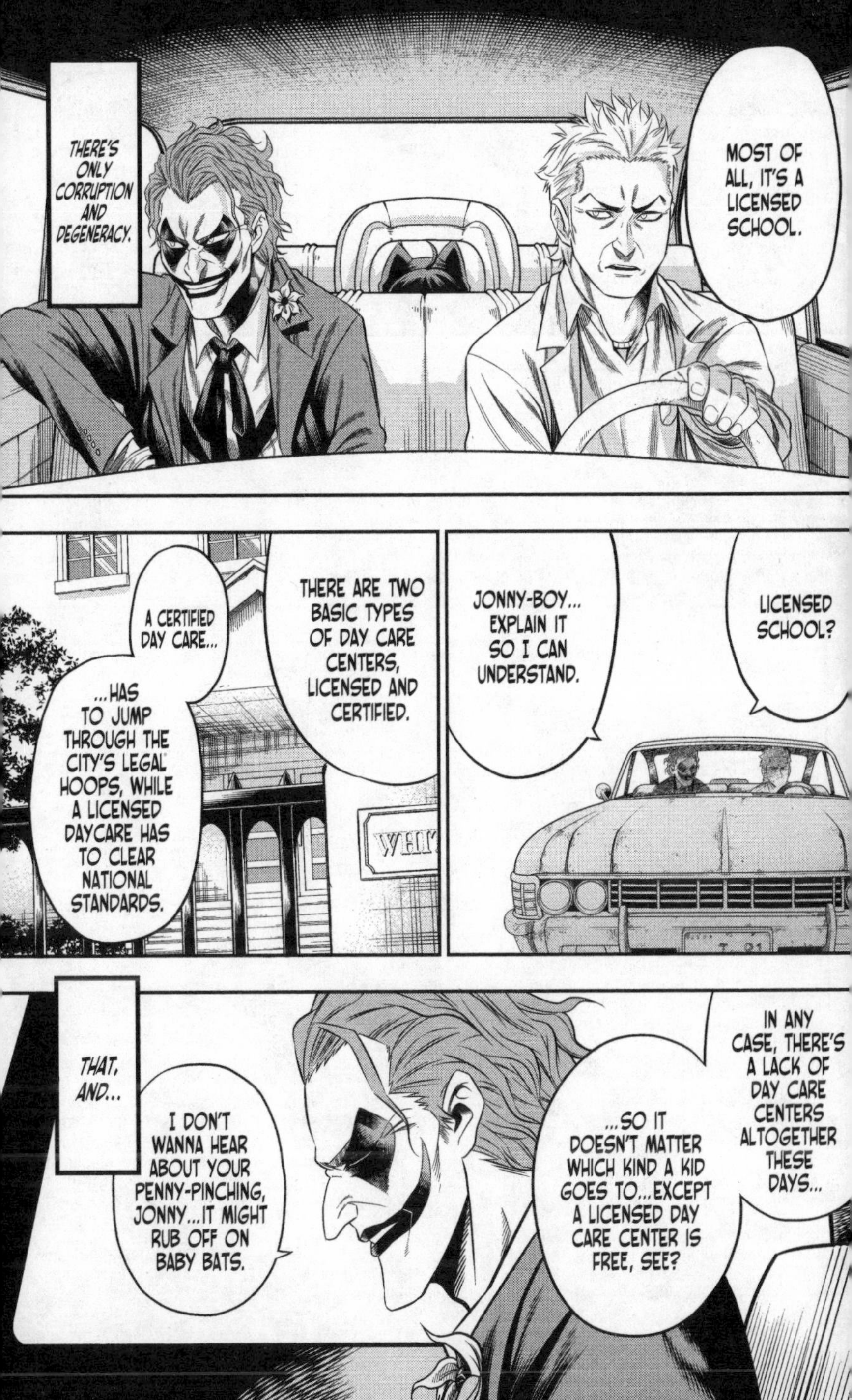
MOST OF ALL, IT'S A LICENSED SCHOOL.
THERE'S ONLY CORRUPTION AND DEGENERACY.
LICENSED SCHOOL?
JONNY-BOY... EXPLAIN IT SO I CAN UNDERSTAND.
THERE ARE TWO BASIC TYPES OF DAY CARE CENTERS, LICENSED AND CERTIFIED.
A CERTIFIED DAY CARE...
...HAS TO JUMP THROUGH THE CITY'S LEGAL HOOPS, WHILE A LICENSED DAYCARE HAS TO CLEAR NATIONAL STANDARDS.
IN ANY CASE, THERE'S A LACK OF DAY CARE CENTERS ALTOGETHER THESE DAYS...
...SO IT DOESN'T MATTER WHICH KIND A KID GOES TO...EXCEPT A LICENSED DAY CARE CENTER IS FREE, SEE?
I DON'T WANNA HEAR ABOUT YOUR PENNY-PINCHING, JONNY...IT MIGHT RUB OFF ON BABY BATS.
THAT. AND...

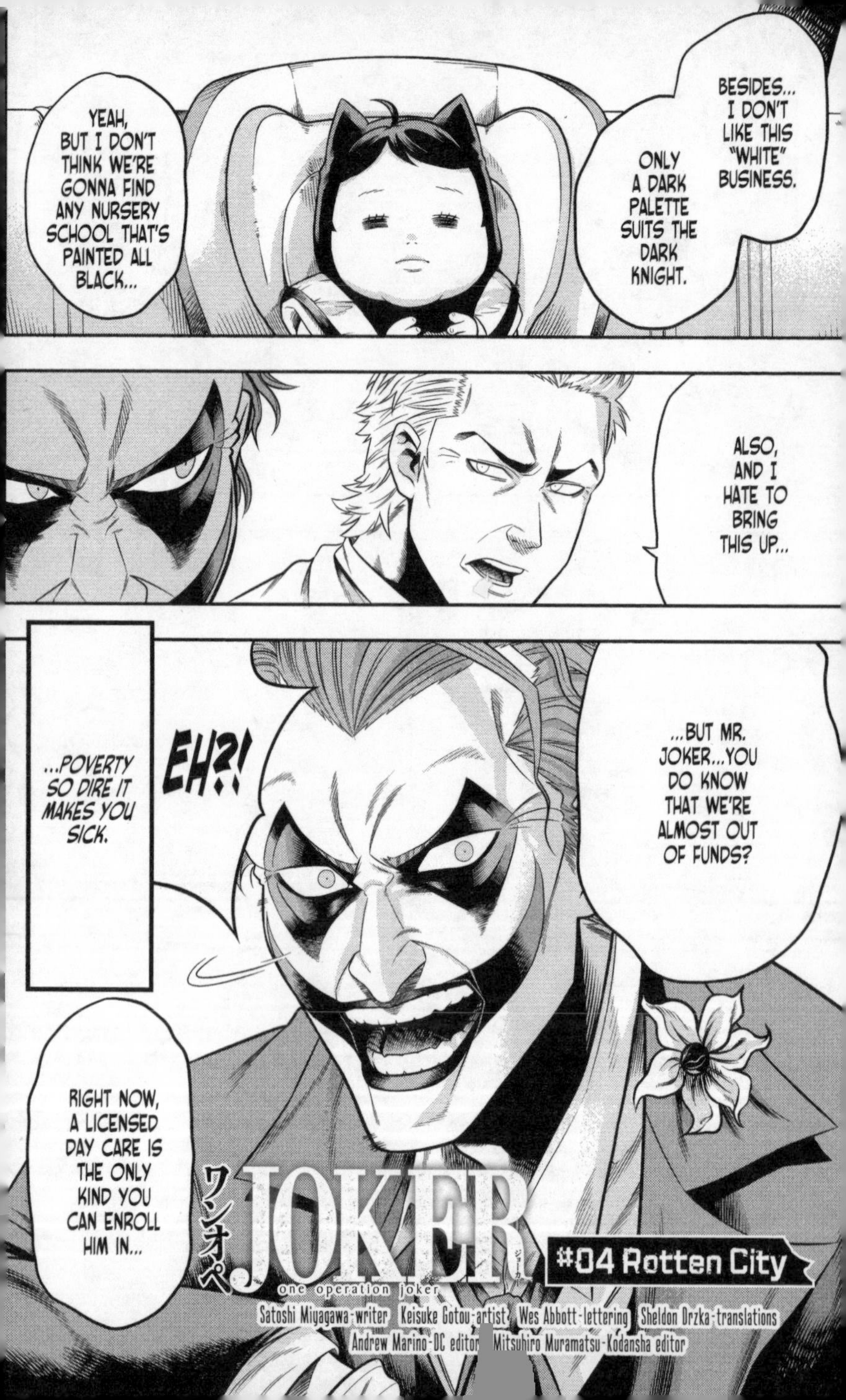
BESIDES... I DON'T LIKE THIS "WHITE" BUSINESS.
ONLY A DARK PALETTE SUITS THE DARK KNIGHT.
YEAH, BUT I DON'T THINK WE'RE GONNA FIND ANY NURSERY SCHOOL THAT'S PAINTED ALL BLACK...
ALSO, AND I HATE TO BRING THIS UP...
...BUT MR. JOKER...YOU DO KNOW THAT WE'RE ALMOST OUT OF FUNDS?
EH?!
...POVERTY SO DIRE IT MAKES YOU SICK.
RIGHT NOW, A LICENSED DAY CARE IS THE ONLY KIND YOU CAN ENROLL HIM IN...
ワンオペ JOKER ジョーカー
one operation joker
#04 Rotten City
Satoshi Miyagawa-writer Keisuke Gotou-artist Wes Abbott-lettering Sheldon Drzka-translations
Andrew Marino-DC editor Mitsuhiro Muramatsu-Kodansha editor

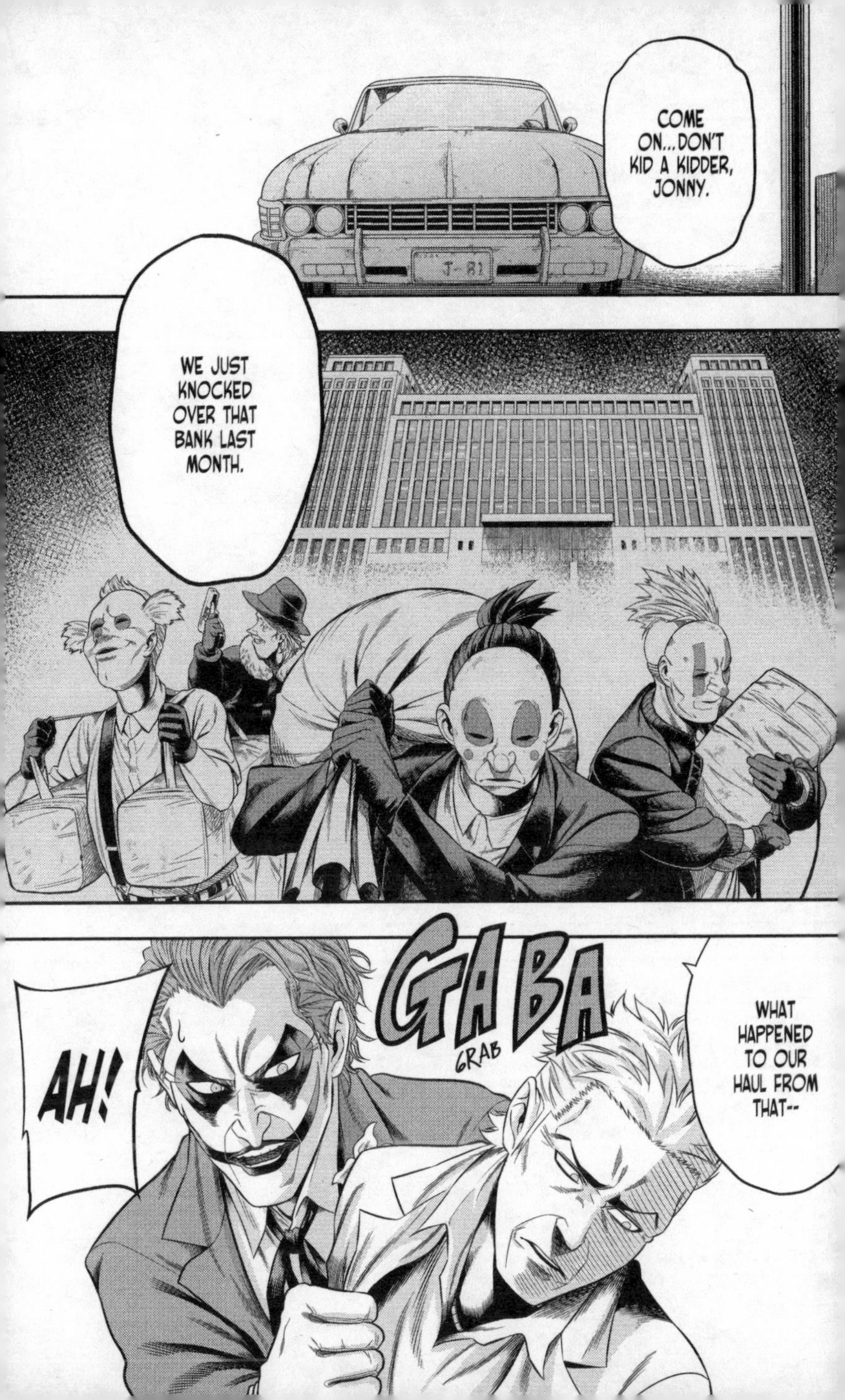
COME ON...DON'T KID A KIDDER, JONNY.
WE JUST KNOCKED OVER THAT BANK LAST MONTH.
WHAT HAPPENED TO OUR HAUL FROM THAT--
GA BA
GRAB
AH!

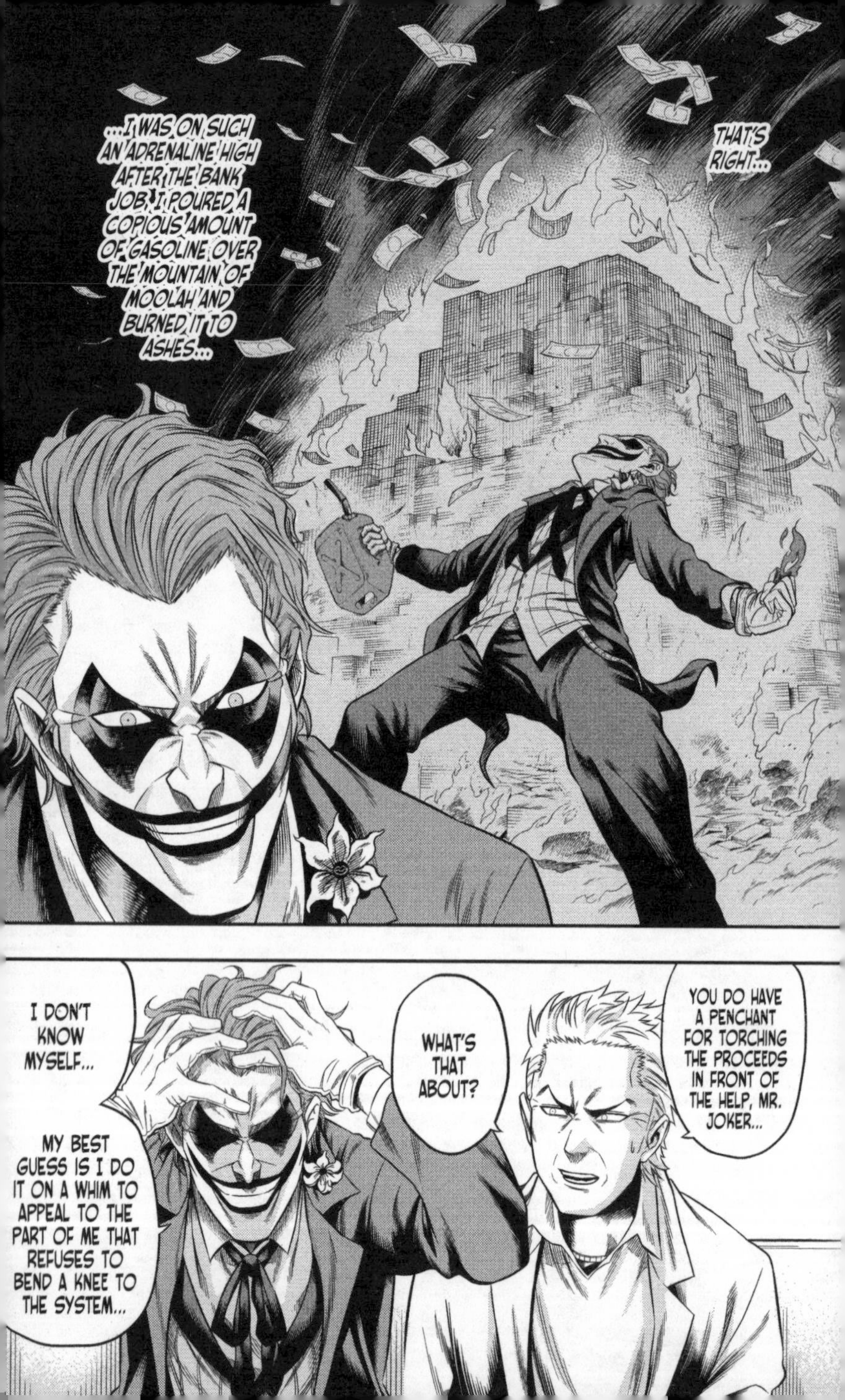
THAT'S RIGHT...
...I WAS ON SUCH AN ADRENALINE HIGH AFTER THE BANK JOB, I POURED A COPIOUS AMOUNT OF GASOLINE OVER THE MOUNTAIN OF MOOLAH AND BURNED IT TO ASHES...
YOU DO HAVE A PENCHANT FOR TORCHING THE PROCEEDS IN FRONT OF THE HELP, MR. JOKER...
WHAT'S THAT ABOUT?
I DON'T KNOW MYSELF...
MY BEST GUESS IS I DO IT ON A WHIM TO APPEAL TO THE PART OF ME THAT REFUSES TO BEND A KNEE TO THE SYSTEM...

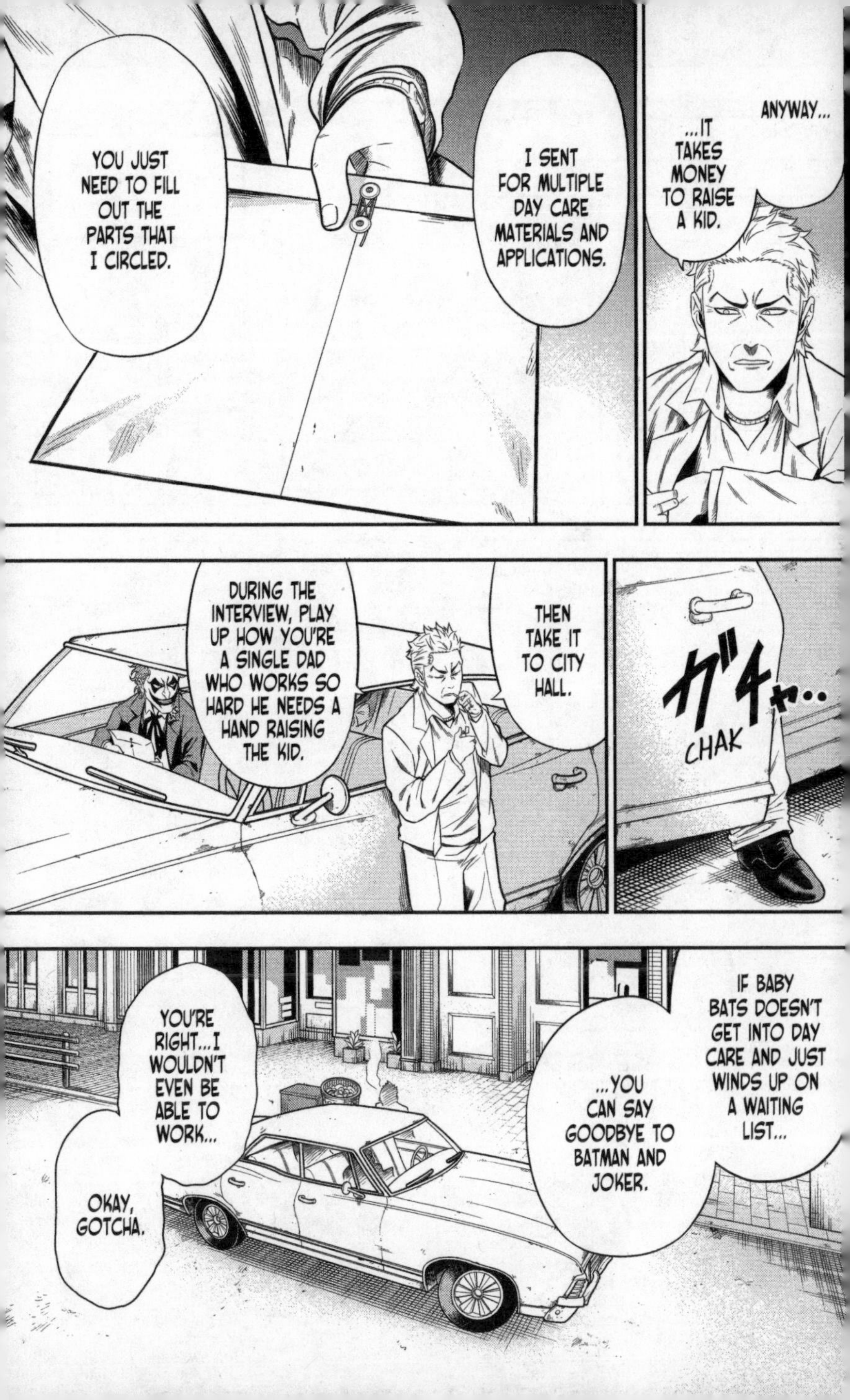
ANYWAY...
...IT TAKES MONEY TO RAISE A KID.
I SENT FOR MULTIPLE DAY CARE MATERIALS AND APPLICATIONS.
YOU JUST NEED TO FILL OUT THE PARTS THAT I CIRCLED.
ガチャ..
CHAK
THEN TAKE IT TO CITY HALL.
DURING THE INTERVIEW, PLAY UP HOW YOU'RE A SINGLE DAD WHO WORKS SO HARD HE NEEDS A HAND RAISING THE KID.
IF BABY BATS DOESN'T GET INTO DAY CARE AND JUST WINDS UP ON A WAITING LIST...
...YOU CAN SAY GOODBYE TO BATMAN AND JOKER.
YOU'RE RIGHT...I WOULDN'T EVEN BE ABLE TO WORK...
OKAY, GOTCHA.

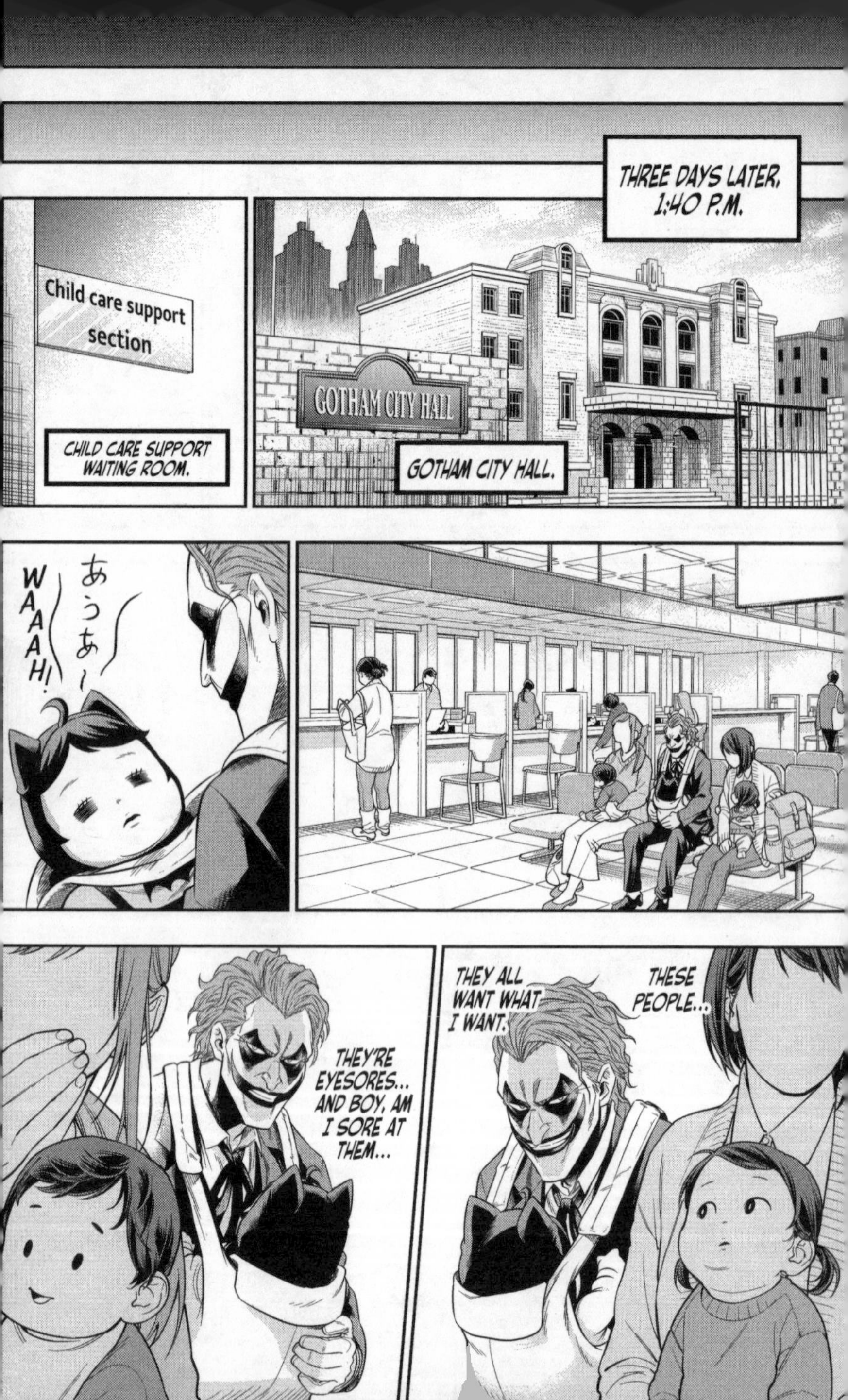
THREE DAYS LATER, 1:40 P.M.
GOTHAM CITY HALL
GOTHAM CITY HALL.
Child care support section
CHILD CARE SUPPORT WAITING ROOM.
あうあ~
WAAAAH!
THESE PEOPLE...
THEY ALL WANT WHAT I WANT.
THEY'RE EYESORES... AND BOY, AM I SORE AT THEM...

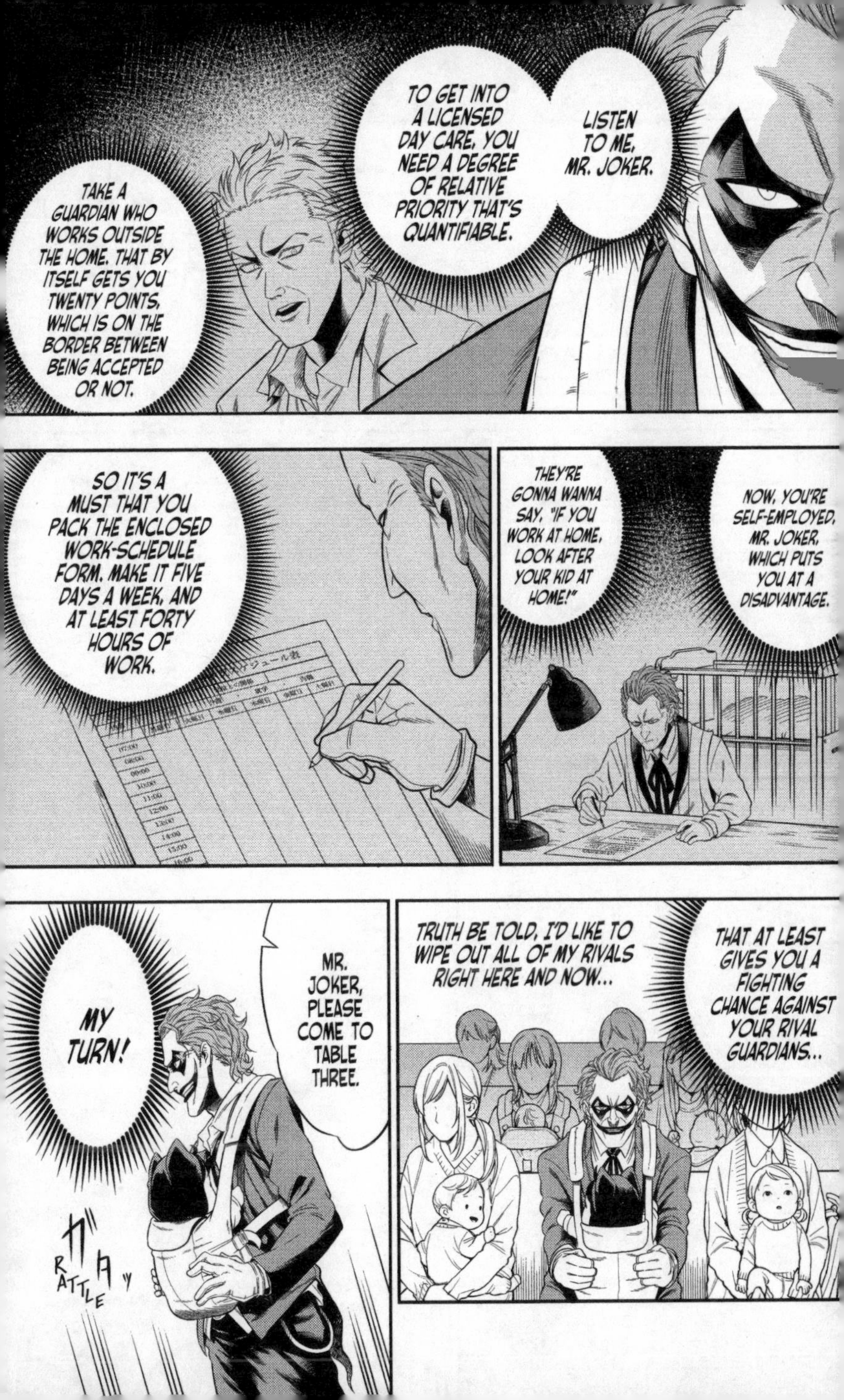
LISTEN TO ME, MR. JOKER.
TO GET INTO A LICENSED DAY CARE, YOU NEED A DEGREE OF RELATIVE PRIORITY THAT'S QUANTIFIABLE.
TAKE A GUARDIAN WHO WORKS OUTSIDE THE HOME. THAT BY ITSELF GETS YOU TWENTY POINTS, WHICH IS ON THE BORDER BETWEEN BEING ACCEPTED OR NOT.
NOW, YOU'RE SELF-EMPLOYED, MR. JOKER, WHICH PUTS YOU AT A DISADVANTAGE.
THEY'RE GONNA WANNA SAY, "IF YOU WORK AT HOME, LOOK AFTER YOUR KID AT HOME!"
SO IT'S A MUST THAT YOU PACK THE ENCLOSED WORK-SCHEDULE FORM. MAKE IT FIVE DAYS A WEEK, AND AT LEAST FORTY HOURS OF WORK.
THAT AT LEAST GIVES YOU A FIGHTING CHANCE AGAINST YOUR RIVAL GUARDIANS...
TRUTH BE TOLD, I'D LIKE TO WIPE OUT ALL OF MY RIVALS RIGHT HERE AND NOW...
MR. JOKER, PLEASE COME TO TABLE THREE.
MY TURN!
ガタッ
RATTLE

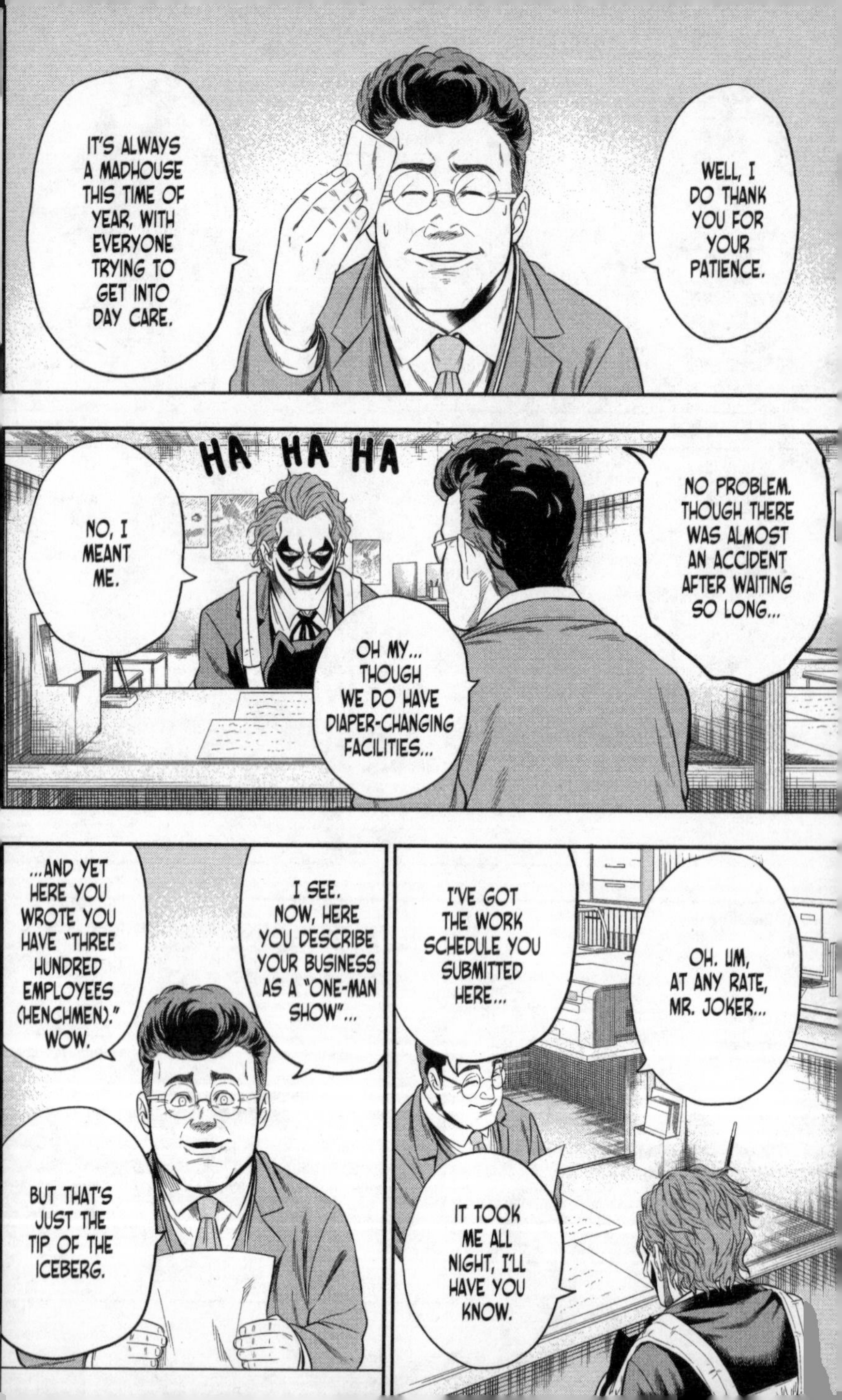
WELL, I DO THANK YOU FOR YOUR PATIENCE.
IT'S ALWAYS A MADHOUSE THIS TIME OF YEAR, WITH EVERYONE TRYING TO GET INTO DAY CARE.
NO PROBLEM. THOUGH THERE WAS ALMOST AN ACCIDENT AFTER WAITING SO LONG...
HA HA HA
NO, I MEANT ME.
OH MY... THOUGH WE DO HAVE DIAPER-CHANGING FACILITIES...
OH. UM, AT ANY RATE, MR. JOKER...
I'VE GOT THE WORK SCHEDULE YOU SUBMITTED HERE...
IT TOOK ME ALL NIGHT, I'LL HAVE YOU KNOW.
I SEE. NOW, HERE YOU DESCRIBE YOUR BUSINESS AS A "ONE-MAN SHOW"...
...AND YET HERE YOU WROTE YOU HAVE "THREE HUNDRED EMPLOYEES (HENCHMEN)." WOW.
BUT THAT'S JUST THE TIP OF THE ICEBERG.

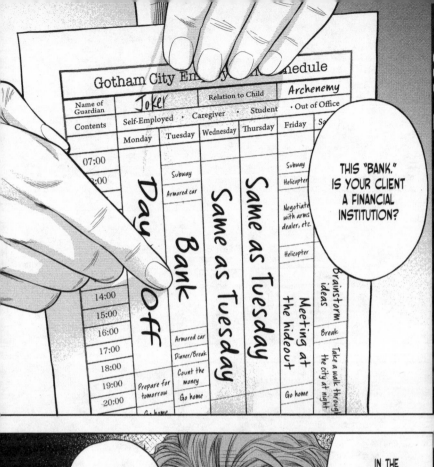

Gotham City Em... ...hedule

Name of Guardian	Joker		Relation to Child		Archenemy	
Contents	Self-Employed	·	Caregiver	· Student	· Out of Office	
	Monday	Tuesday	Wednesday	Thursday	Friday	Sa...
07:00					Subway	
?:00		Subway			Helicopter	
	Day Off	Armored car	Same as Tuesday	Same as Tuesday	Negotiate with arms dealer, etc.	
		Bank			Helicopter	
14:00						Brainstorm ideas
15:00						
16:00		Armored car				Break
17:00		Dinner/Break			Meeting at the hideout	
18:00		Count the money				Take a walk through the city at night
19:00	Prepare for tomorrow					
20:00		Go home			Go home	
	Go home					

THIS "BANK." IS YOUR CLIENT A FINANCIAL INSTITUTION?

IN THE FIRST PLACE, I DON'T QUITE UNDERSTAND THE NATURE OF YOUR BUSINESS...

IF THE TYPE OF WORK YOU DO IS UNCLEAR, I CAN'T GRANT YOU ANY POINTS...

HE'S GOT ME CORNERED!

DOKI
THUMP
DOKI
THUMP

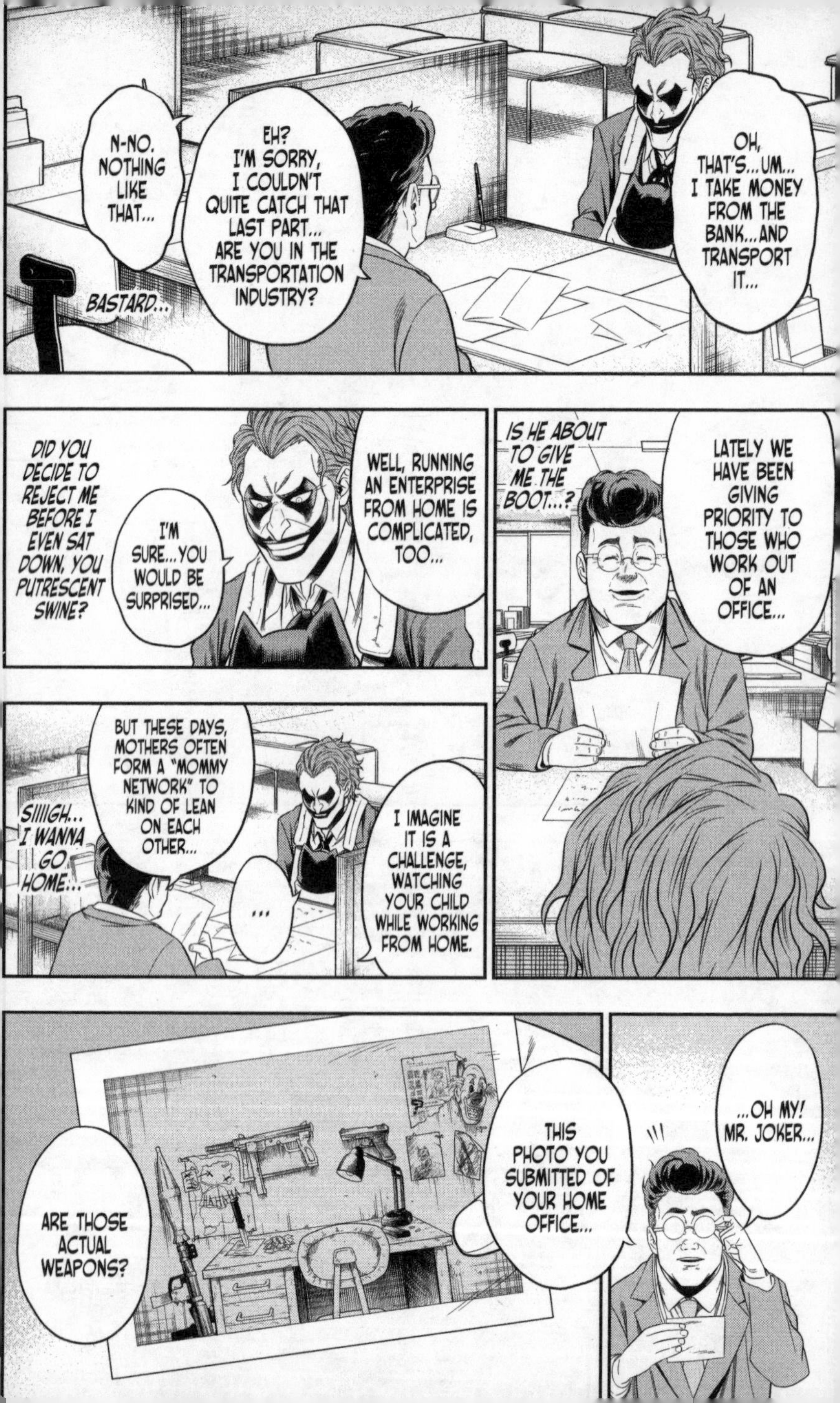

OH, THAT'S...UM... I TAKE MONEY FROM THE BANK...AND TRANSPORT IT...
EH? I'M SORRY, I COULDN'T QUITE CATCH THAT LAST PART... ARE YOU IN THE TRANSPORTATION INDUSTRY?
N-NO. NOTHING LIKE THAT...
BASTARD...
LATELY WE HAVE BEEN GIVING PRIORITY TO THOSE WHO WORK OUT OF AN OFFICE...
IS HE ABOUT TO GIVE ME THE BOOT...?
WELL, RUNNING AN ENTERPRISE FROM HOME IS COMPLICATED, TOO...
I'M SURE...YOU WOULD BE SURPRISED...
DID YOU DECIDE TO REJECT ME BEFORE I EVEN SAT DOWN, YOU PUTRESCENT SWINE?
I IMAGINE IT IS A CHALLENGE, WATCHING YOUR CHILD WHILE WORKING FROM HOME.
...
BUT THESE DAYS, MOTHERS OFTEN FORM A "MOMMY NETWORK" TO KIND OF LEAN ON EACH OTHER...
SIIIGH... I WANNA GO HOME...
...OH MY! MR. JOKER...
THIS PHOTO YOU SUBMITTED OF YOUR HOME OFFICE...
ARE THOSE ACTUAL WEAPONS?

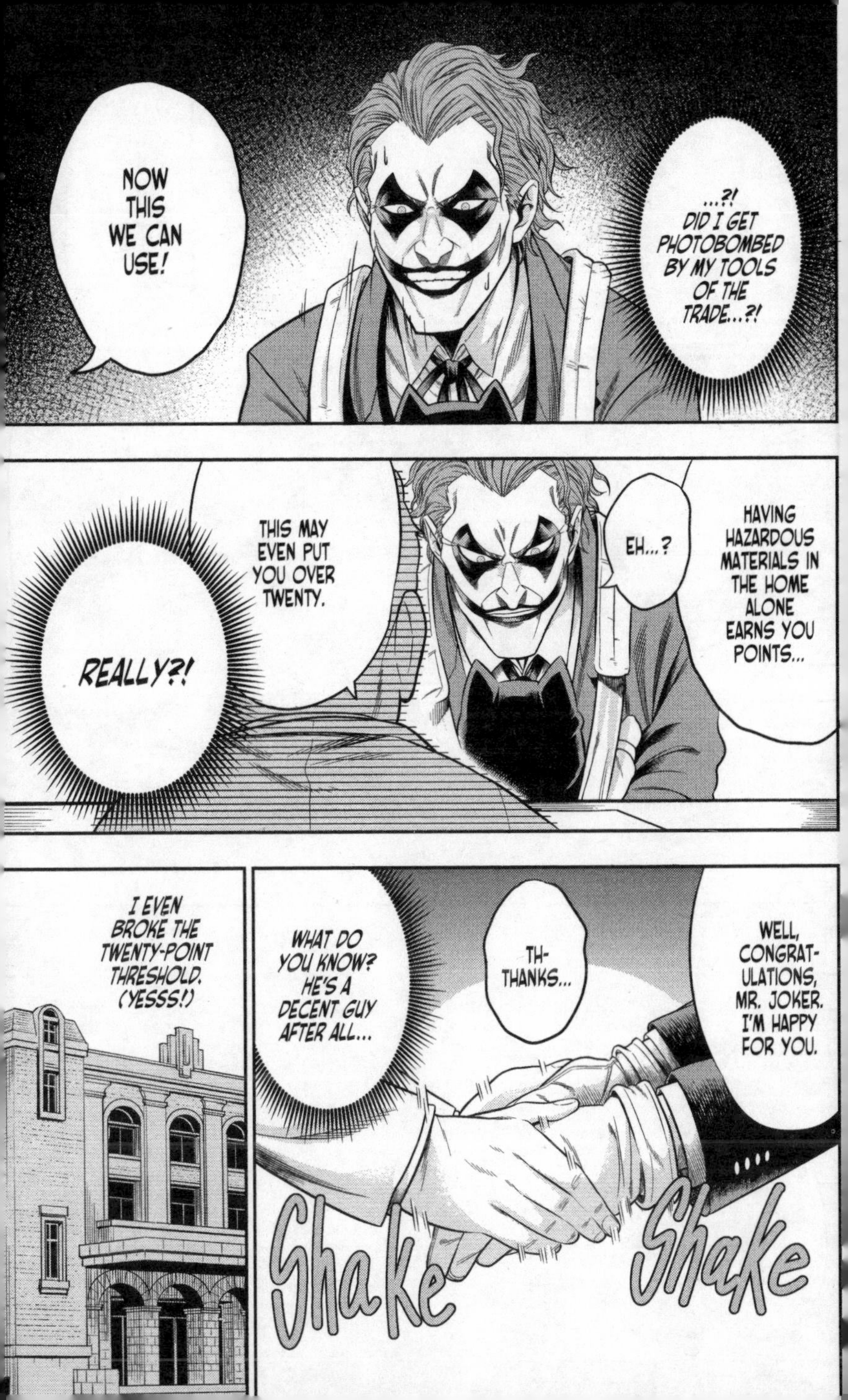
...?! DID I GET PHOTOBOMBED BY MY TOOLS OF THE TRADE...?!
NOW THIS WE CAN USE!
HAVING HAZARDOUS MATERIALS IN THE HOME ALONE EARNS YOU POINTS...
EH...?
THIS MAY EVEN PUT YOU OVER TWENTY.
REALLY?!
WELL, CONGRAT-ULATIONS, MR. JOKER. I'M HAPPY FOR YOU.
TH- THANKS...
WHAT DO YOU KNOW? HE'S A DECENT GUY AFTER ALL...
...
Shake Shake
I EVEN BROKE THE TWENTY-POINT THRESHOLD. (YESSS!)

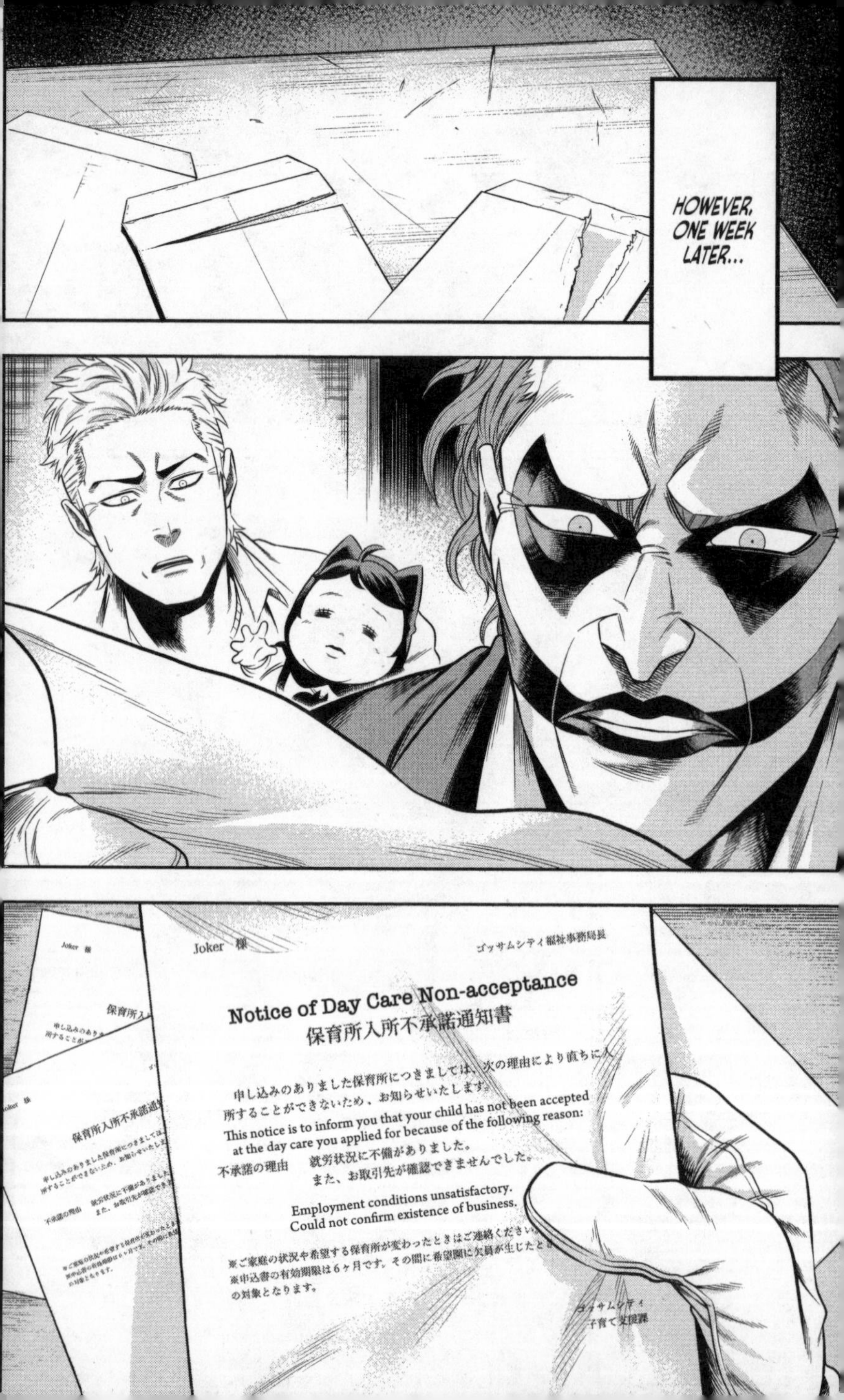
HOWEVER, ONE WEEK LATER...
Joker 様
ゴッサムシティ福祉事務局長
Notice of Day Care Non-acceptance
保育所入所不承諾通知書
申し込みのありました保育所につきましては、次の理由により直ちに入
所することができないため、お知らせいたします。
This notice is to inform you that your child has not been accepted
at the day care you applied for because of the following reason:
不承諾の理由　就労状況に不備がありました。
また、お取引先が確認できませんでした。
Employment conditions unsatisfactory.
Could not confirm existence of business.
※ご家庭の状況や希望する保育所が変わったときはご連絡ください。
※申込書の有効期限は6ヶ月です。その間に希望園に欠員が生じたと
の対象となります。
子育て支援課

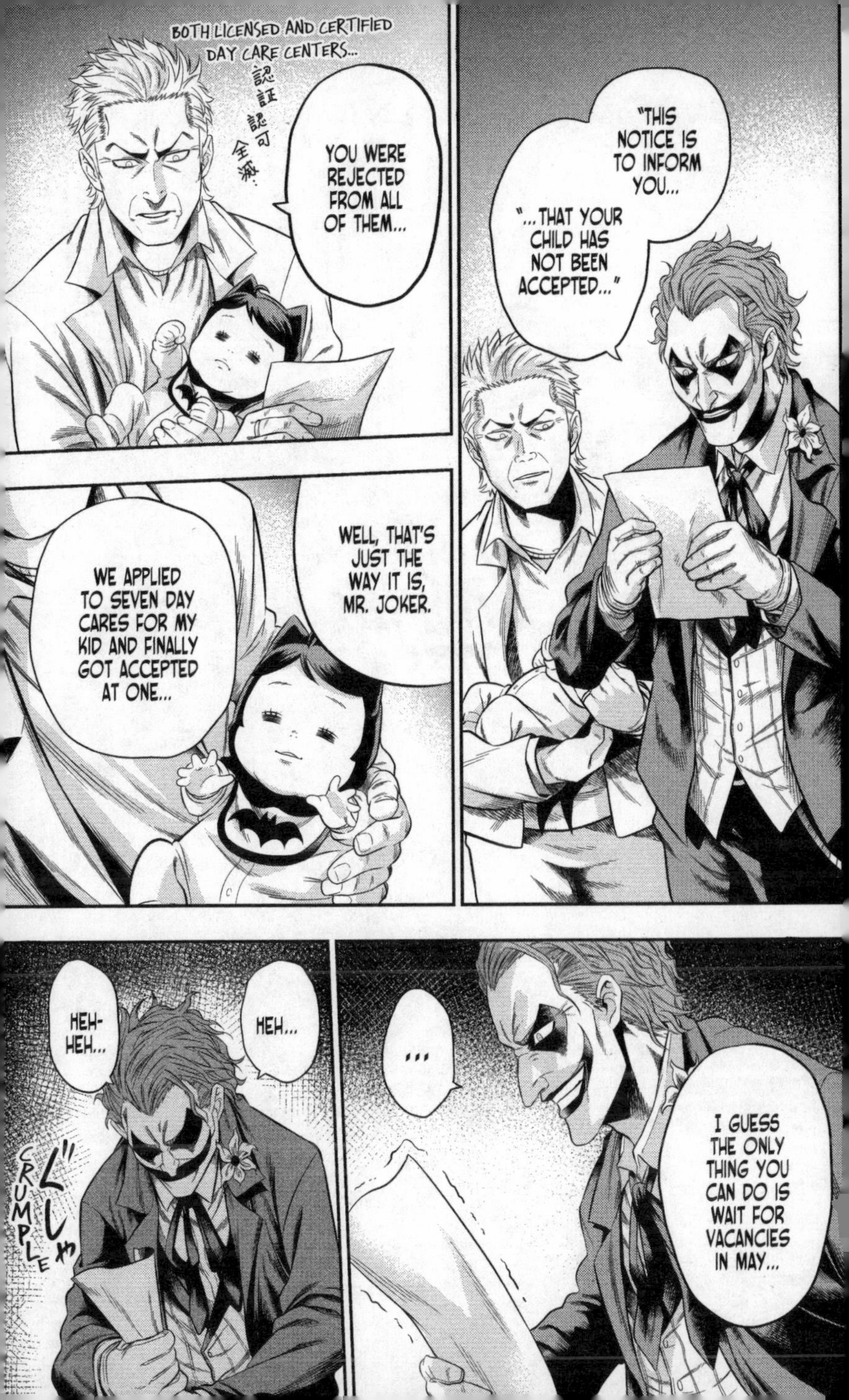
"THIS NOTICE IS TO INFORM YOU...
"...THAT YOUR CHILD HAS NOT BEEN ACCEPTED..."
BOTH LICENSED AND CERTIFIED DAY CARE CENTERS...
認証 認可 全滅…
YOU WERE REJECTED FROM ALL OF THEM...
WELL, THAT'S JUST THE WAY IT IS, MR. JOKER.
WE APPLIED TO SEVEN DAY CARES FOR MY KID AND FINALLY GOT ACCEPTED AT ONE...
...
I GUESS THE ONLY THING YOU CAN DO IS WAIT FOR VACANCIES IN MAY...
HEH...
HEH-HEH...
CRUMPLE
ぐしゃ

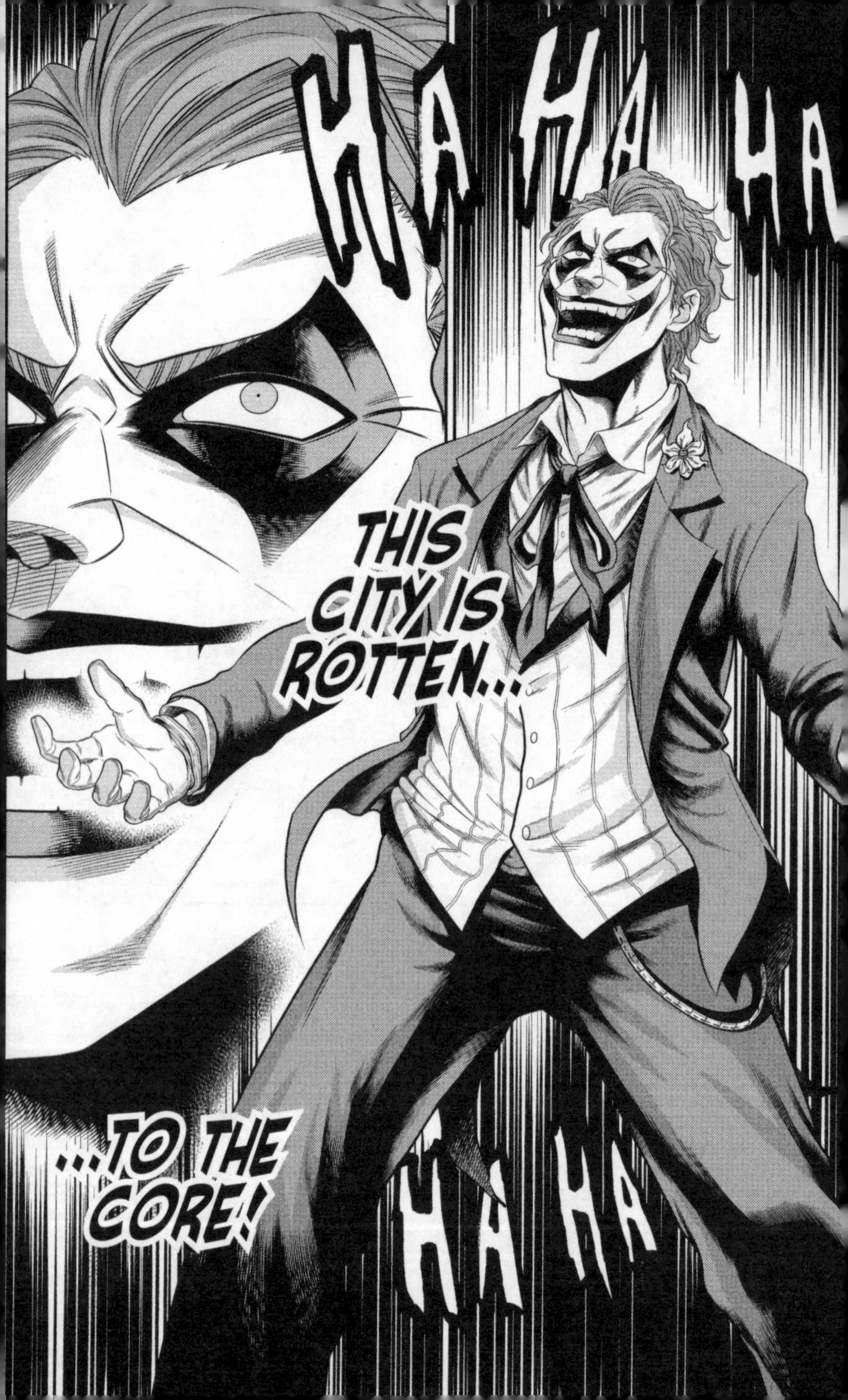
HA HA HA HA
THIS CITY IS ROTTEN...
HA HA HA
...TO THE CORE!

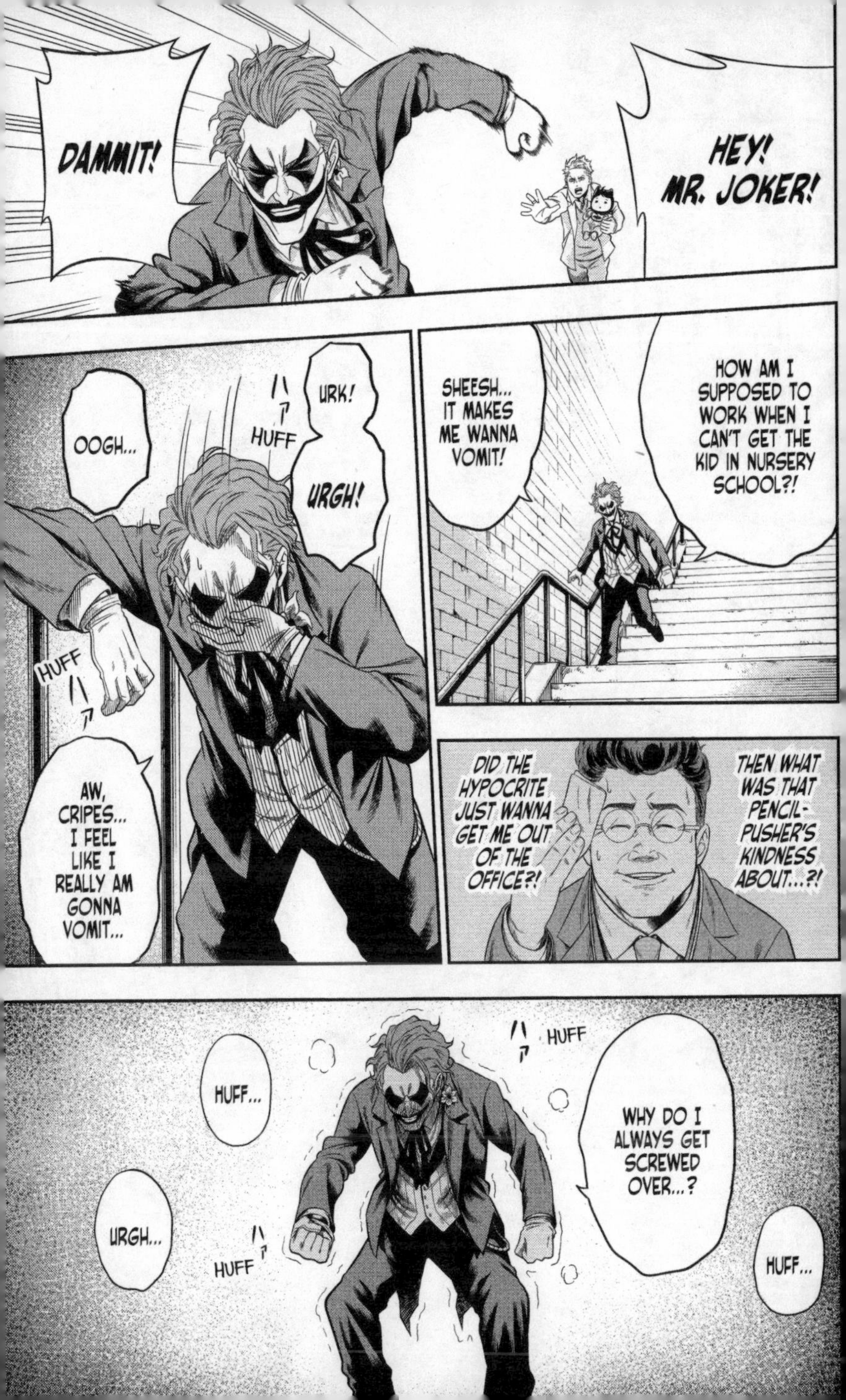
HEY! MR. JOKER!
DAMMIT!
HOW AM I SUPPOSED TO WORK WHEN I CAN'T GET THE KID IN NURSERY SCHOOL?!
SHEESH... IT MAKES ME WANNA VOMIT!
THEN WHAT WAS THAT PENCIL-PUSHER'S KINDNESS ABOUT...?!
DID THE HYPOCRITE JUST WANNA GET ME OUT OF THE OFFICE?!
URK!
ハァ HUFF
OOGH...
URGH!
HUFF ハァ
AW, CRIPES... I FEEL LIKE I REALLY AM GONNA VOMIT...
ハァ HUFF
WHY DO I ALWAYS GET SCREWED OVER...?
HUFF...
HUFF...
ハァ HUFF
URGH...

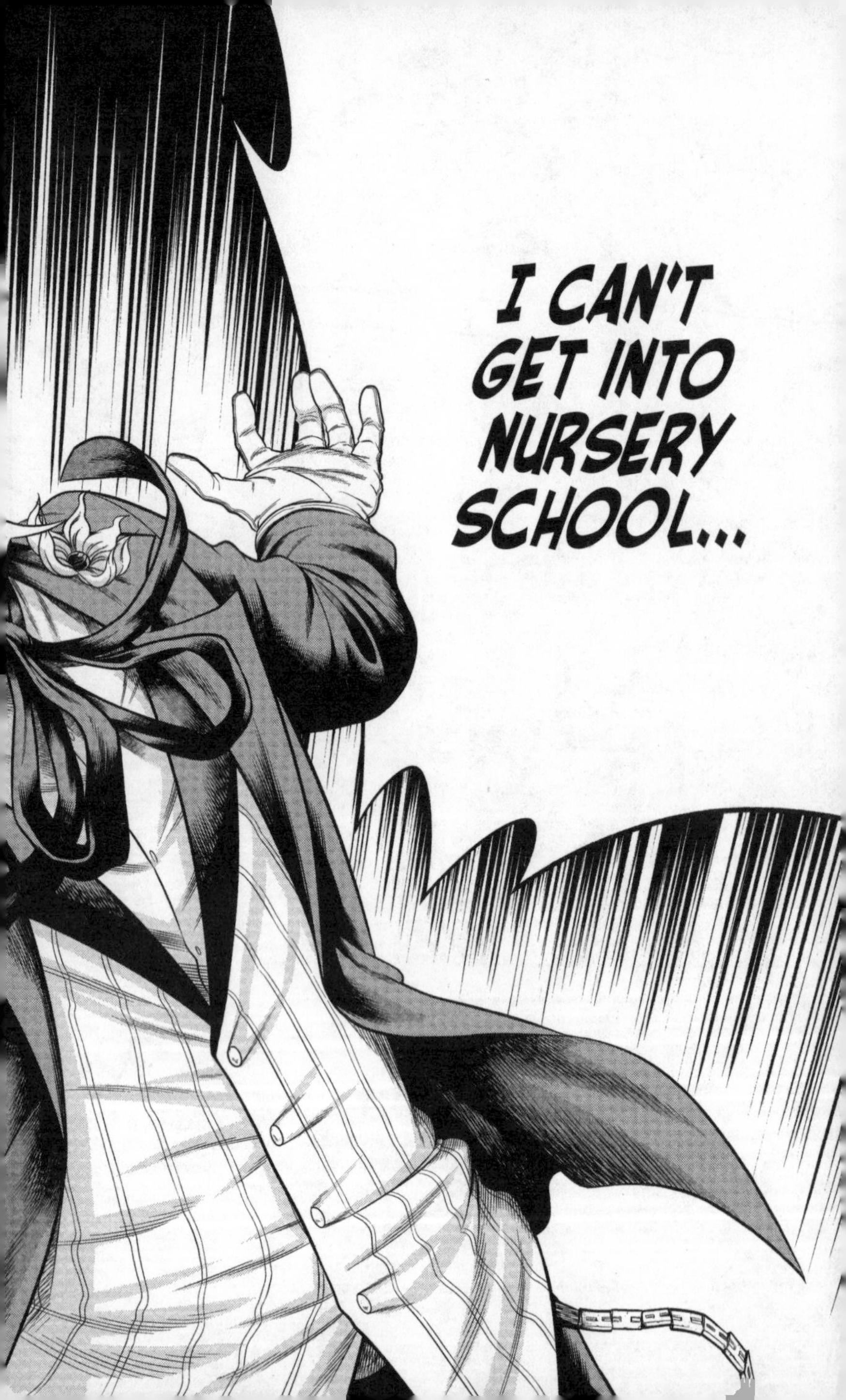
I CAN'T GET INTO NURSERY SCHOOL...

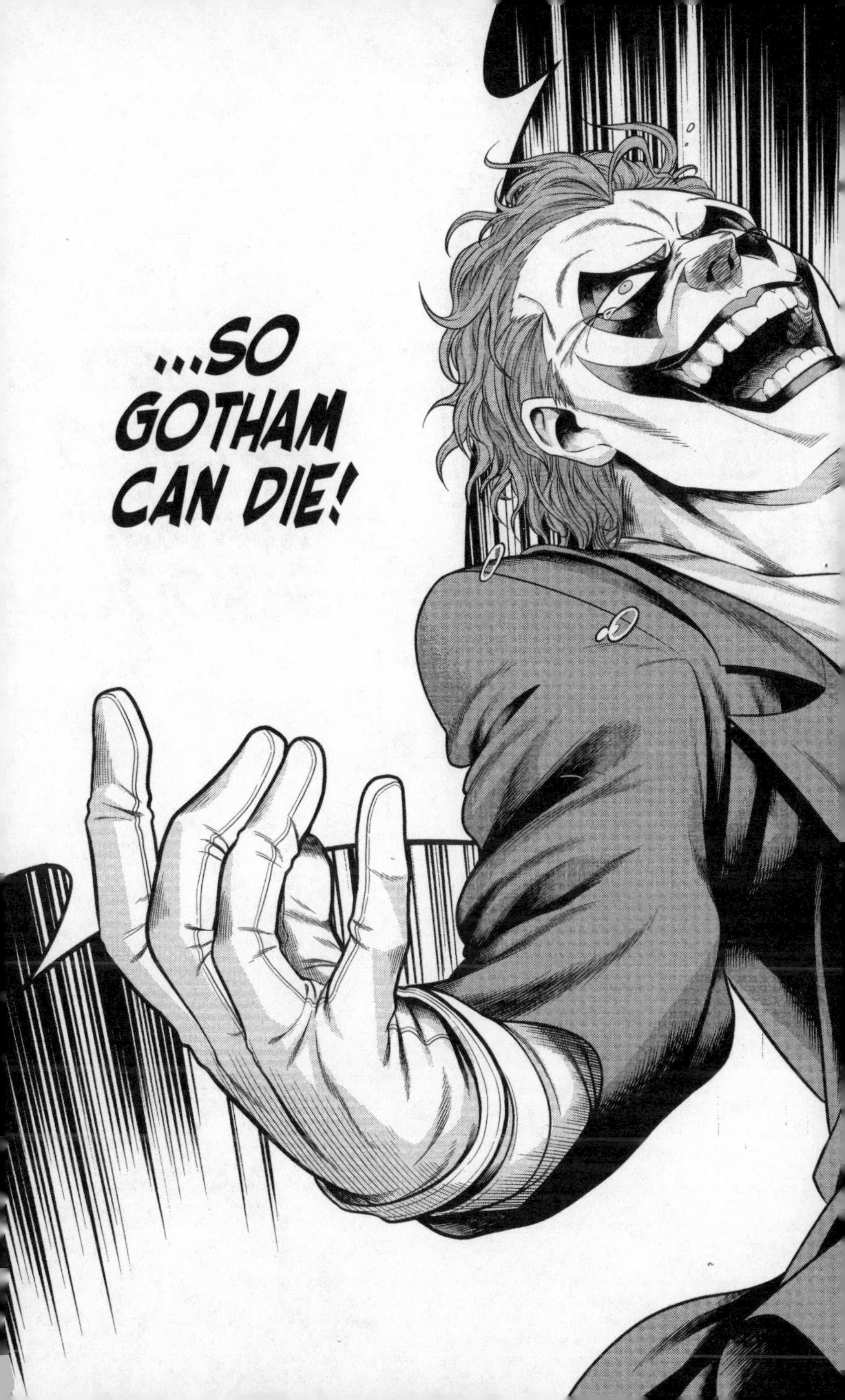
...SO GOTHAM CAN DIE!

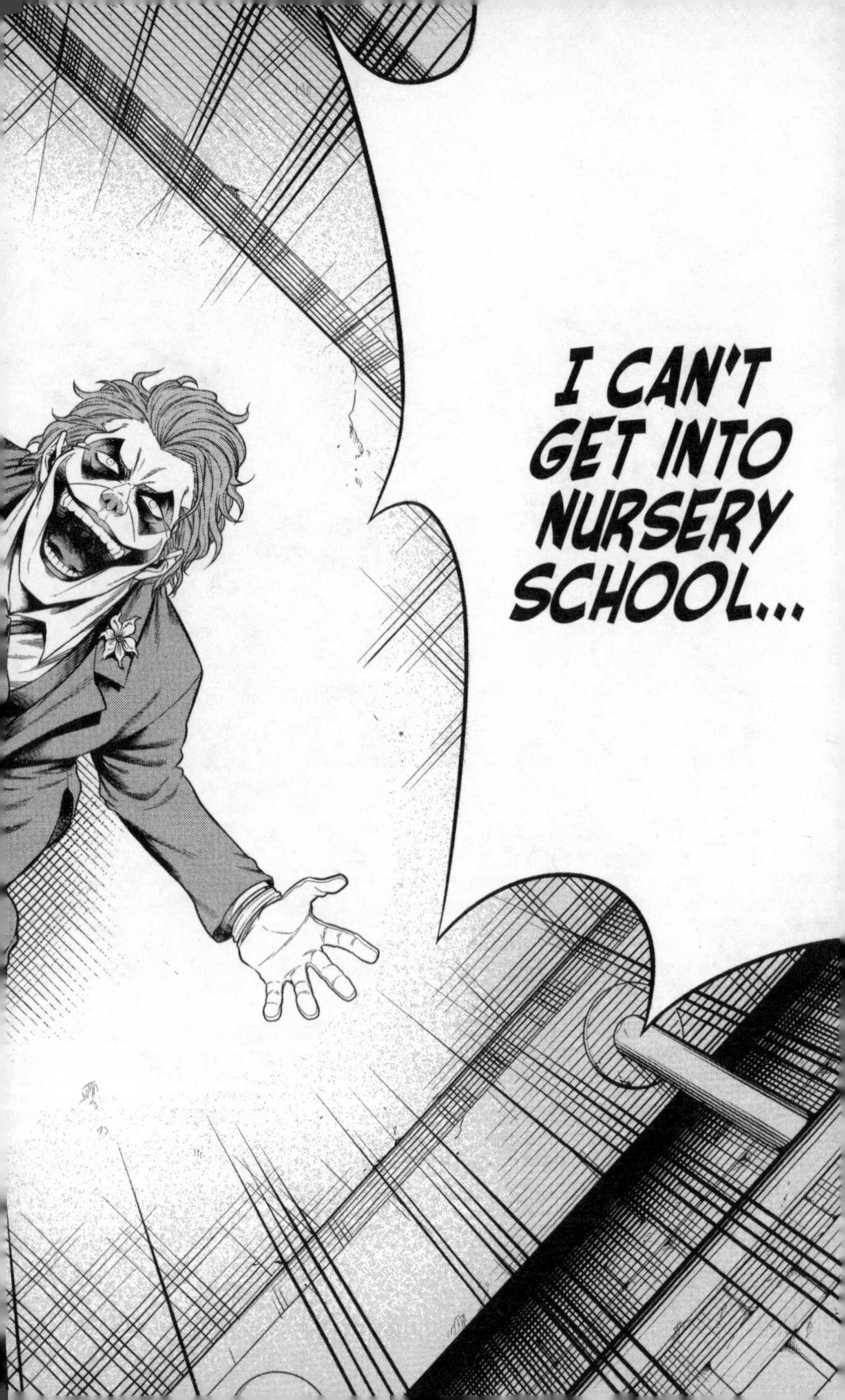
I CAN'T GET INTO NURSERY SCHOOL...

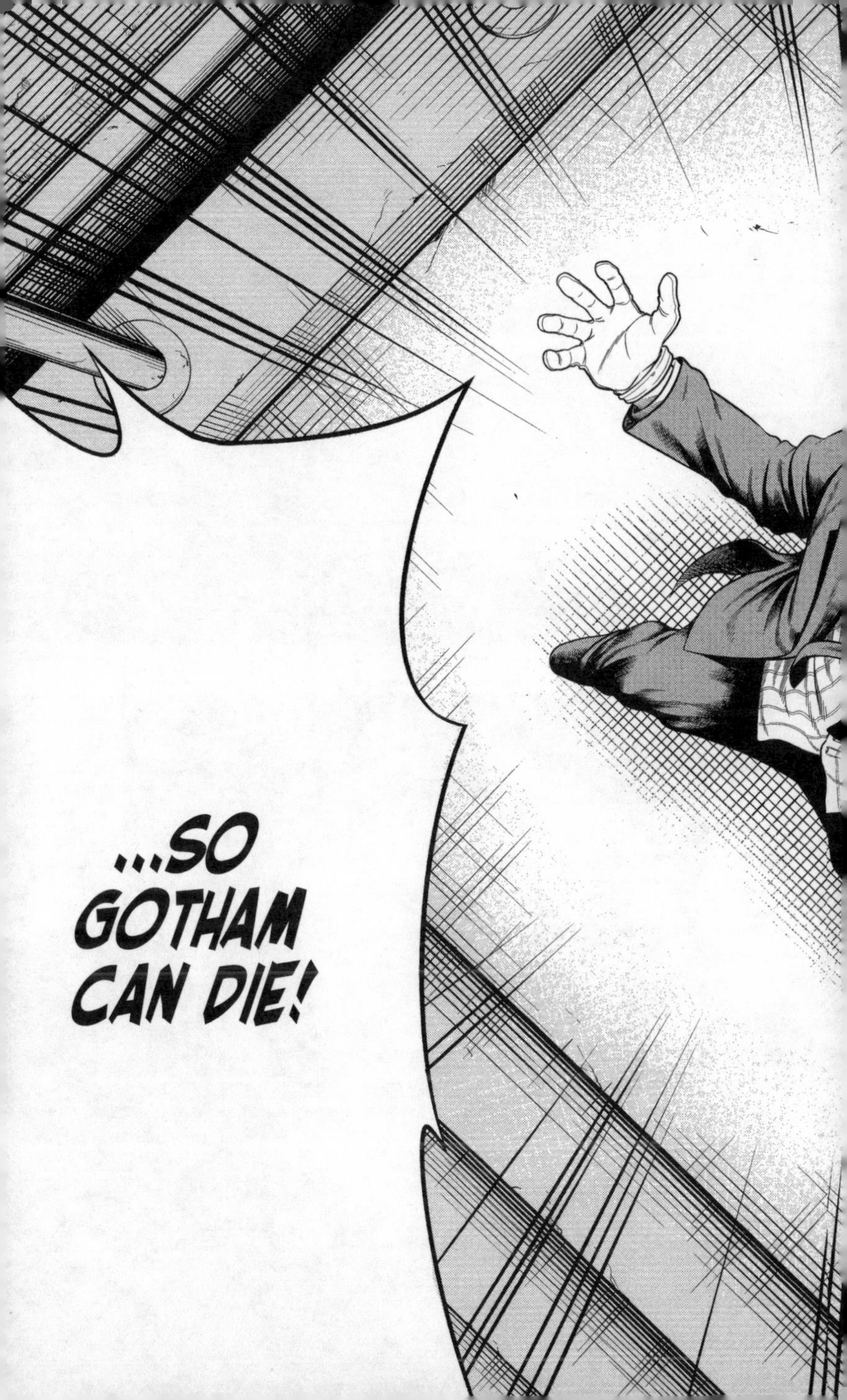
...SO GOTHAM CAN DIE!

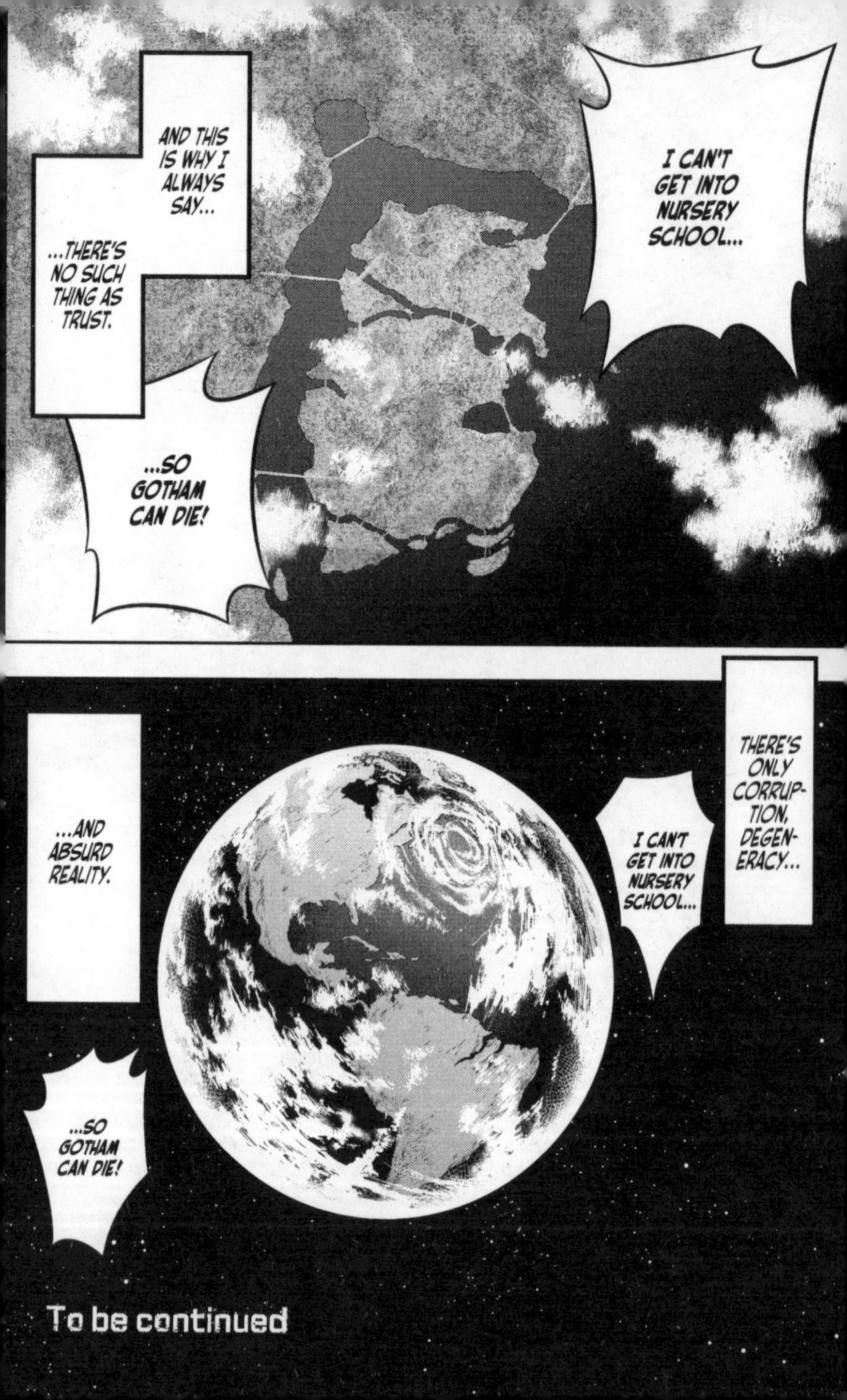
I CAN'T GET INTO NURSERY SCHOOL...
AND THIS IS WHY I ALWAYS SAY...
...THERE'S NO SUCH THING AS TRUST.
...SO GOTHAM CAN DIE!
THERE'S ONLY CORRUPTION, DEGENERACY...
I CAN'T GET INTO NURSERY SCHOOL...
...AND ABSURD REALITY.
...SO GOTHAM CAN DIE!
To be continued

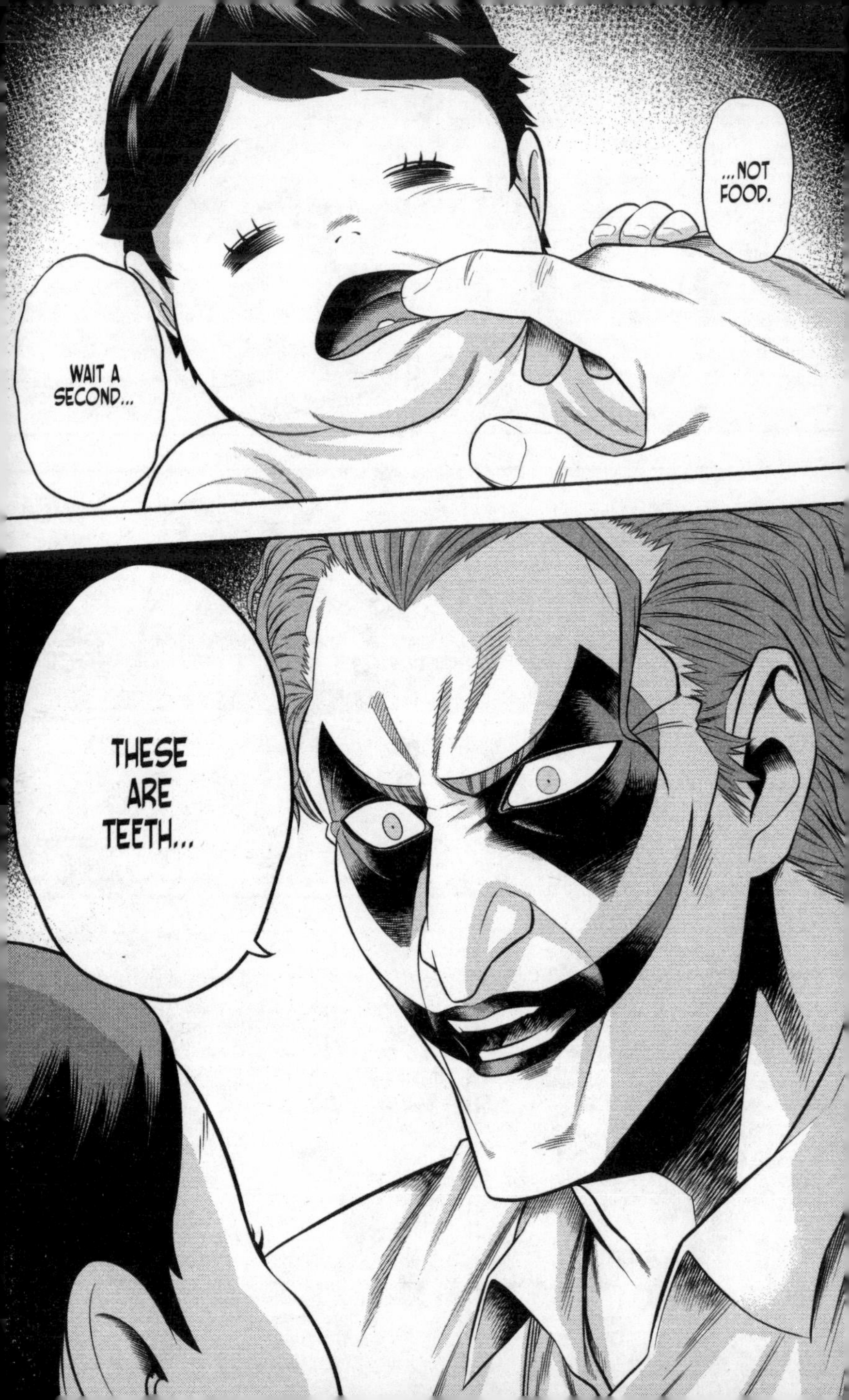
...NOT FOOD.
WAIT A SECOND...
THESE ARE TEETH...

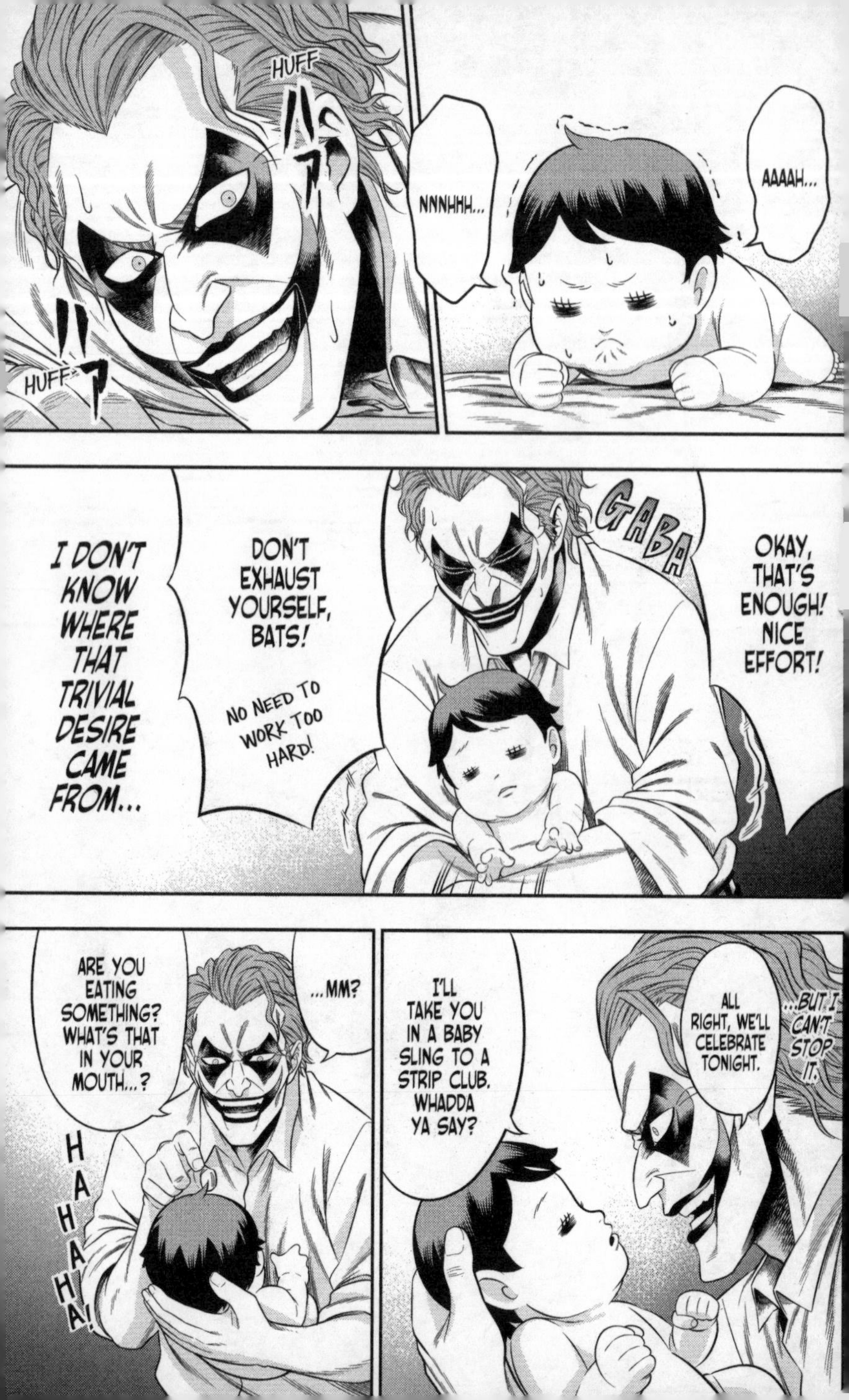
AAAAH...
NNNHHH...
HUFF
HUFF
OKAY, THAT'S ENOUGH! NICE EFFORT!
GABA
DON'T EXHAUST YOURSELF, BATS!
NO NEED TO WORK TOO HARD!
I DON'T KNOW WHERE THAT TRIVIAL DESIRE CAME FROM...
...BUT I CAN'T STOP IT.
ALL RIGHT, WE'LL CELEBRATE TONIGHT.
I'LL TAKE YOU IN A BABY SLING TO A STRIP CLUB. WHADDA YA SAY?
...MM?
ARE YOU EATING SOMETHING? WHAT'S THAT IN YOUR MOUTH...?
HAHAHA!

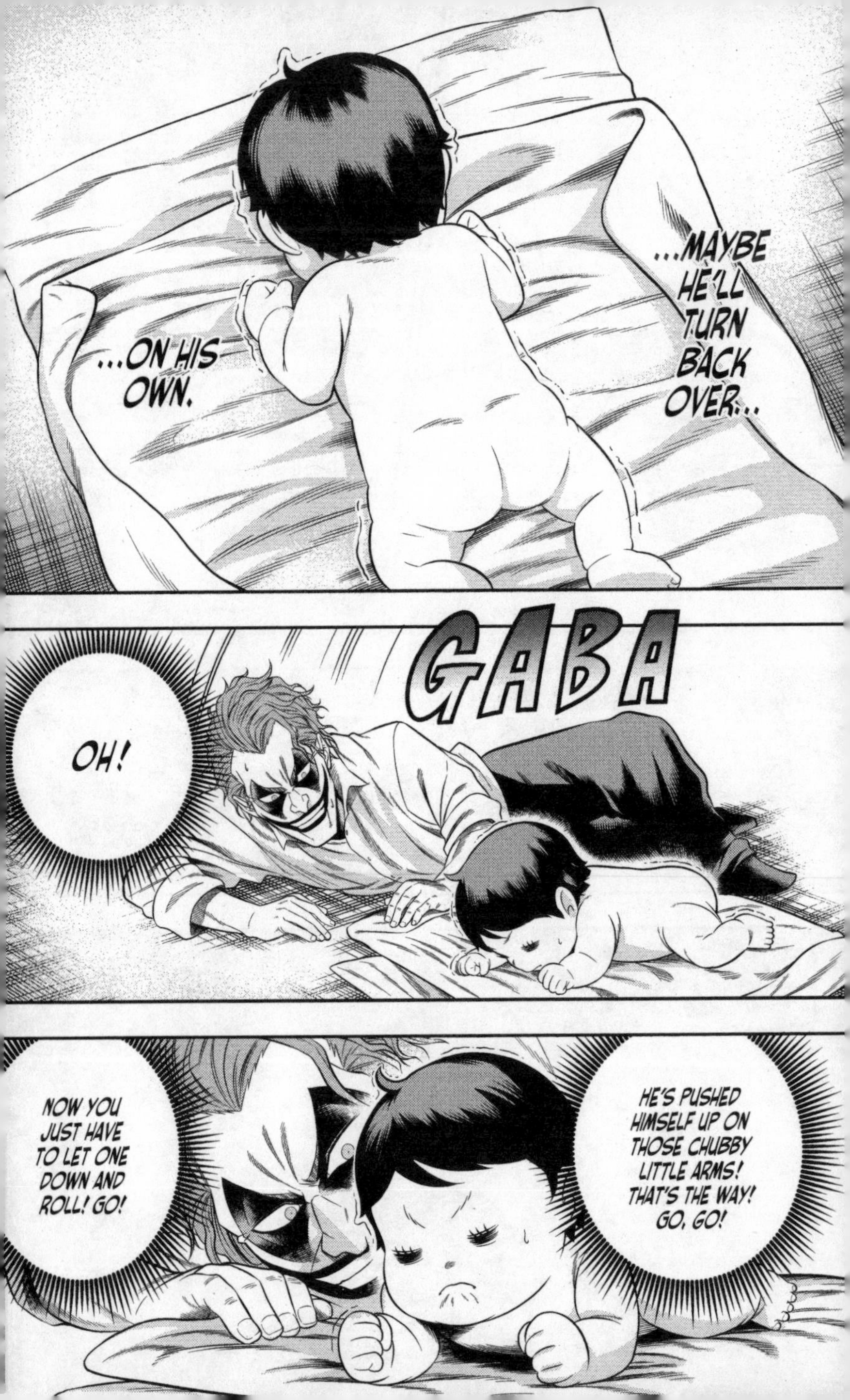
...MAYBE HE'LL TURN BACK OVER...
...ON HIS OWN.
GABA
OH!
HE'S PUSHED HIMSELF UP ON THOSE CHUBBY LITTLE ARMS! THAT'S THE WAY! GO, GO!
NOW YOU JUST HAVE TO LET ONE DOWN AND ROLL! GO!

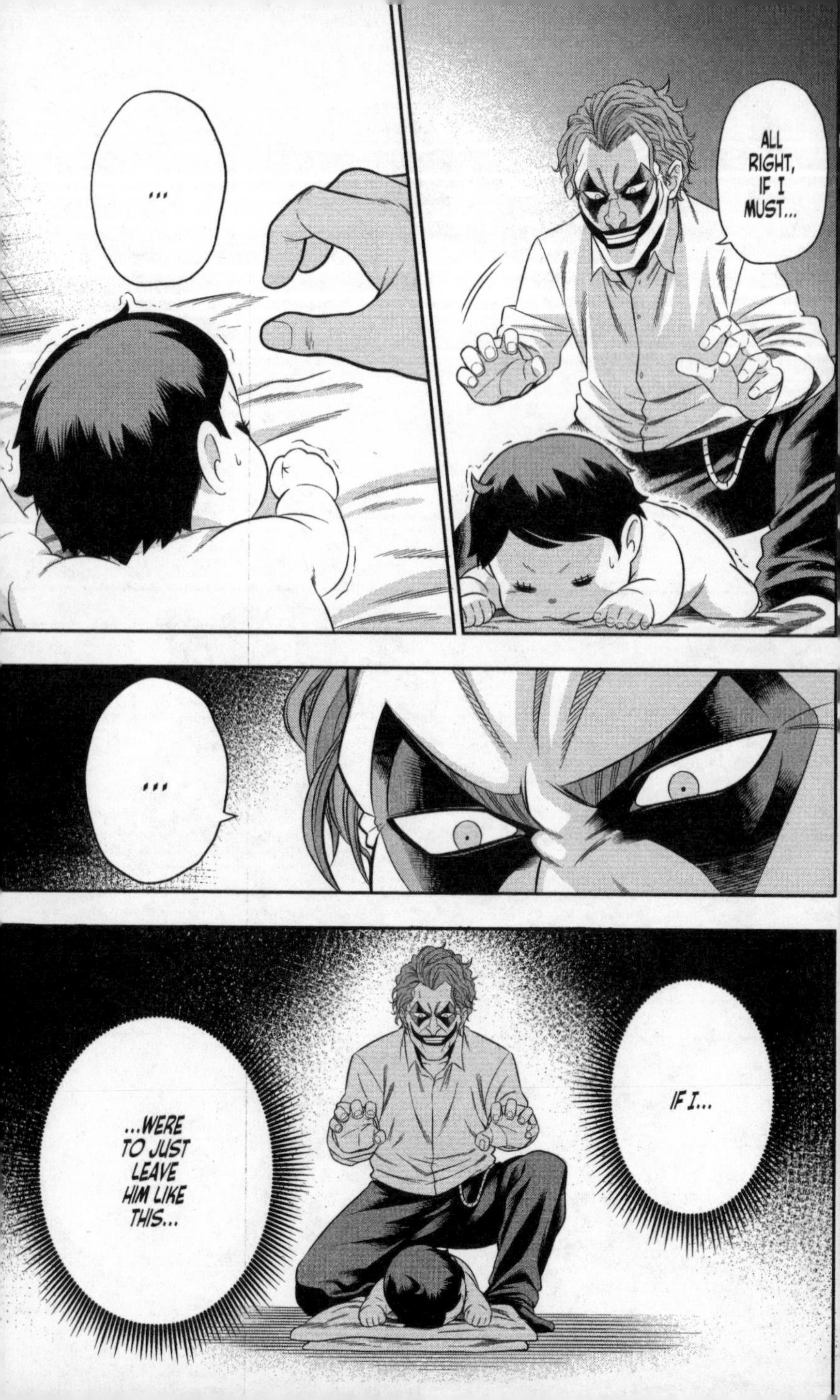
ALL RIGHT, IF I MUST...
...
...
IF I...
...WERE TO JUST LEAVE HIM LIKE THIS...

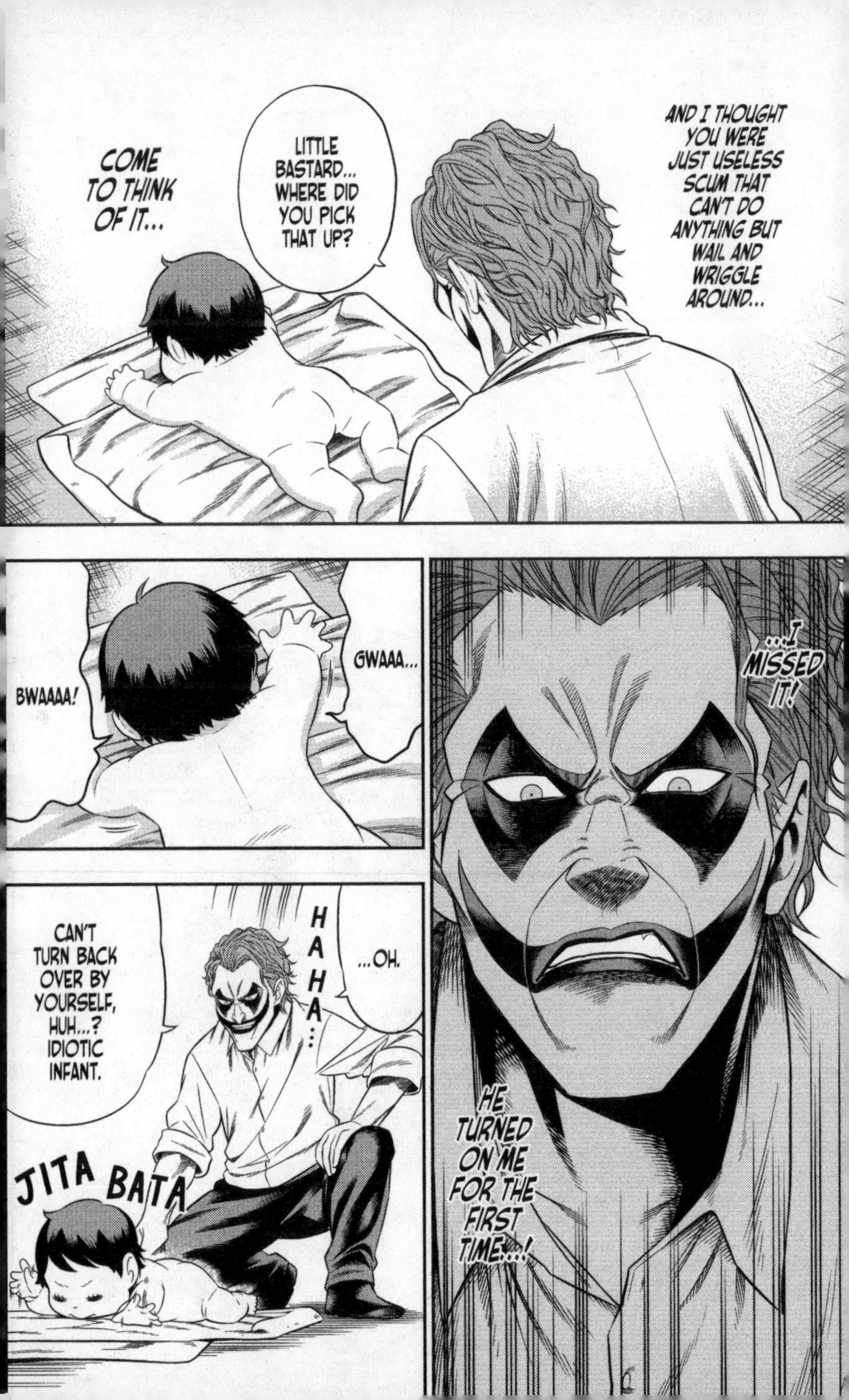
AND I THOUGHT YOU WERE JUST USELESS SCUM THAT CAN'T DO ANYTHING BUT WAIL AND WRIGGLE AROUND...
LITTLE BASTARD... WHERE DID YOU PICK THAT UP?
COME TO THINK OF IT...
...I MISSED IT!
HE TURNED ON ME FOR THE FIRST TIME...!
GWAAA...
BWAAAA!
...OH.
HAHA...
CAN'T TURN BACK OVER BY YOURSELF, HUH...? IDIOTIC INFANT.
JITA BATA

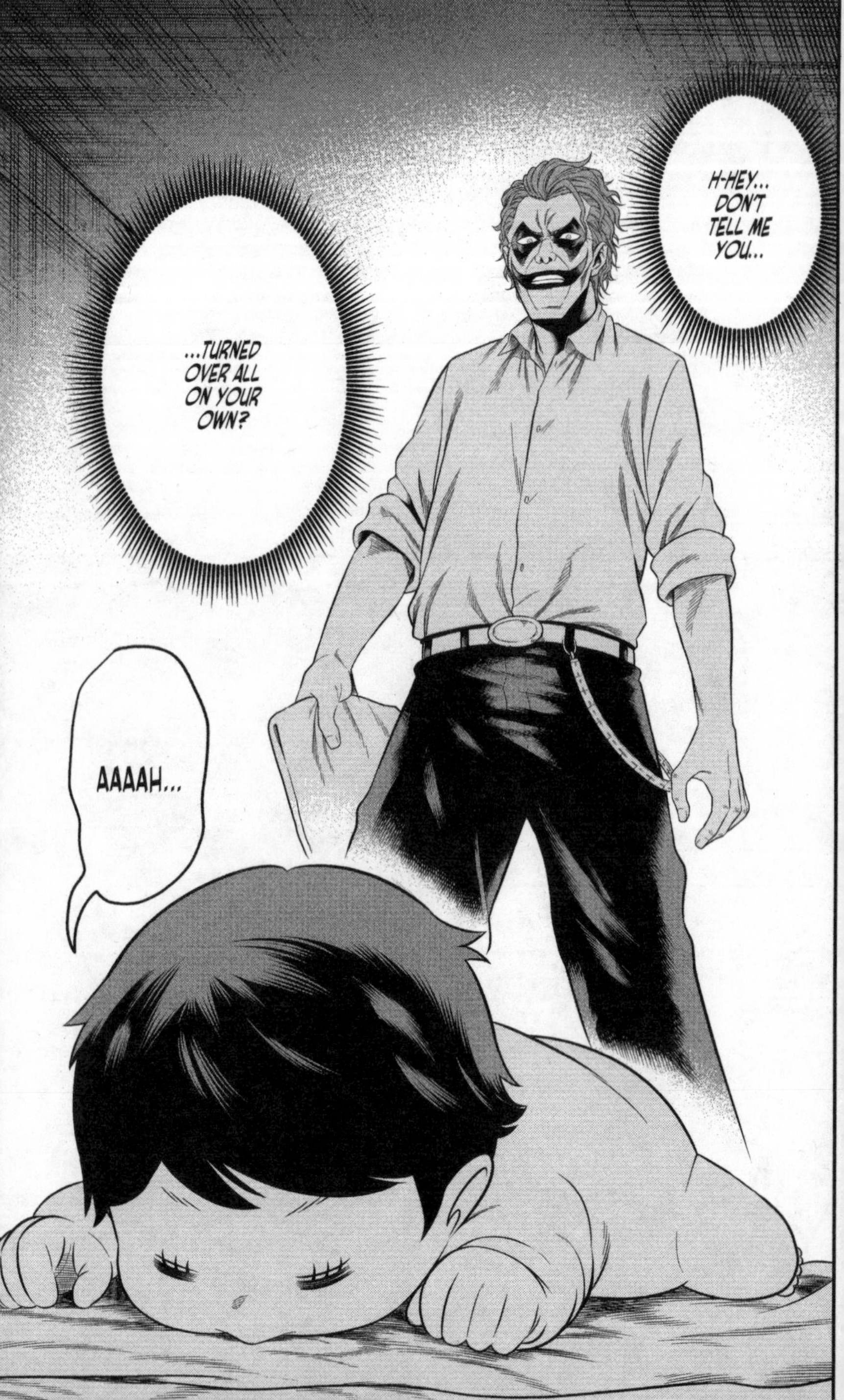
H-HEY... DON'T TELL ME YOU...
...TURNED OVER ALL ON YOUR OWN?
AAAAH...

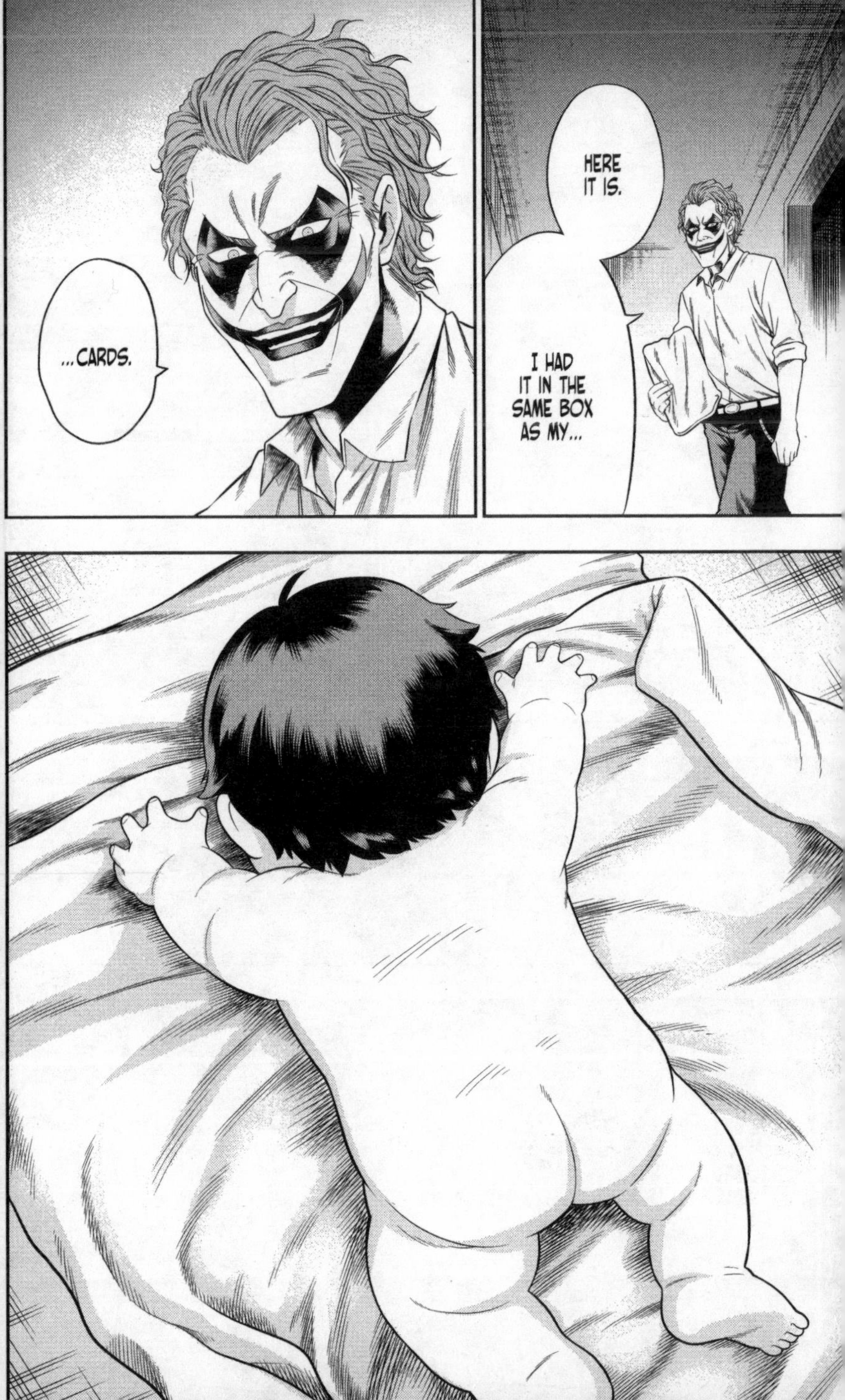
HERE IT IS.
I HAD IT IN THE SAME BOX AS MY...
...CARDS.

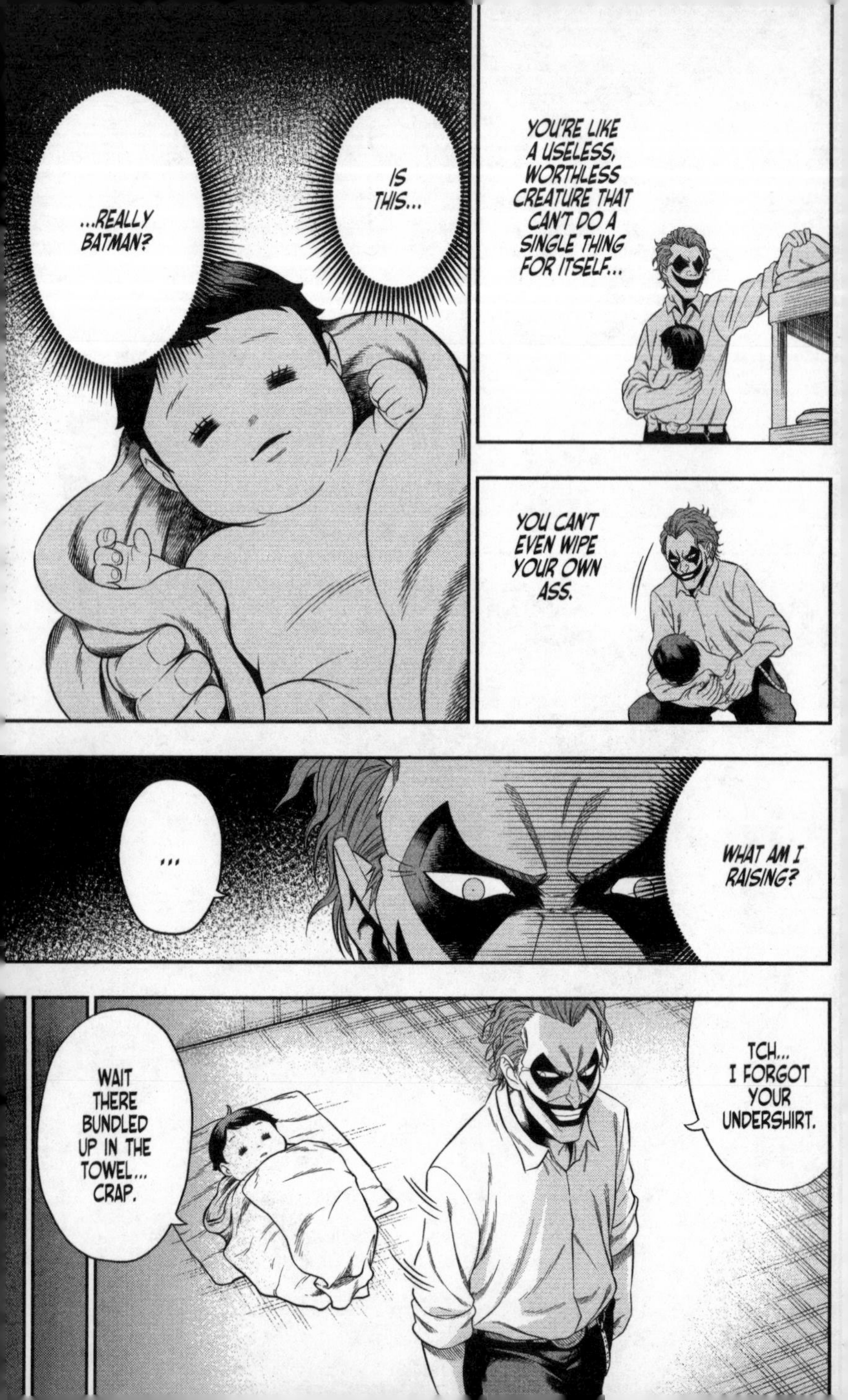
YOU'RE LIKE A USELESS, WORTHLESS CREATURE THAT CAN'T DO A SINGLE THING FOR ITSELF...
YOU CAN'T EVEN WIPE YOUR OWN ASS.
IS THIS...
...REALLY BATMAN?
WHAT AM I RAISING?
...
TCH... I FORGOT YOUR UNDERSHIRT.
WAIT THERE BUNDLED UP IN THE TOWEL... CRAP.

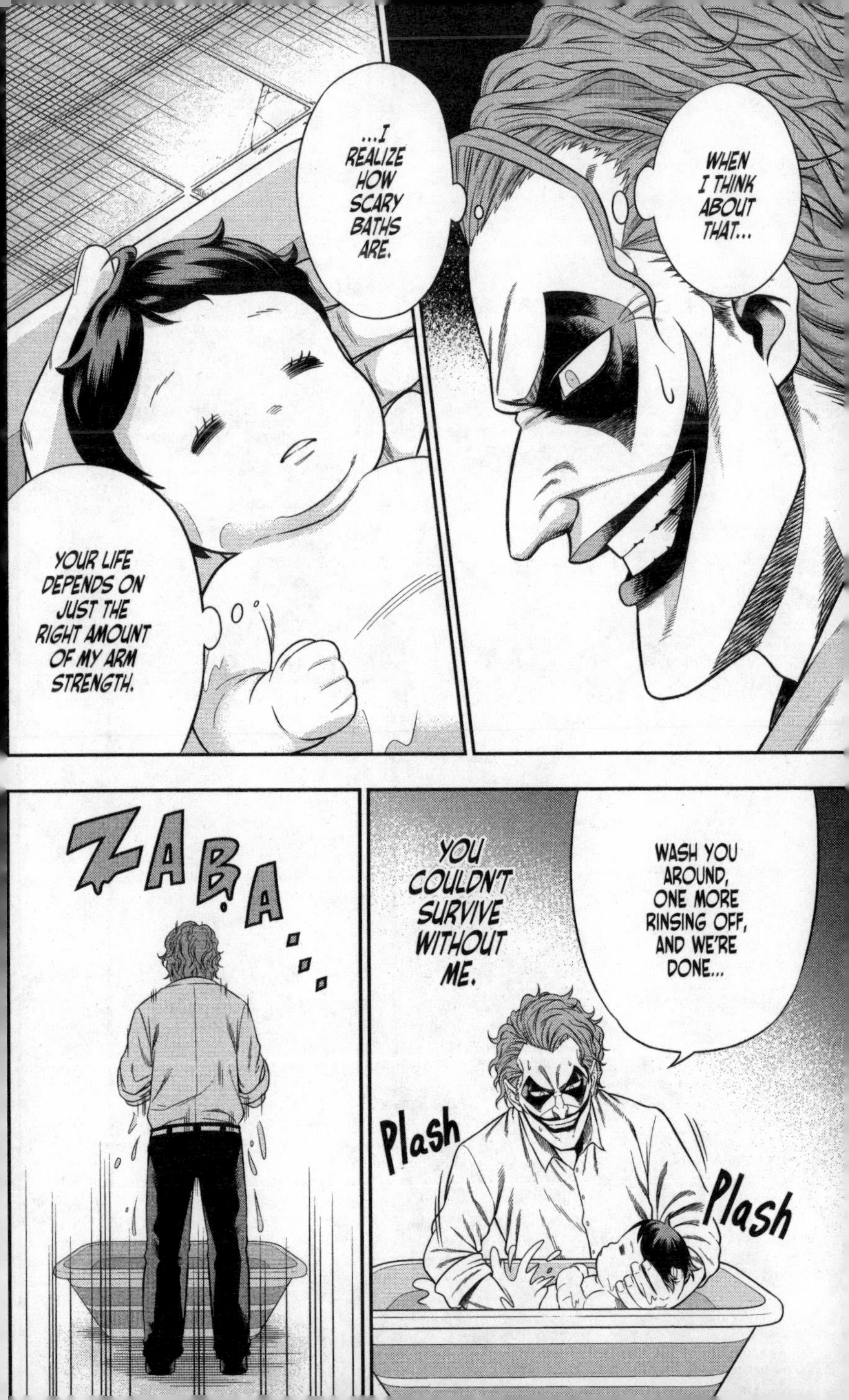
WHEN I THINK ABOUT THAT...
...I REALIZE HOW SCARY BATHS ARE.
YOUR LIFE DEPENDS ON JUST THE RIGHT AMOUNT OF MY ARM STRENGTH.
WASH YOU AROUND, ONE MORE RINSING OFF, AND WE'RE DONE...
YOU COULDN'T SURVIVE WITHOUT ME.
Plash
Plash
ZABA...

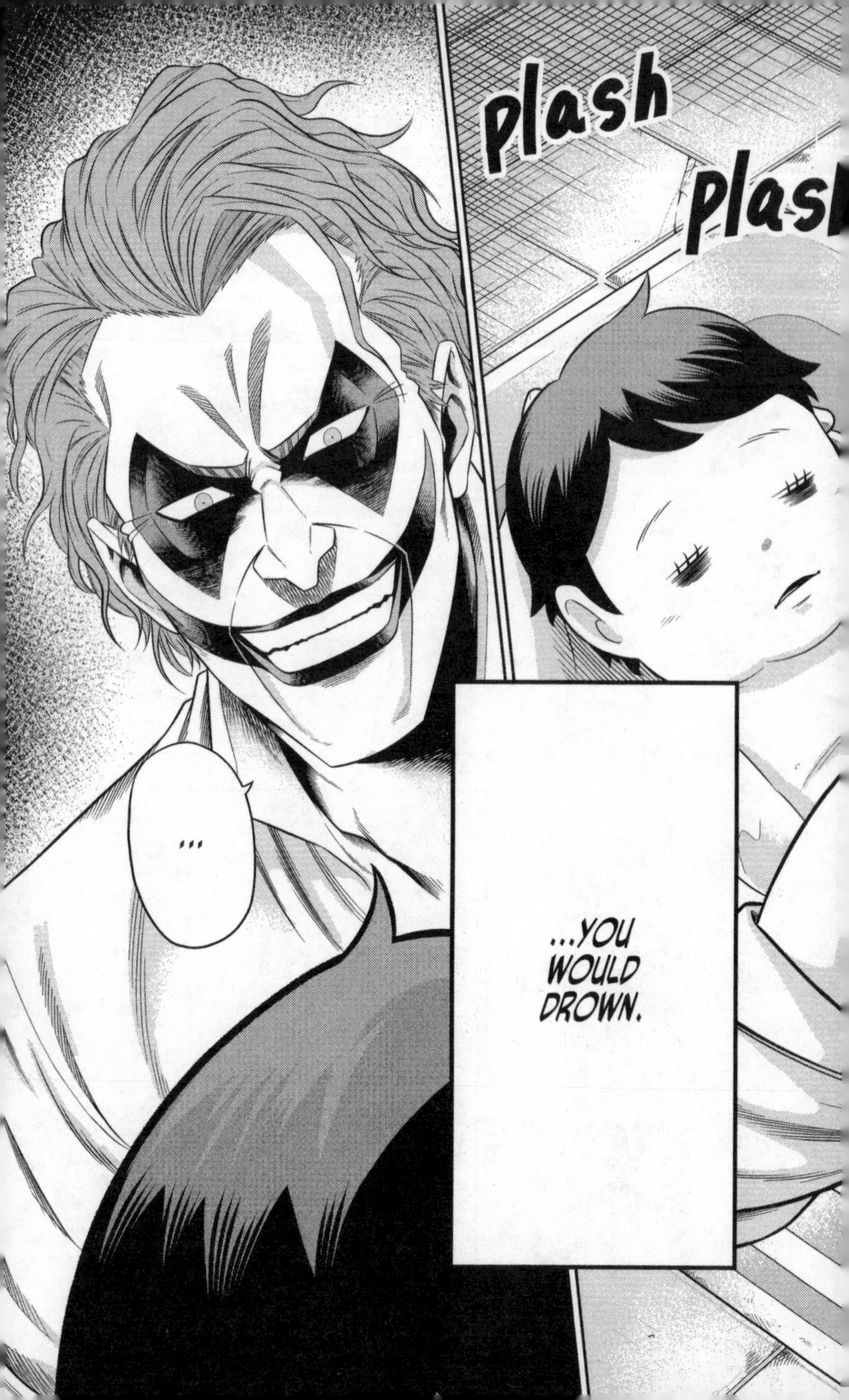
Plash
Plas
...YOU WOULD DROWN.
...

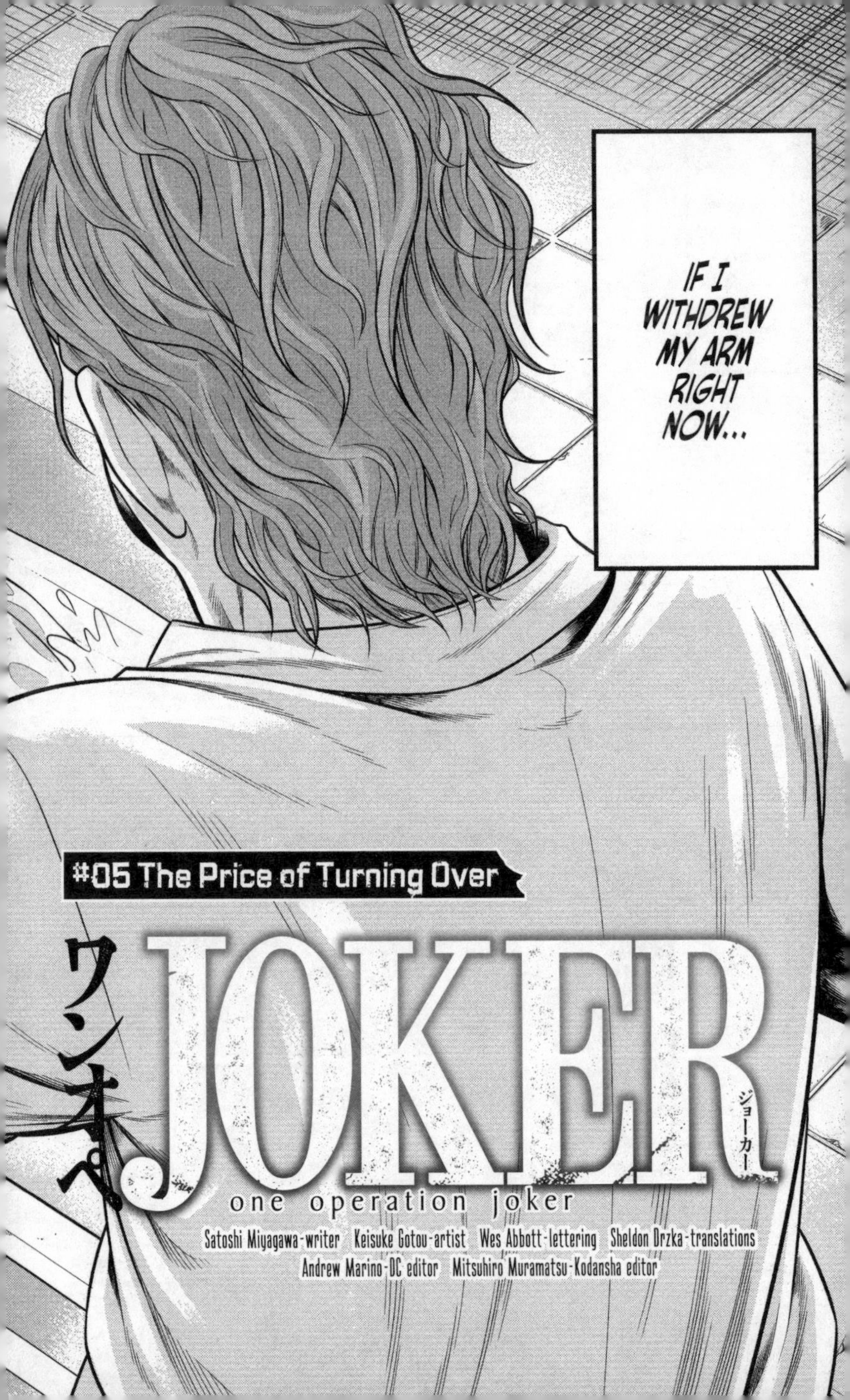
IF I WITHDREW MY ARM RIGHT NOW...
#05 The Price of Turning Over
ワンオペ JOKER ジョーカー
one operation joker
Satoshi Miyagawa-writer Keisuke Gotou-artist Wes Abbott-lettering Sheldon Drzka-translations
Andrew Marino-DC editor Mitsuhiro Muramatsu-Kodansha editor

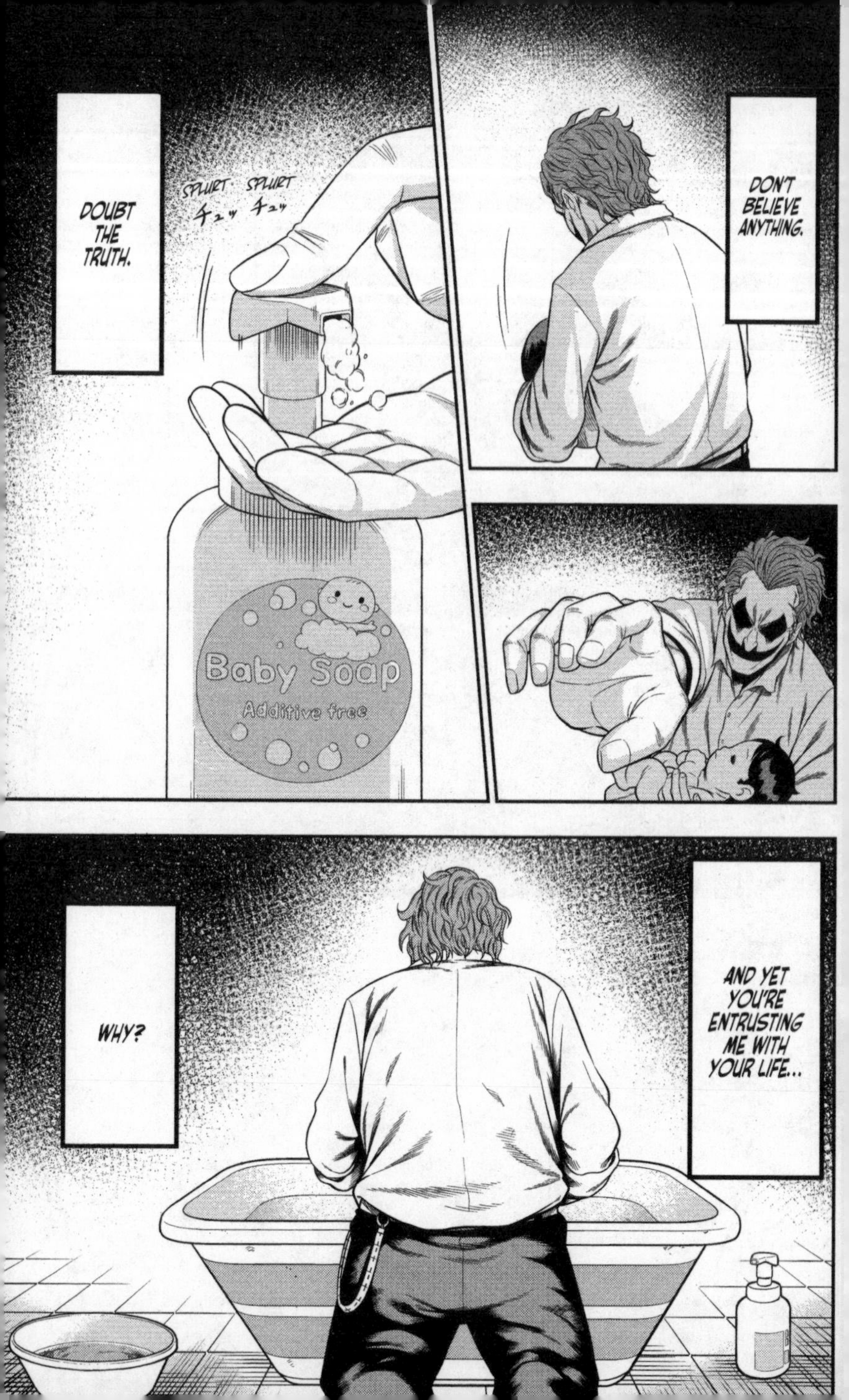
DON'T BELIEVE ANYTHING.
DOUBT THE TRUTH.
SPLURT SPLURT
チュッ チュッ
Baby Soap
Additive free
AND YET YOU'RE ENTRUSTING ME WITH YOUR LIFE...
WHY?

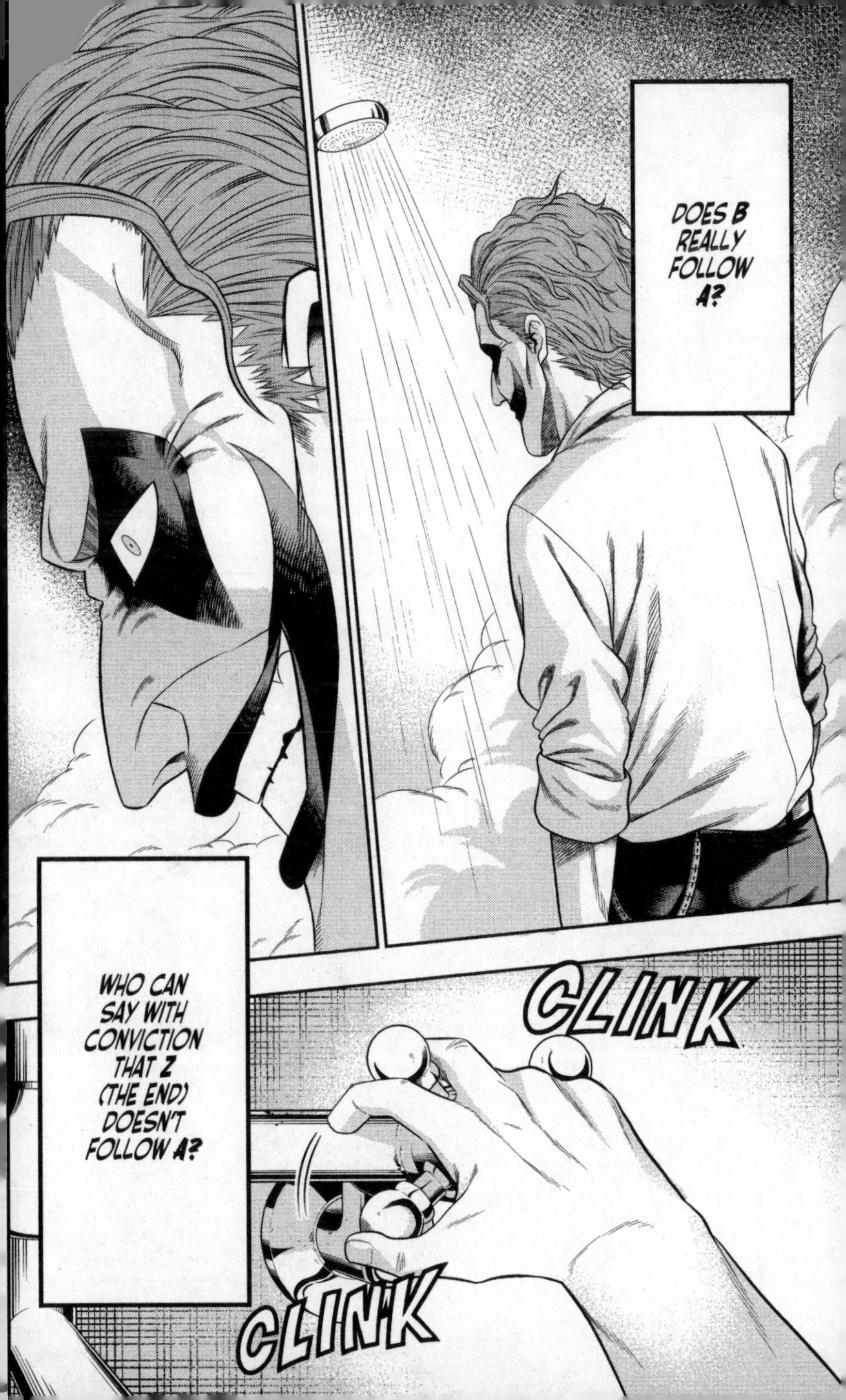
DOES B REALLY FOLLOW A?
CLINK
WHO CAN SAY WITH CONVICTION THAT Z (THE END) DOESN'T FOLLOW A?
CLINK

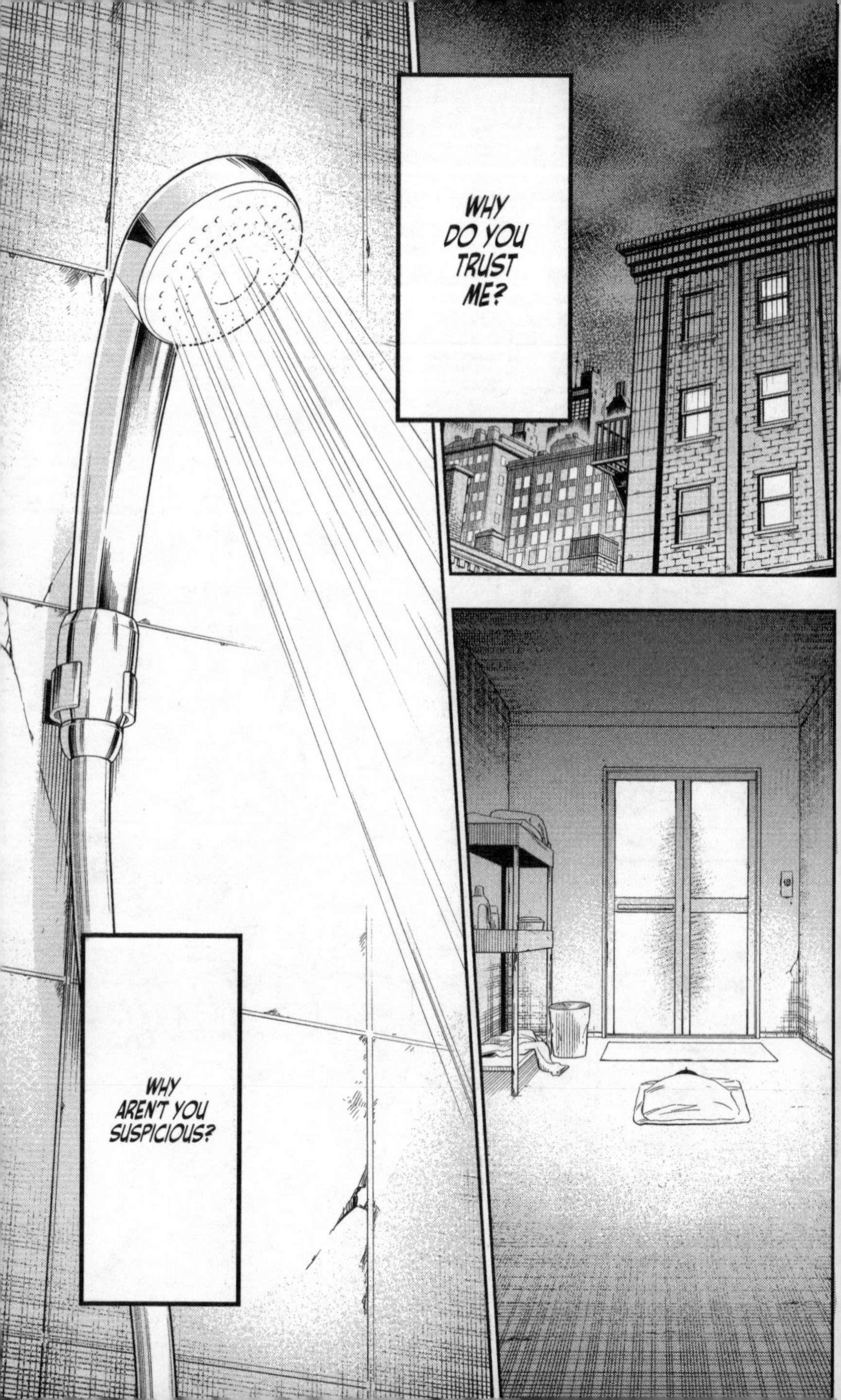
WHY DO YOU TRUST ME?
WHY AREN'T YOU SUSPICIOUS?

ワンオペ JOKER

one operation joker vol. 1

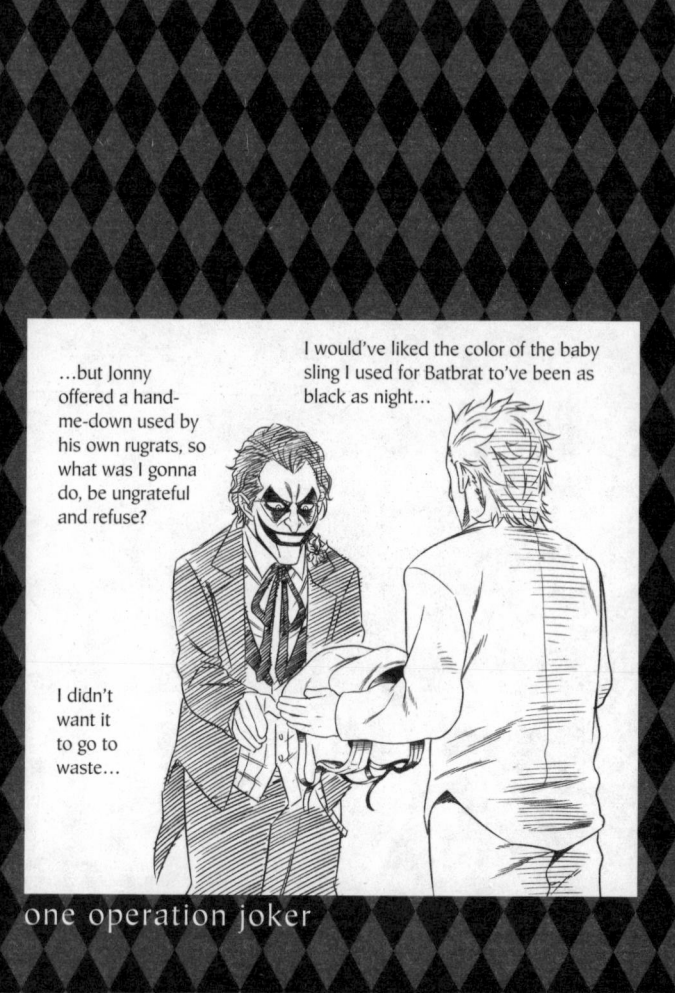

I would've liked the color of the baby sling I used for Batbrat to've been as black as night...
...but Jonny offered a hand-me-down used by his own rugrats, so what was I gonna do, be ungrateful and refuse?
I didn't want it to go to waste...

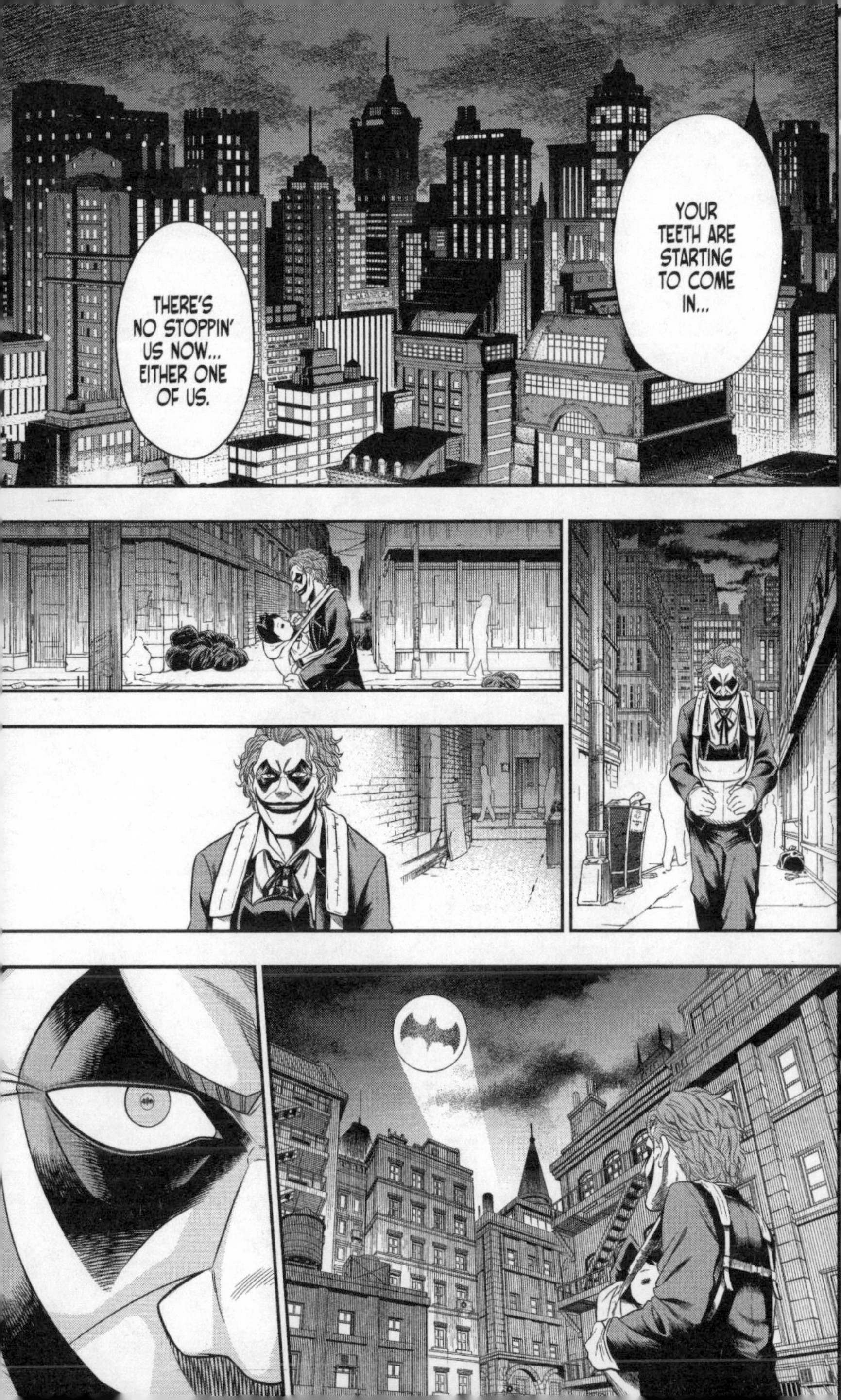
YOUR TEETH ARE STARTING TO COME IN...
THERE'S NO STOPPIN' US NOW... EITHER ONE OF US.

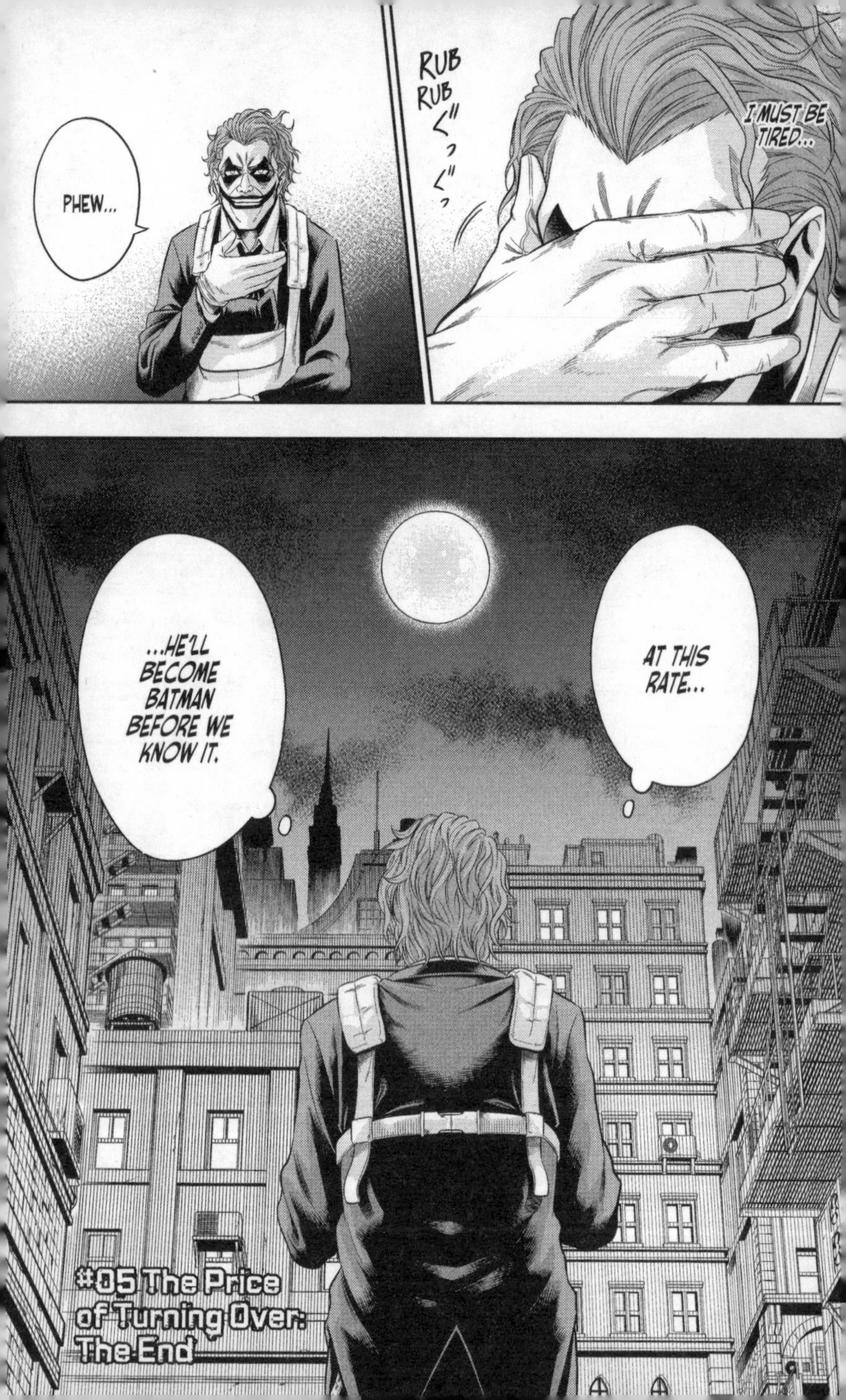
I MUST BE TIRED...
RUB RUB
ぐっぐっ
PHEW...
AT THIS RATE...
...HE'LL BECOME BATMAN BEFORE WE KNOW IT.
#05 The Price of Turning Over: The End

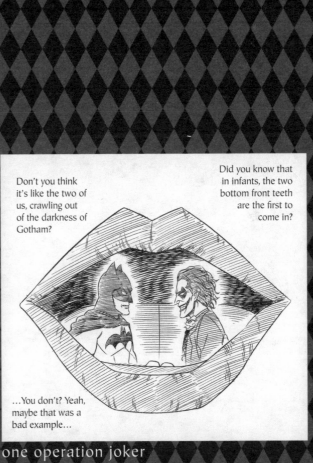

Did you know that in infants, the two bottom front teeth are the first to come in?
Don't you think it's like the two of us, crawling out of the darkness of Gotham?
...You don't? Yeah, maybe that was a bad example...

one operation joker

ワンオペ**JOKER**

one operation joker   vol. 1

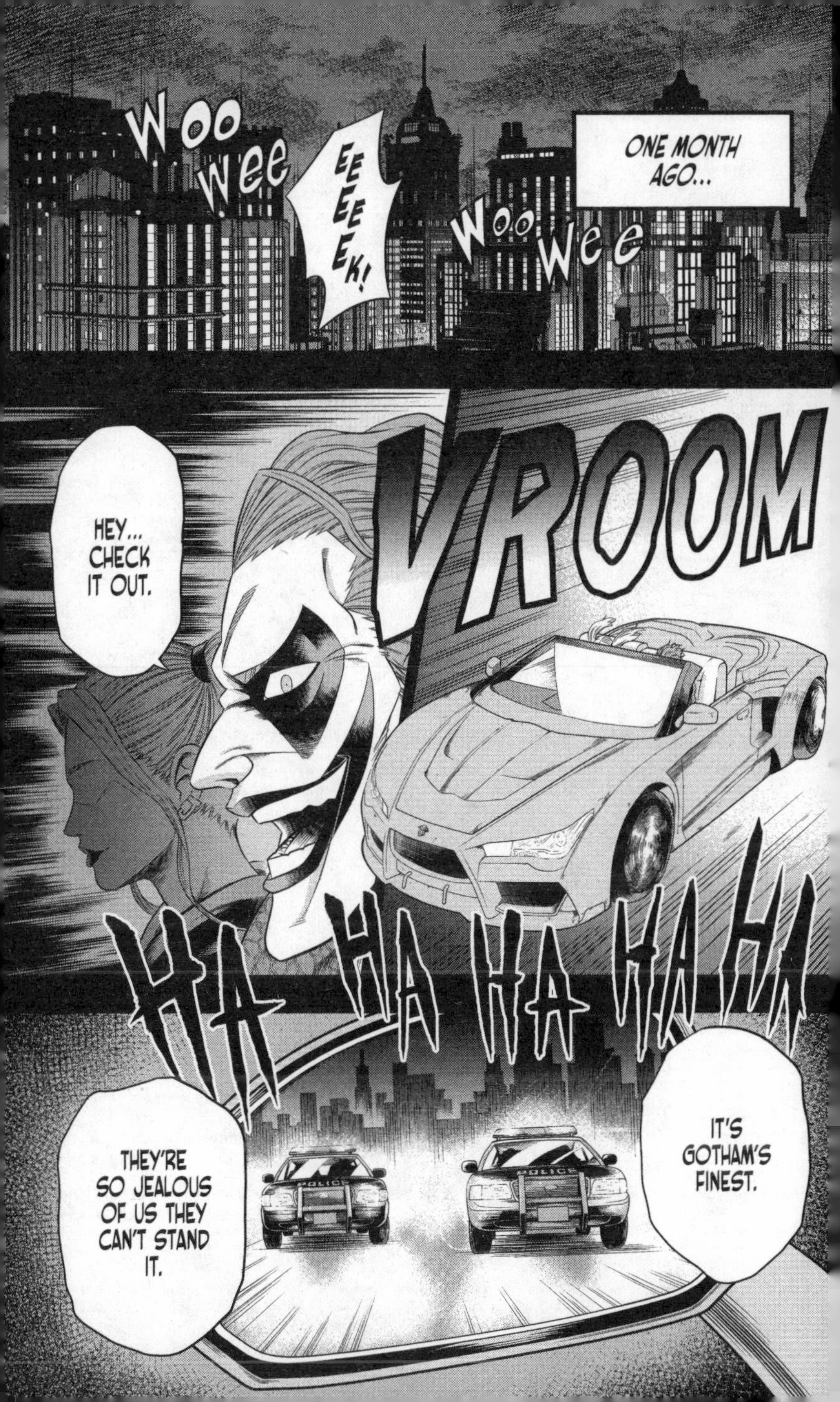
ONE MONTH AGO...
WOO WEE
EEEEEK!
WOO WEE
VROOM
HEY... CHECK IT OUT.
HA HA HA HA HA
IT'S GOTHAM'S FINEST.
THEY'RE SO JEALOUS OF US THEY CAN'T STAND IT.

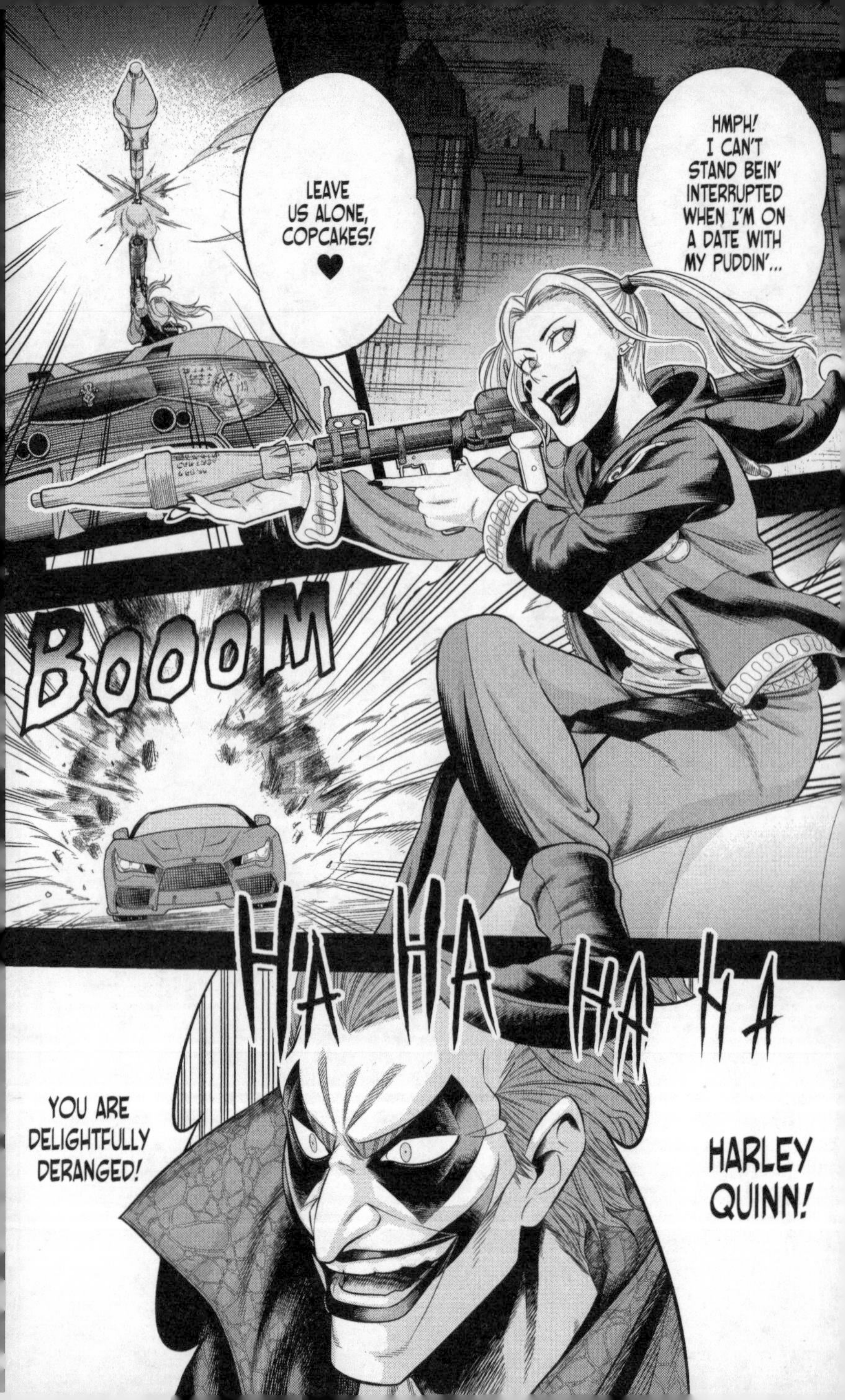
HMPH! I CAN'T STAND BEIN' INTERRUPTED WHEN I'M ON A DATE WITH MY PUDDIN'...
LEAVE US ALONE, COPCAKES! ♥
BOOOM
HA HA HA HA
HARLEY QUINN!
YOU ARE DELIGHTFULLY DERANGED!

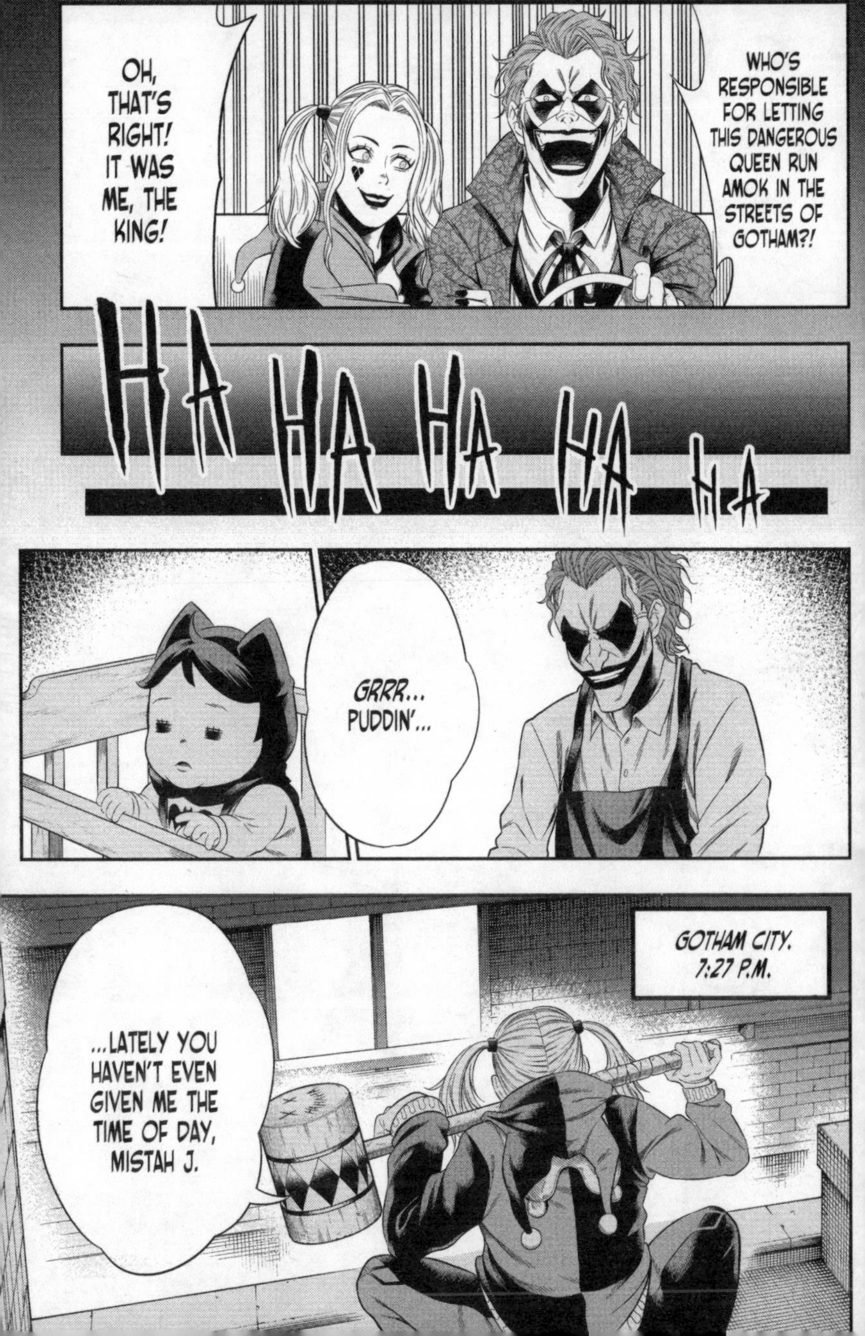
WHO'S RESPONSIBLE FOR LETTING THIS DANGEROUS QUEEN RUN AMOK IN THE STREETS OF GOTHAM?!
OH, THAT'S RIGHT! IT WAS ME, THE KING!
HA HA HA HA HA
GRRR... PUDDIN'...
GOTHAM CITY. 7:27 P.M.
...LATELY YOU HAVEN'T EVEN GIVEN ME THE TIME OF DAY, MISTAH J.

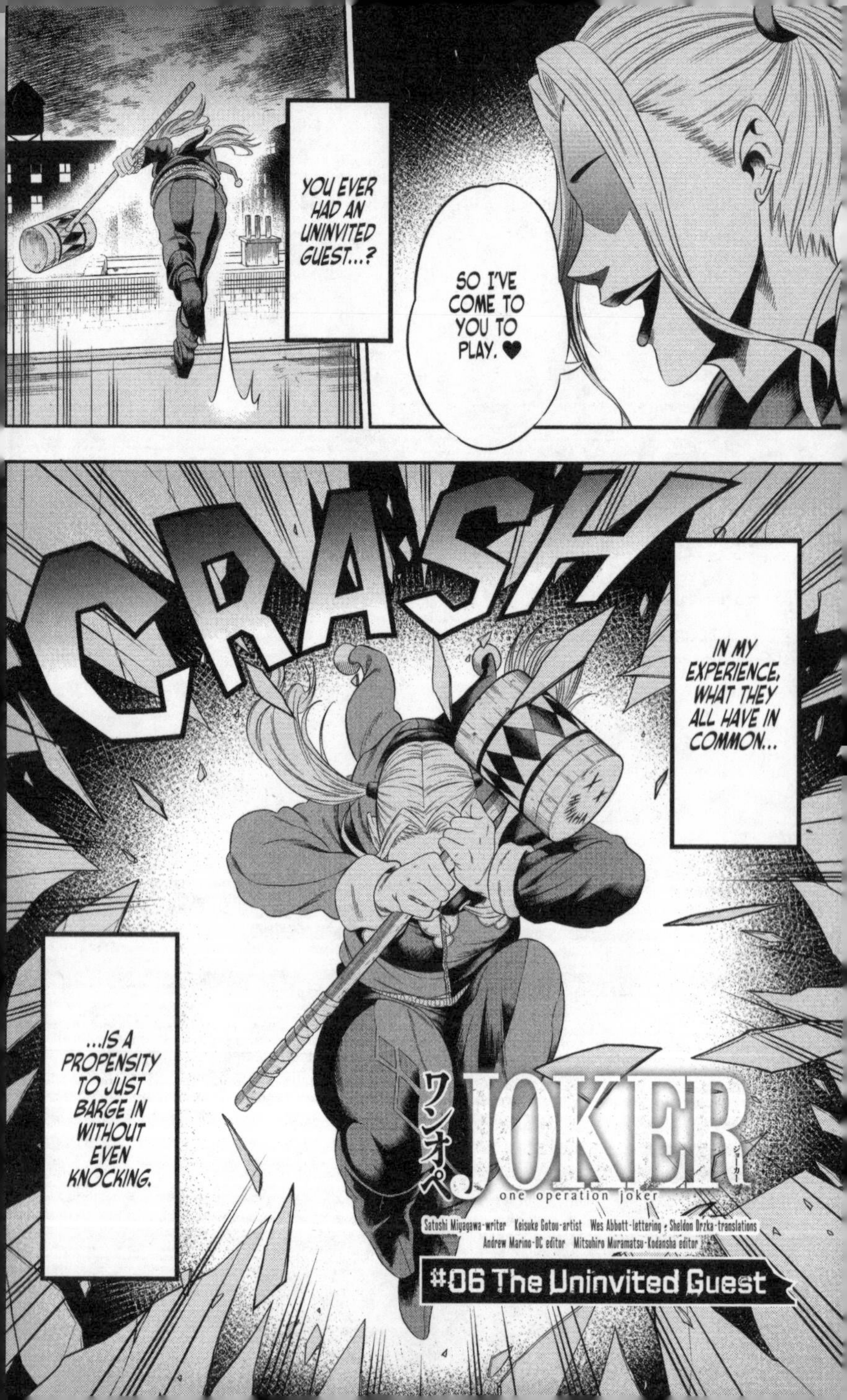
YOU EVER HAD AN UNINVITED GUEST...?
SO I'VE COME TO YOU TO PLAY. ♥
CRASH
IN MY EXPERIENCE, WHAT THEY ALL HAVE IN COMMON...
...IS A PROPENSITY TO JUST BARGE IN WITHOUT EVEN KNOCKING.
ワンオペ JOKER ジョーカー
one operation joker
Satoshi Miyagawa-writer Keisuke Gotou-artist Wes Abbott-lettering Sheldon Drzka-translations
Andrew Marino-DC editor Mitsuhiro Muramatsu-Kodansha editor
#06 The Uninvited Guest

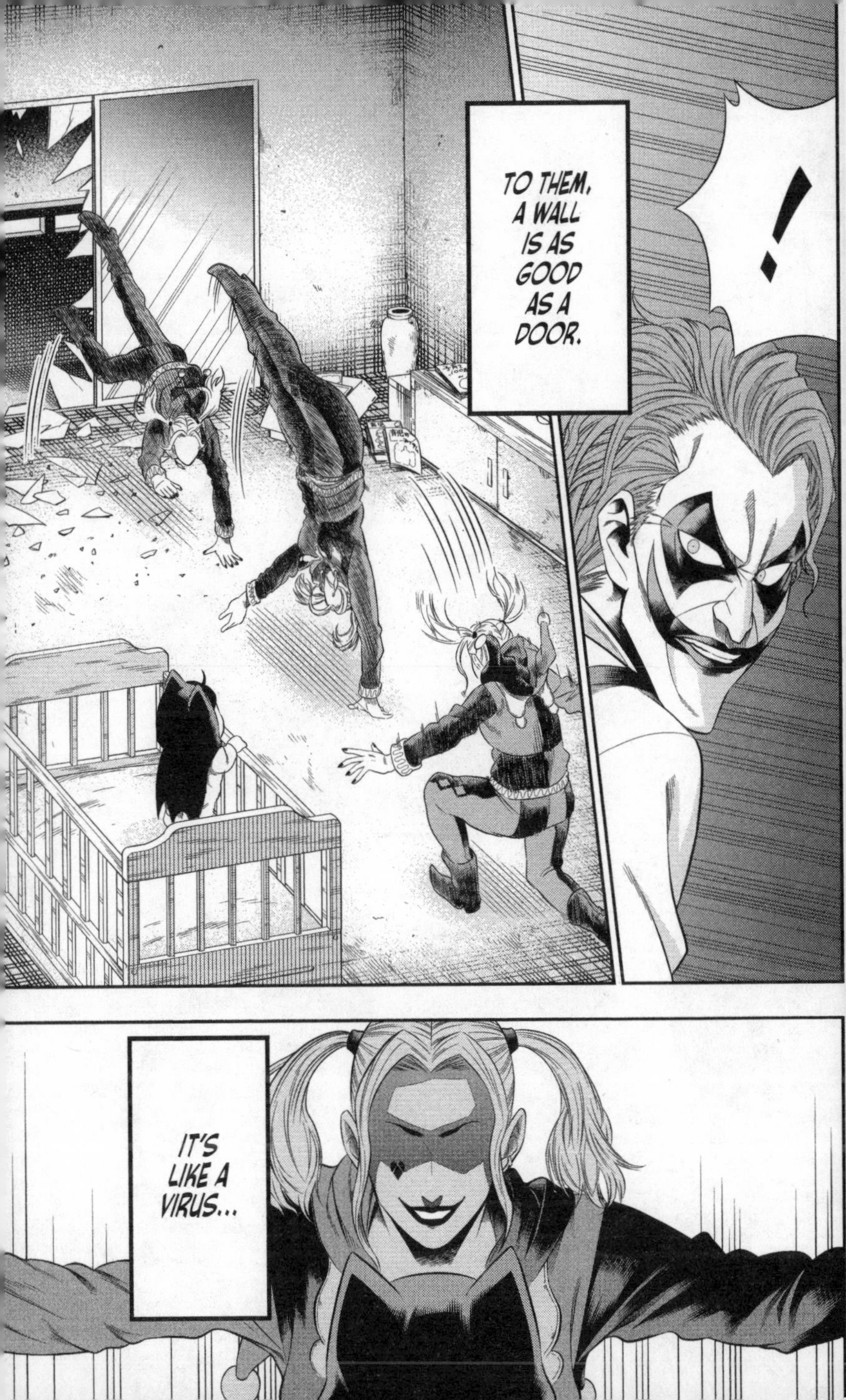
!
TO THEM, A WALL IS AS GOOD AS A DOOR.
IT'S LIKE A VIRUS...

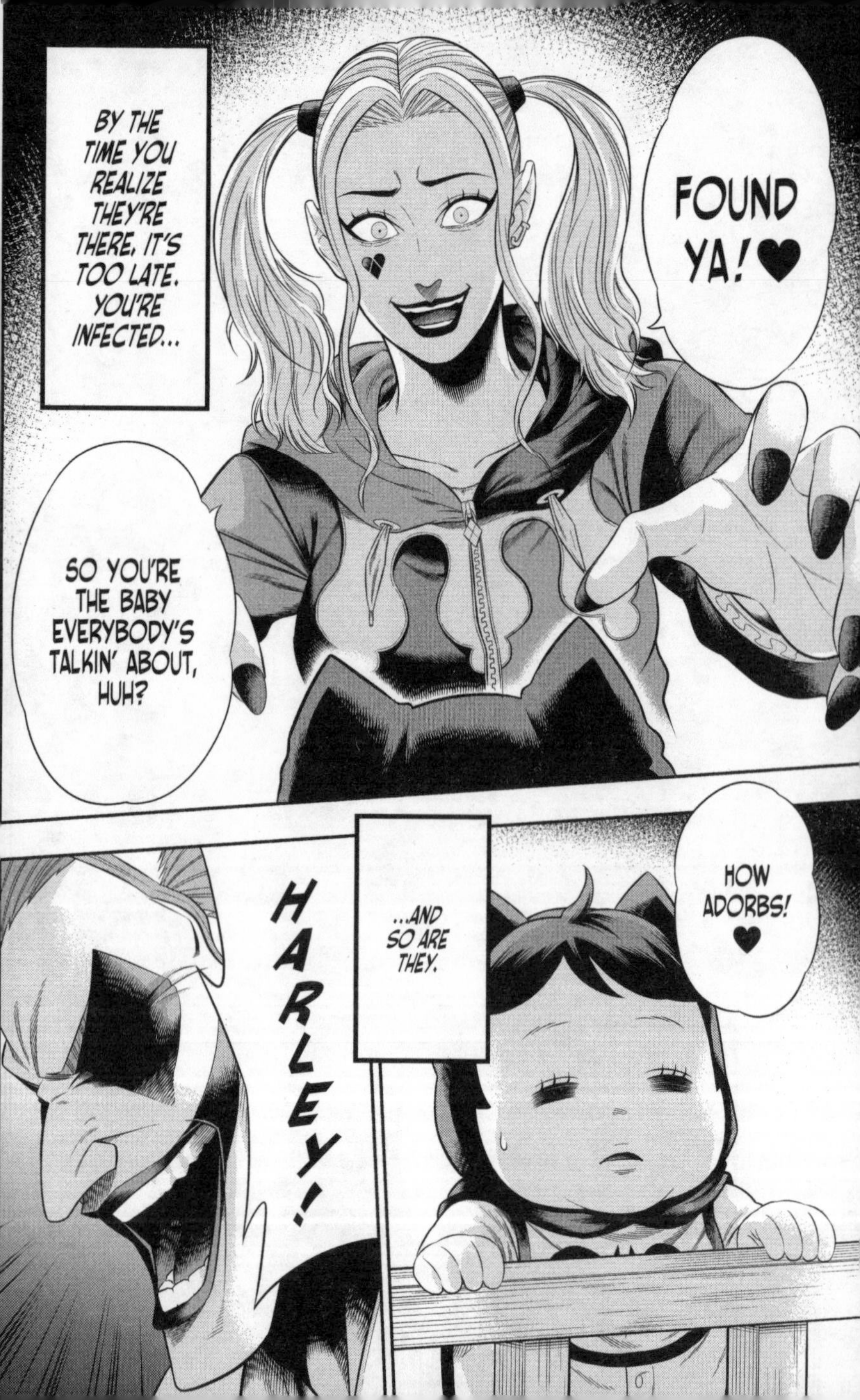
FOUND YA! ♥
BY THE TIME YOU REALIZE THEY'RE THERE, IT'S TOO LATE. YOU'RE INFECTED...
SO YOU'RE THE BABY EVERYBODY'S TALKIN' ABOUT, HUH?
HOW ADORBS! ♥
...AND SO ARE THEY.
HARLEY!!

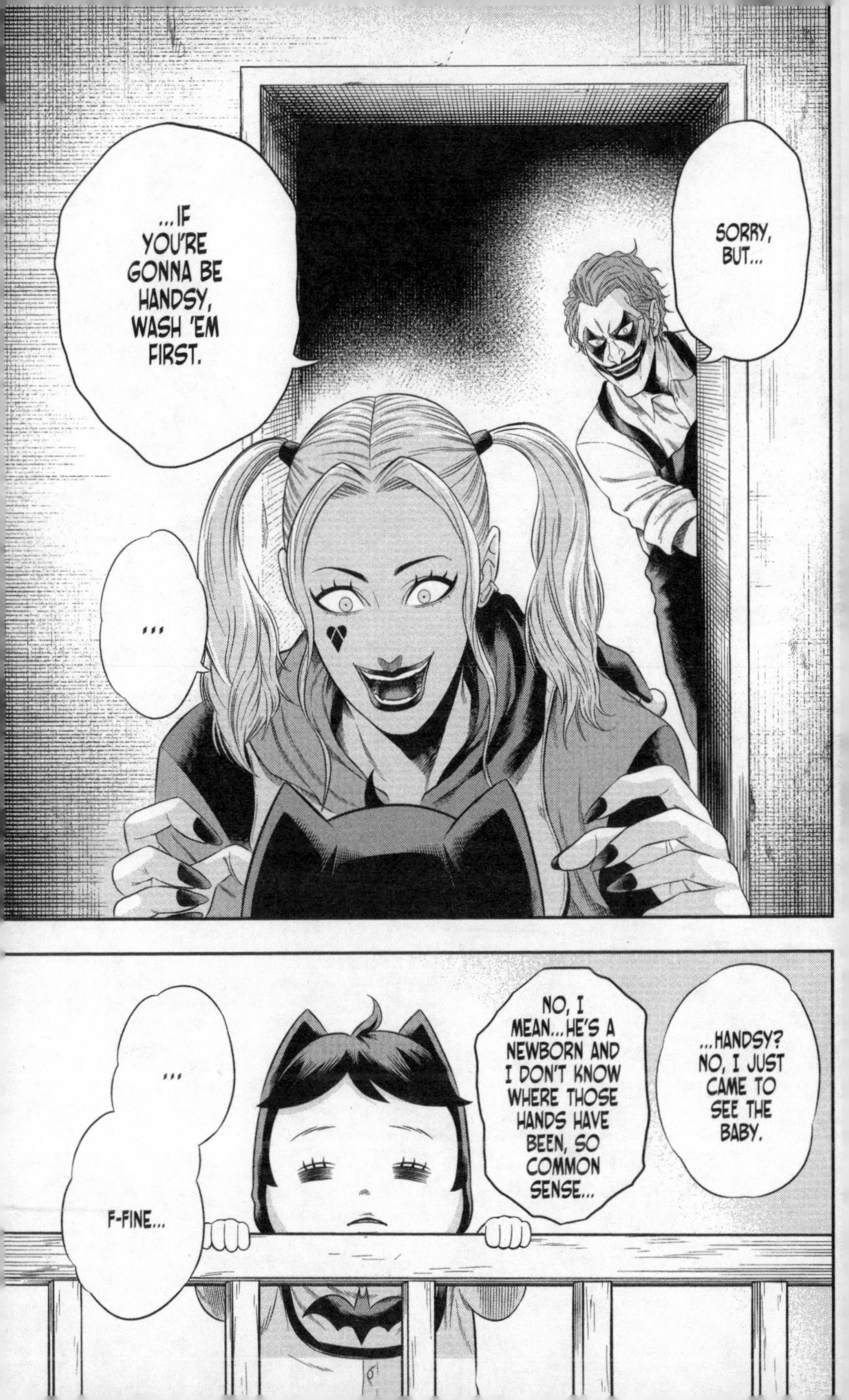
SORRY, BUT...
...IF YOU'RE GONNA BE HANDSY, WASH 'EM FIRST.
...
...HANDSY? NO, I JUST CAME TO SEE THE BABY.
NO, I MEAN...HE'S A NEWBORN AND I DON'T KNOW WHERE THOSE HANDS HAVE BEEN, SO COMMON SENSE...
...
F-FINE...

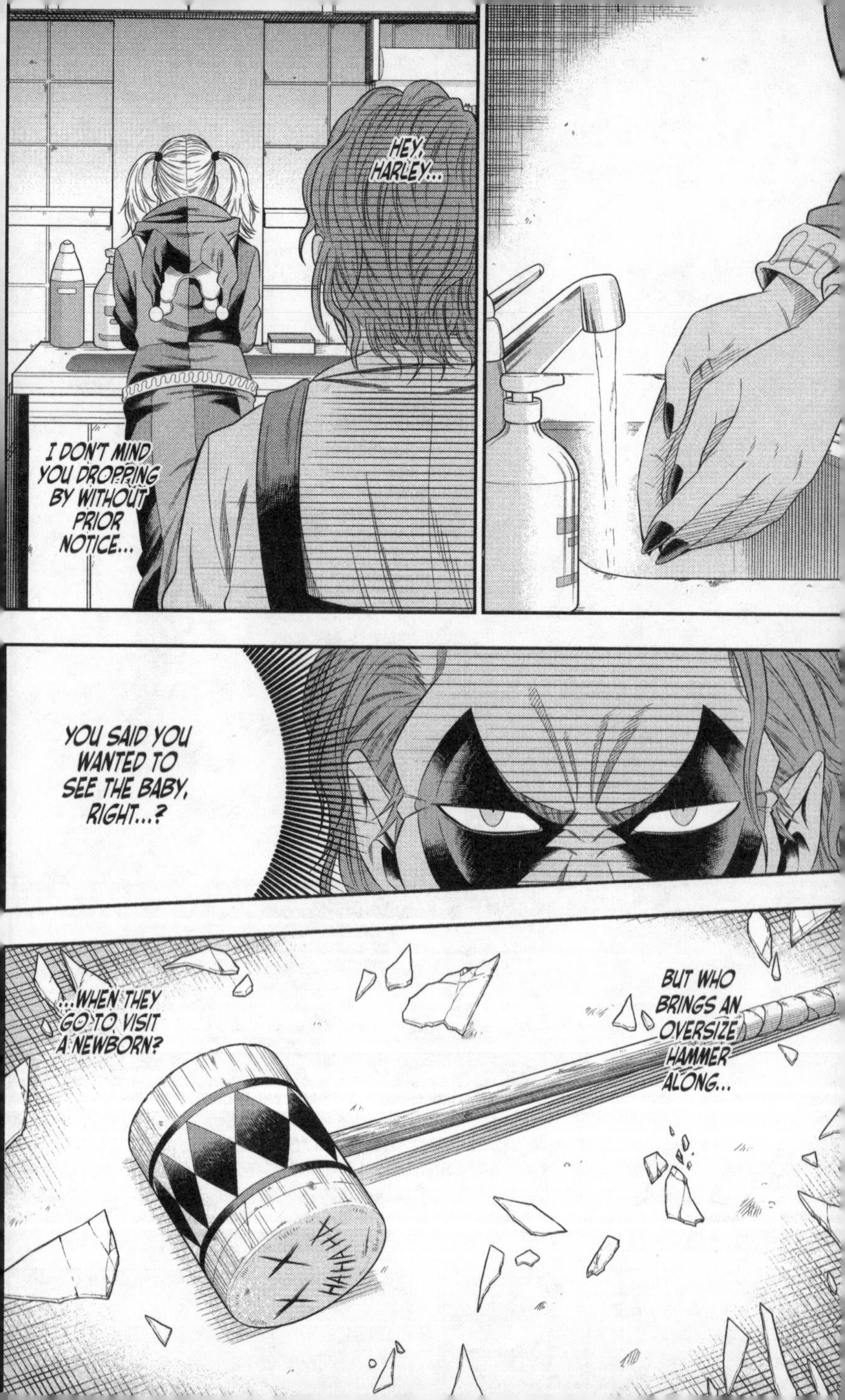
HEY, HARLEY...
I DON'T MIND YOU DROPPING BY WITHOUT PRIOR NOTICE...
YOU SAID YOU WANTED TO SEE THE BABY, RIGHT...?
BUT WHO BRINGS AN OVERSIZE HAMMER ALONG...
...WHEN THEY GO TO VISIT A NEWBORN?

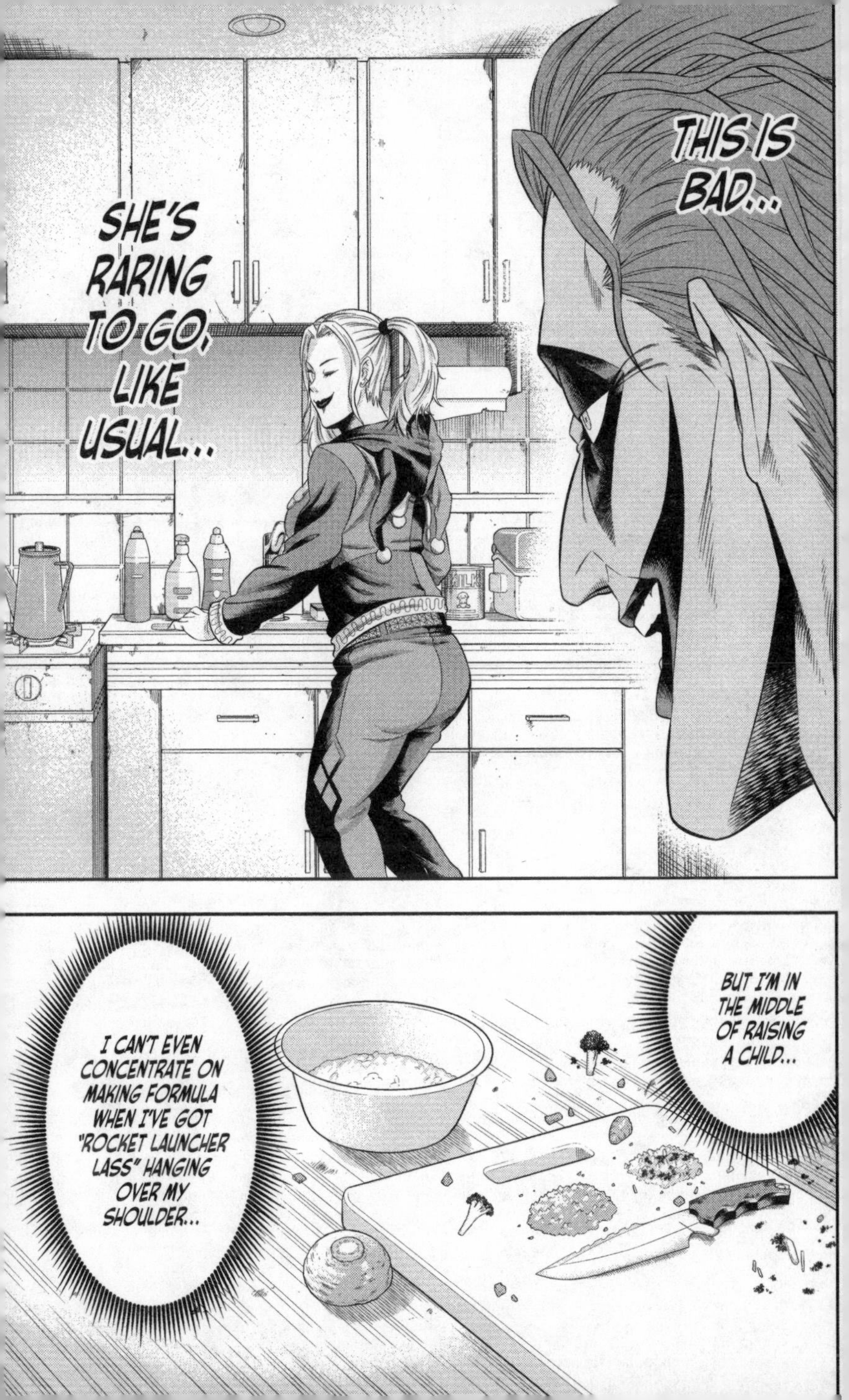
THIS IS BAD...
SHE'S RARING TO GO, LIKE USUAL...
BUT I'M IN THE MIDDLE OF RAISING A CHILD...
I CAN'T EVEN CONCENTRATE ON MAKING FORMULA WHEN I'VE GOT "ROCKET LAUNCHER LASS" HANGING OVER MY SHOULDER...

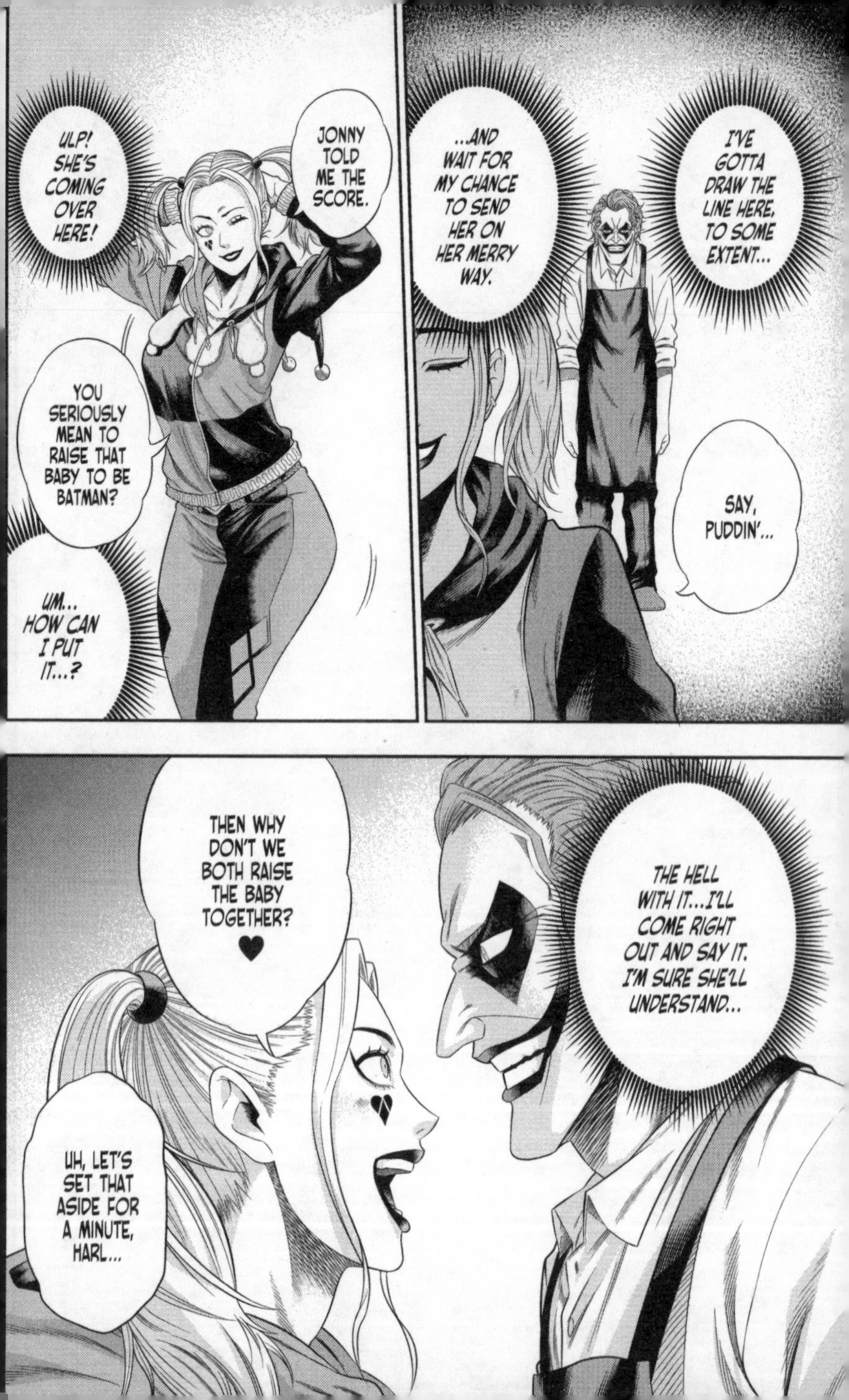
I'VE GOTTA DRAW THE LINE HERE, TO SOME EXTENT...
...AND WAIT FOR MY CHANCE TO SEND HER ON HER MERRY WAY.
SAY, PUDDIN'...
JONNY TOLD ME THE SCORE.
ULP! SHE'S COMING OVER HERE!
YOU SERIOUSLY MEAN TO RAISE THAT BABY TO BE BATMAN?
UM... HOW CAN I PUT IT...?
THE HELL WITH IT...I'LL COME RIGHT OUT AND SAY IT. I'M SURE SHE'LL UNDERSTAND...
THEN WHY DON'T WE BOTH RAISE THE BABY TOGETHER? ♥
UH, LET'S SET THAT ASIDE FOR A MINUTE, HARL...

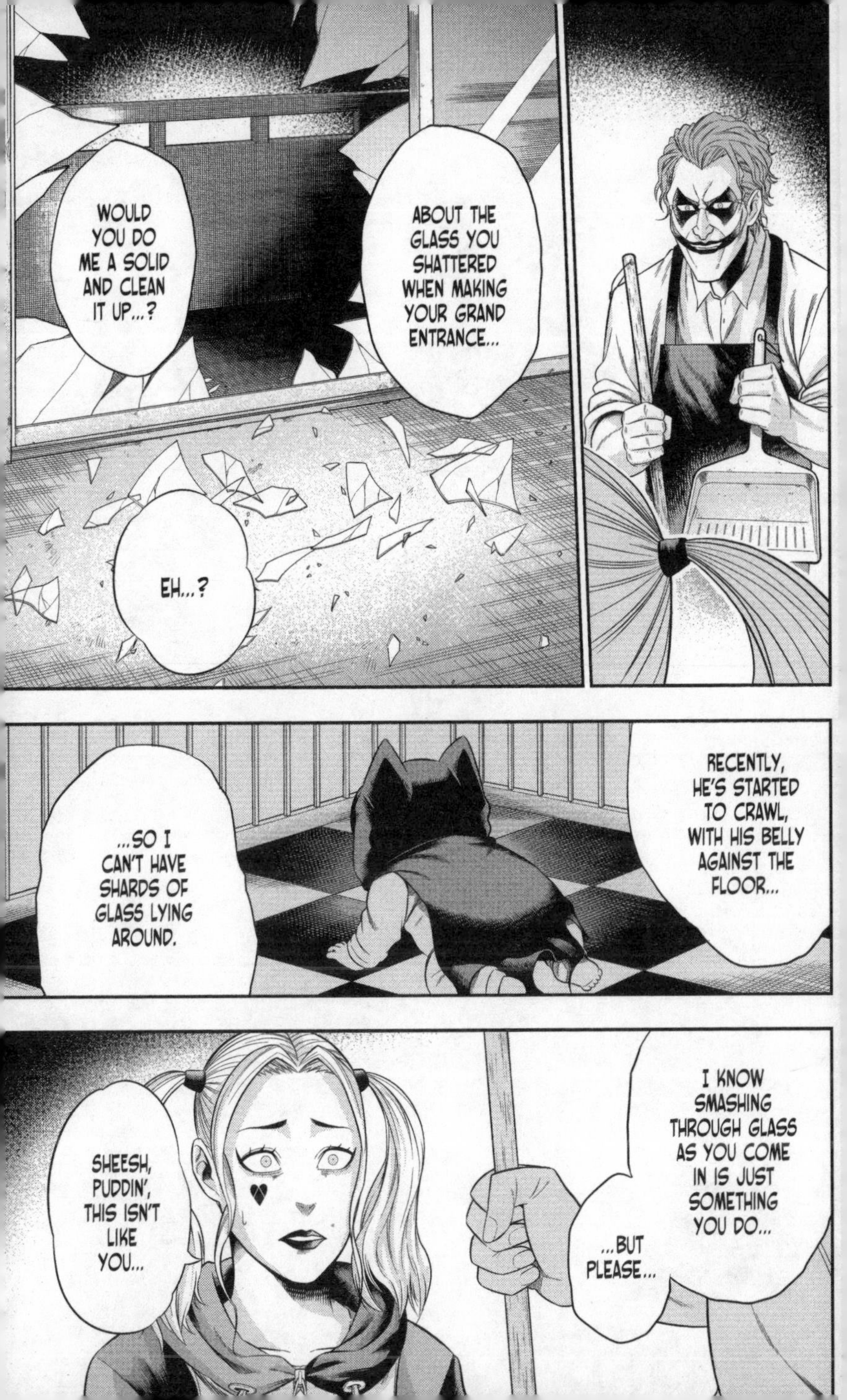
ABOUT THE GLASS YOU SHATTERED WHEN MAKING YOUR GRAND ENTRANCE...
WOULD YOU DO ME A SOLID AND CLEAN IT UP...?
EH...?
RECENTLY, HE'S STARTED TO CRAWL, WITH HIS BELLY AGAINST THE FLOOR...
...SO I CAN'T HAVE SHARDS OF GLASS LYING AROUND.
I KNOW SMASHING THROUGH GLASS AS YOU COME IN IS JUST SOMETHING YOU DO...
...BUT PLEASE...
SHEESH, PUDDIN', THIS ISN'T LIKE YOU...

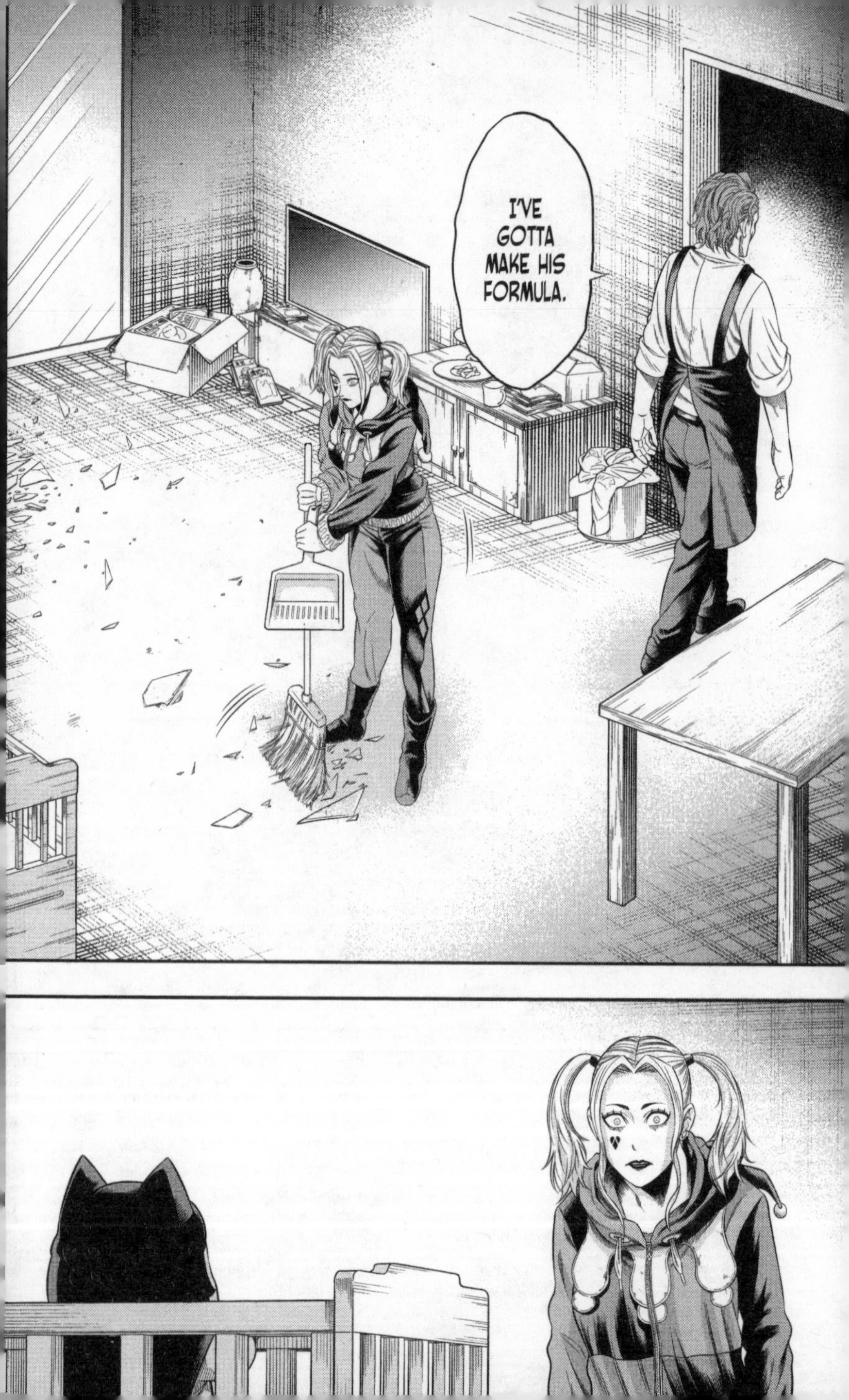
I'VE GOTTA MAKE HIS FORMULA.

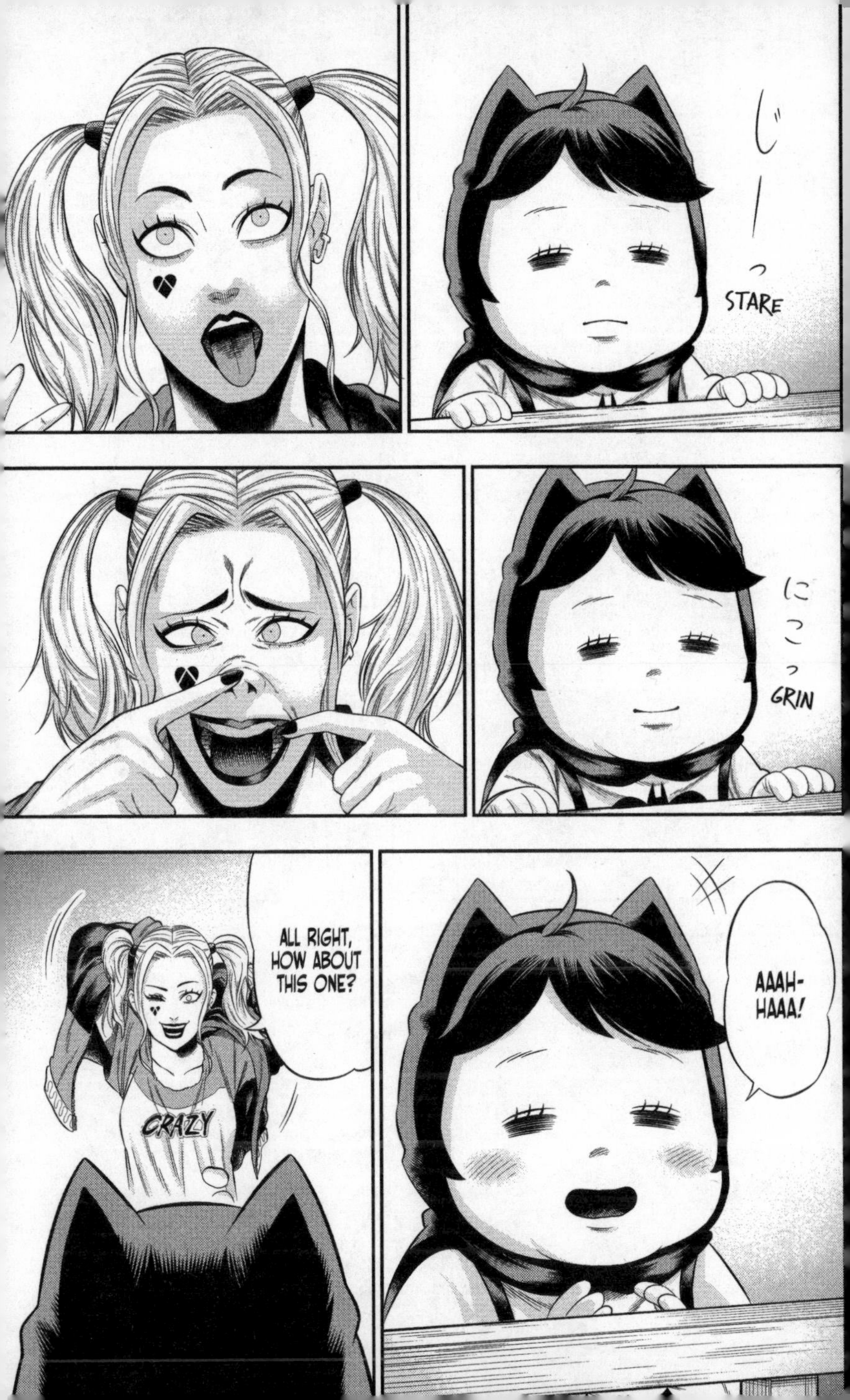
じーっ
STARE
にこっ
GRIN
AAAH-HAAA!
ALL RIGHT, HOW ABOUT THIS ONE?
CRAZY

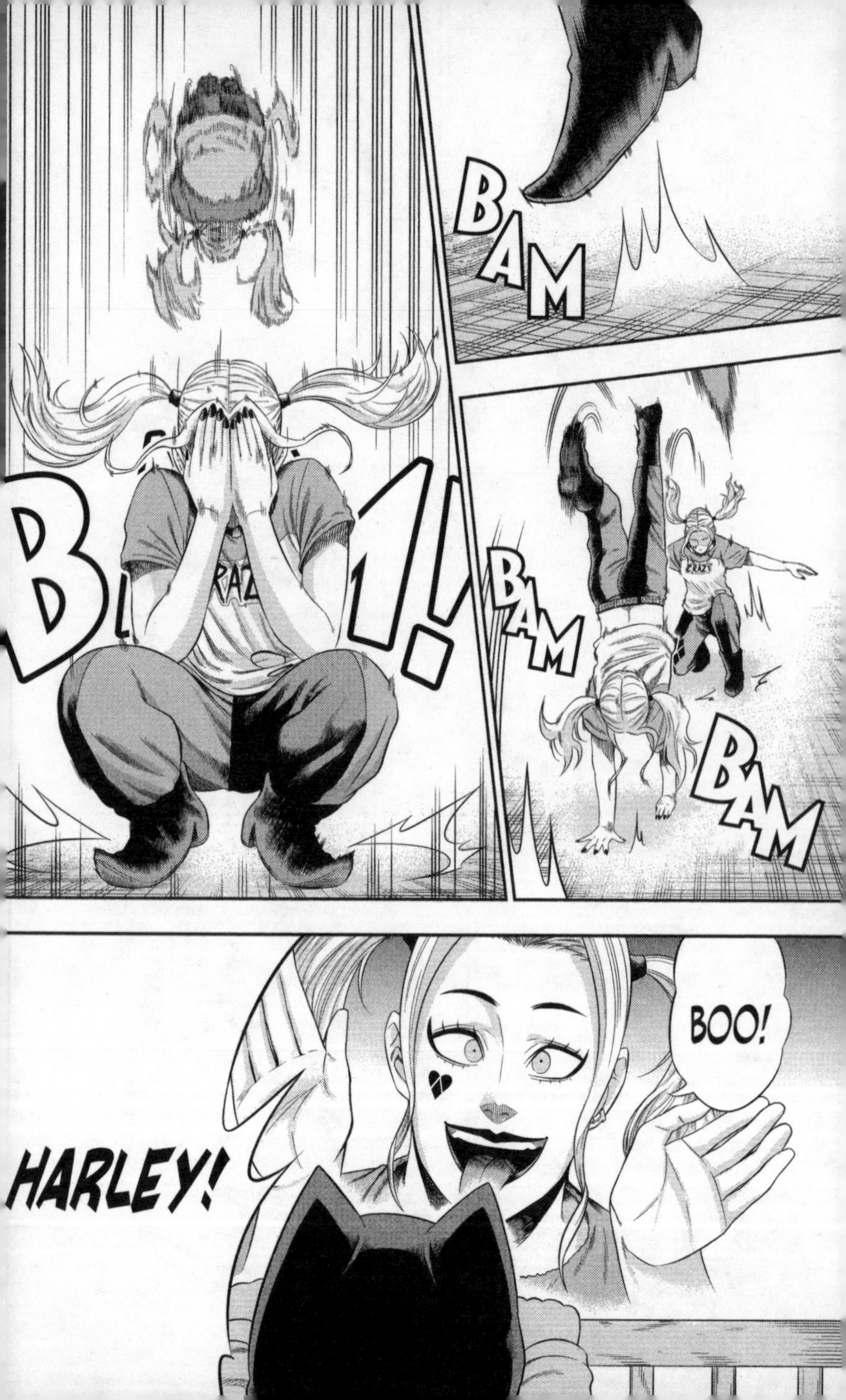
BAM
BAM
CRAZY
BAM
BOO!
HARLEY!

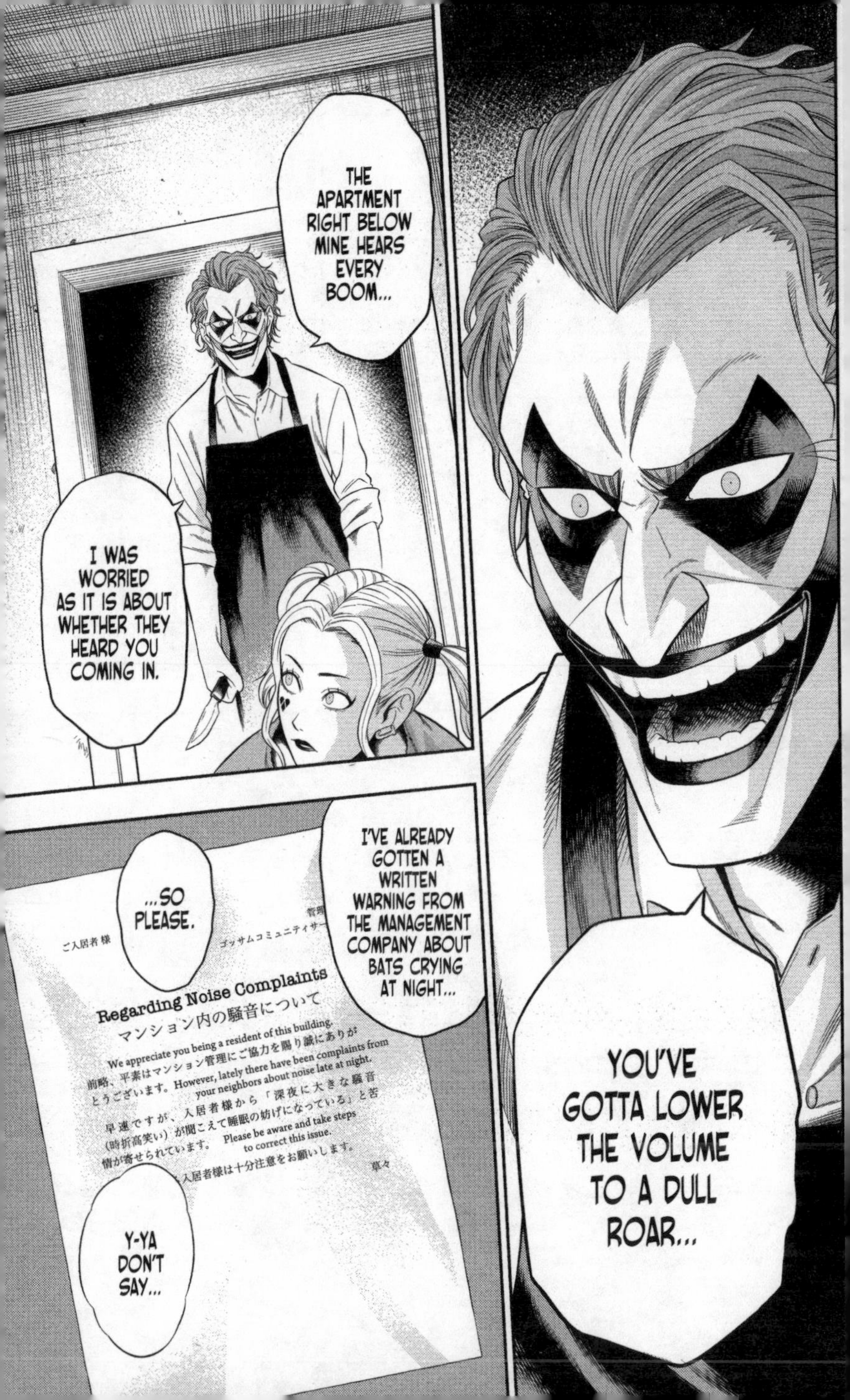
YOU'VE GOTTA LOWER THE VOLUME TO A DULL ROAR...
THE APARTMENT RIGHT BELOW MINE HEARS EVERY BOOM...
I WAS WORRIED AS IT IS ABOUT WHETHER THEY HEARD YOU COMING IN.
I'VE ALREADY GOTTEN A WRITTEN WARNING FROM THE MANAGEMENT COMPANY ABOUT BATS CRYING AT NIGHT...
...SO PLEASE.
ご入居者 様
ゴッサムコミュニティサー
管理
Regarding Noise Complaints
マンション内の騒音について
We appreciate you being a resident of this building.
前略、平素はマンション管理にご協力を賜り誠にありが
とうございます。 However, lately there have been complaints from
your neighbors about noise late at night.
早速ですが、入居者様から「深夜に大きな騒音
（時折高笑い）が聞こえて睡眠の妨げになっている」と苦
情が寄せられています。 Please be aware and take steps
to correct this issue.
入居者様は十分注意をお願いします。
草々
Y-YA DON'T SAY...

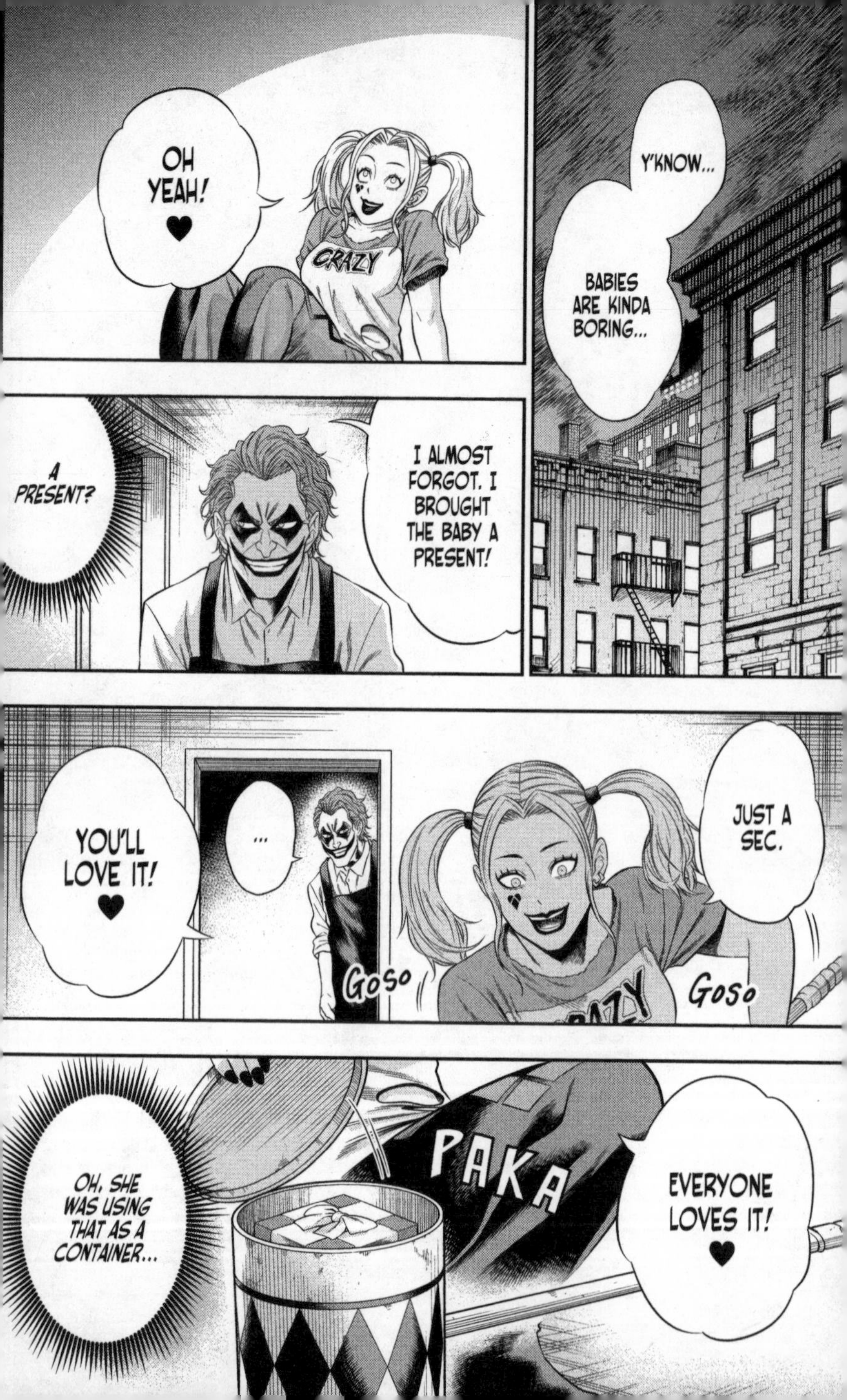
Y'KNOW...
BABIES ARE KINDA BORING...
OH YEAH! ♥
I ALMOST FORGOT. I BROUGHT THE BABY A PRESENT!
A PRESENT?
JUST A SEC.
GOSO
...
YOU'LL LOVE IT! ♥
GOSO
EVERYONE LOVES IT! ♥
PAKA
OH, SHE WAS USING THAT AS A CONTAINER...

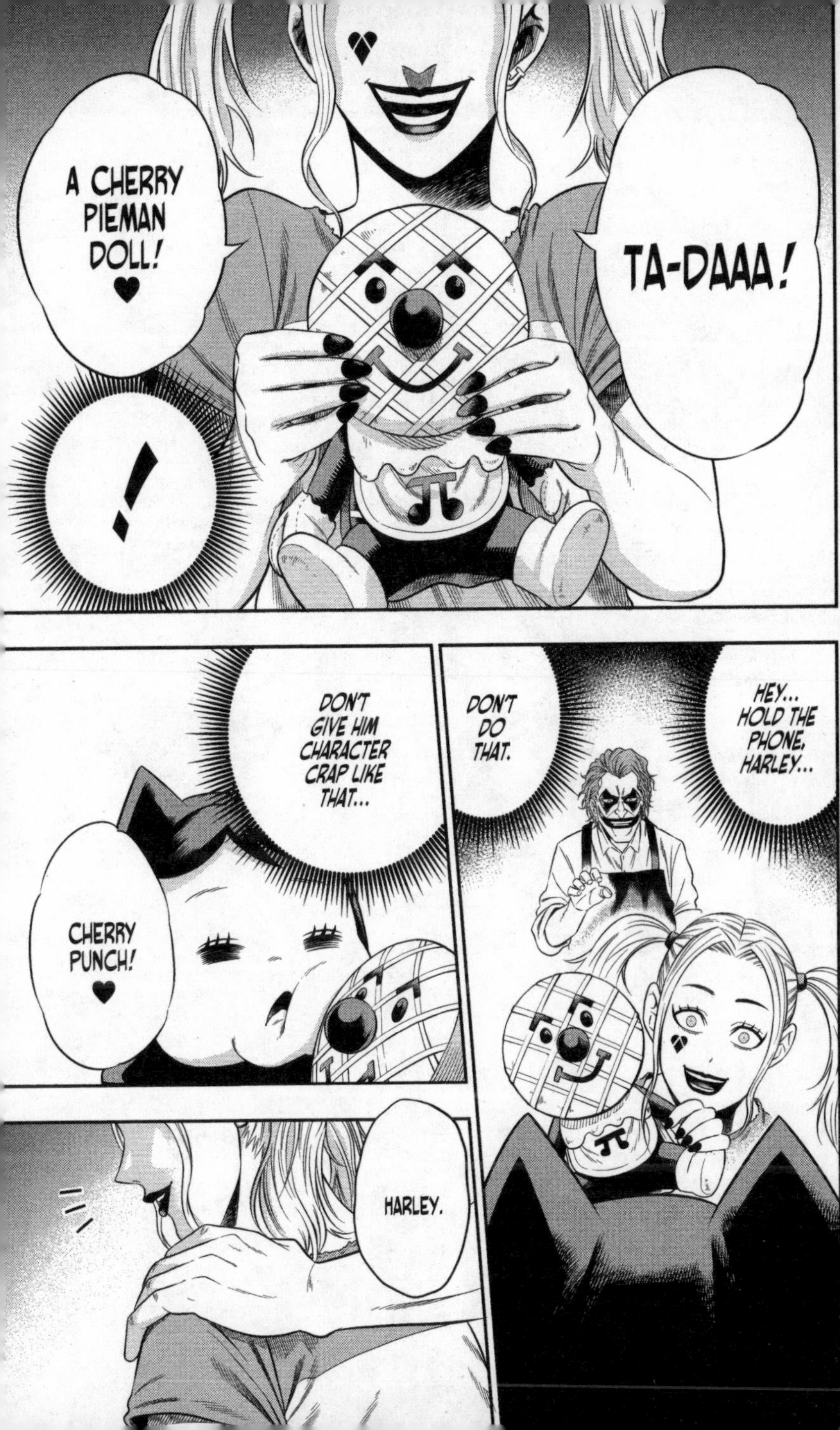
TA-DAAA!
A CHERRY PIEMAN DOLL! ♥
!
HEY... HOLD THE PHONE, HARLEY...
DON'T DO THAT.
DON'T GIVE HIM CHARACTER CRAP LIKE THAT...
CHERRY PUNCH! ♥
HARLEY.

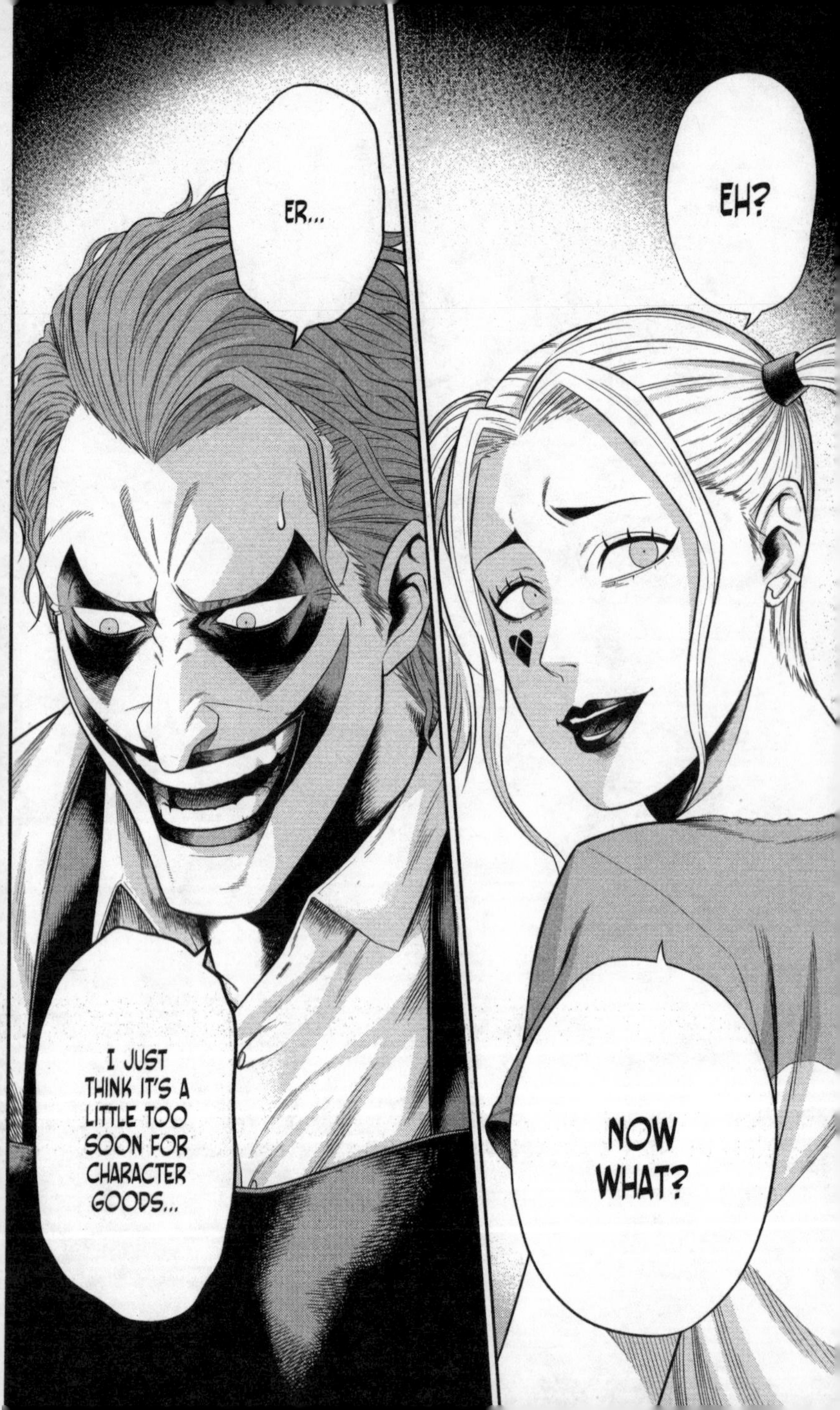
EH?
NOW WHAT?
ER...
I JUST THINK IT'S A LITTLE TOO SOON FOR CHARACTER GOODS...

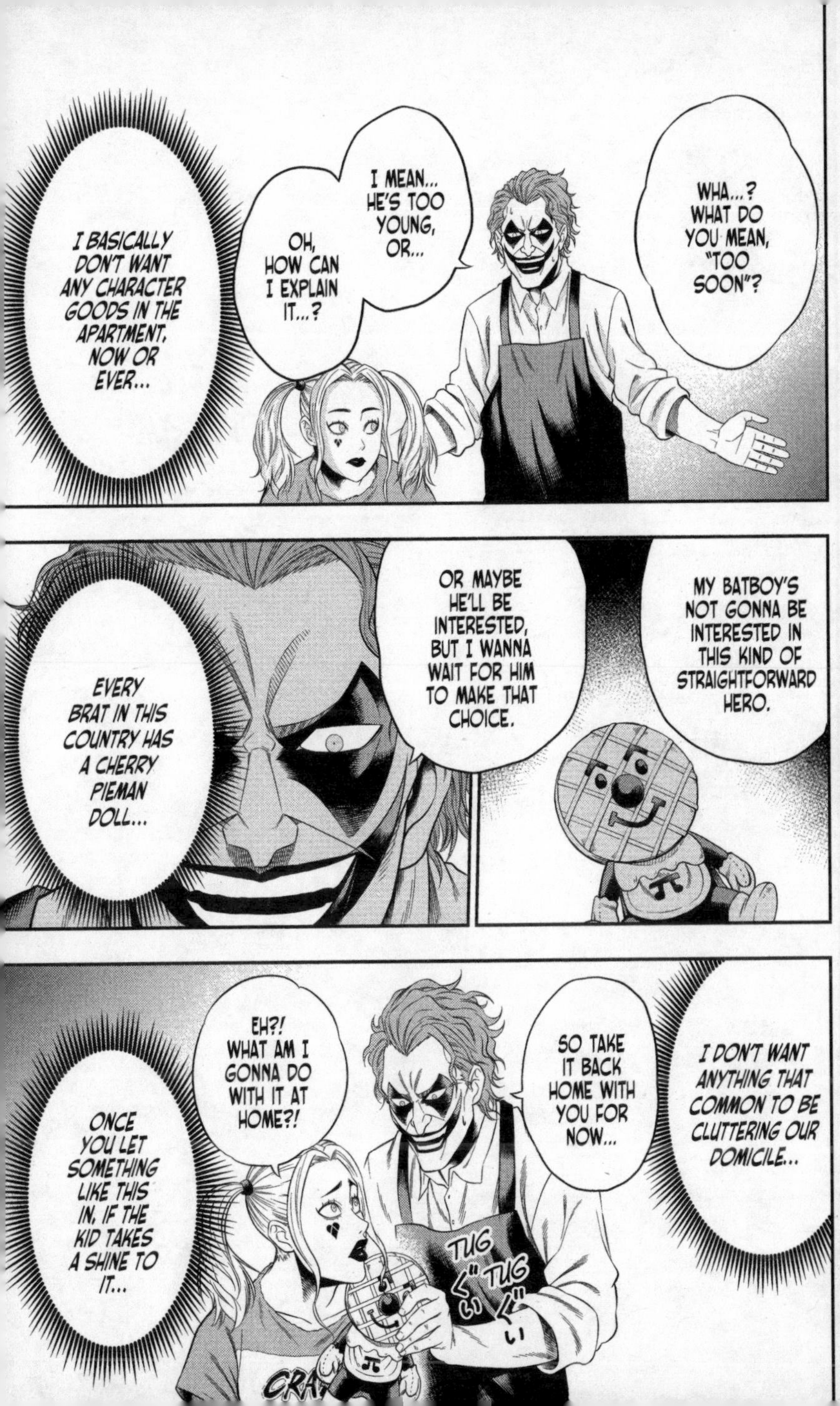
WHA...? WHAT DO YOU MEAN, "TOO SOON"?
I MEAN... HE'S TOO YOUNG, OR...
OH, HOW CAN I EXPLAIN IT...?
I BASICALLY DON'T WANT ANY CHARACTER GOODS IN THE APARTMENT. NOW OR EVER...
MY BATBOY'S NOT GONNA BE INTERESTED IN THIS KIND OF STRAIGHTFORWARD HERO.
OR MAYBE HE'LL BE INTERESTED, BUT I WANNA WAIT FOR HIM TO MAKE THAT CHOICE.
EVERY BRAT IN THIS COUNTRY HAS A CHERRY PIEMAN DOLL...
I DON'T WANT ANYTHING THAT COMMON TO BE CLUTTERING OUR DOMICILE...
SO TAKE IT BACK HOME WITH YOU FOR NOW...
EH?! WHAT AM I GONNA DO WITH IT AT HOME?!
ONCE YOU LET SOMETHING LIKE THIS IN, IF THE KID TAKES A SHINE TO IT...
TUG TUG

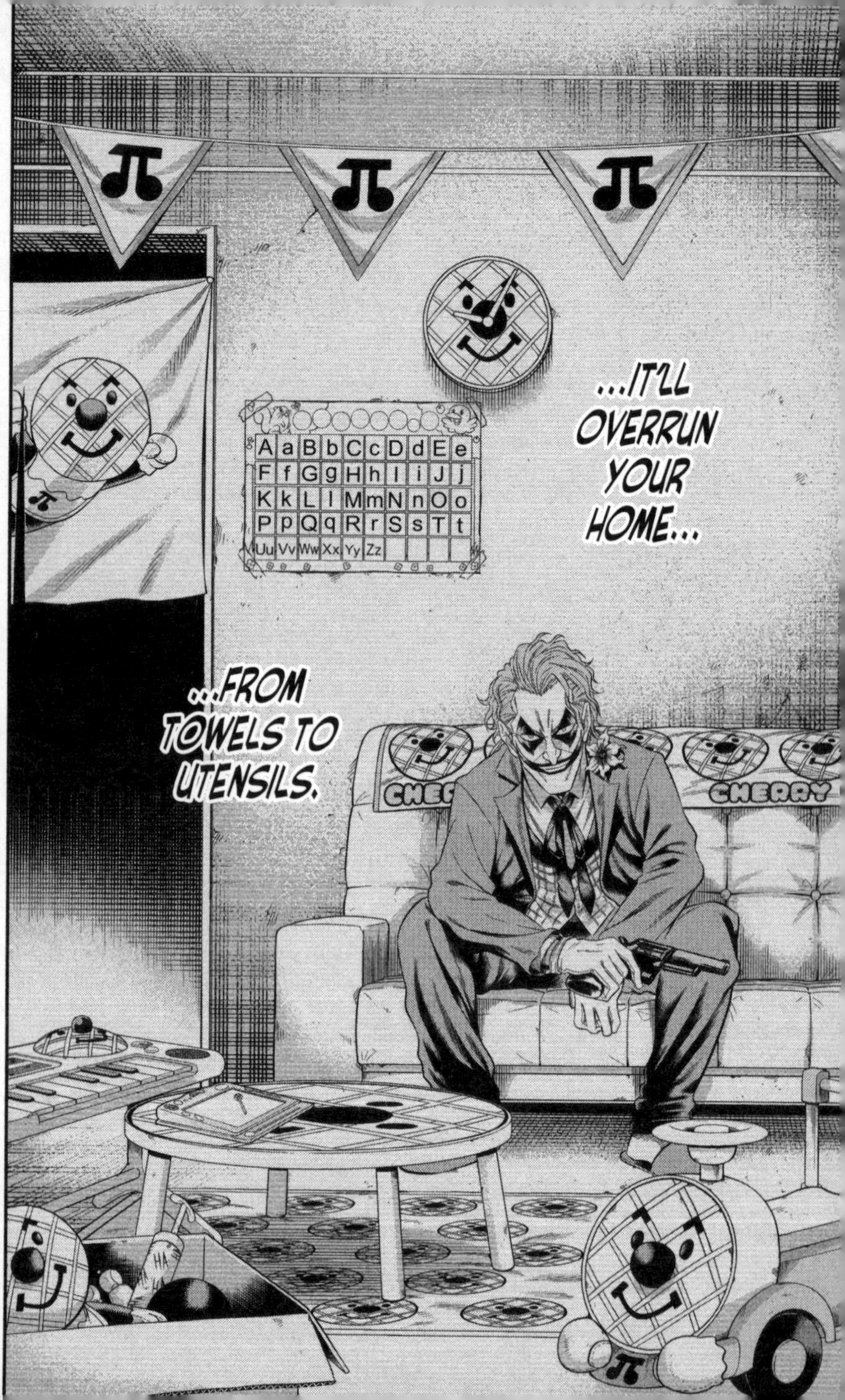
...IT'LL OVERRUN YOUR HOME...
...FROM TOWELS TO UTENSILS.
CHERRY

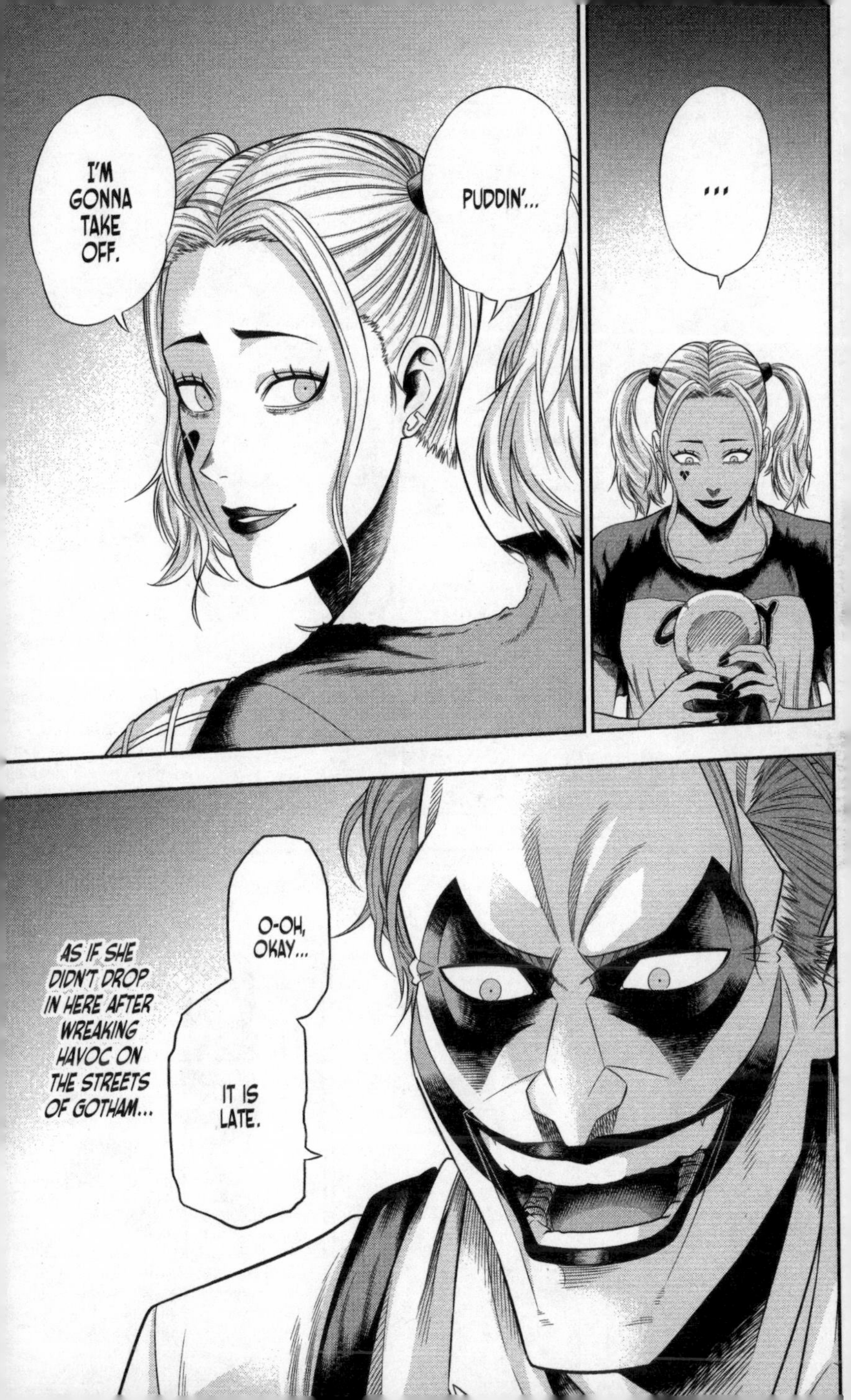
...
PUDDIN'...
I'M GONNA TAKE OFF.
O-OH, OKAY...
IT IS LATE.
AS IF SHE DIDN'T DROP IN HERE AFTER WREAKING HAVOC ON THE STREETS OF GOTHAM...

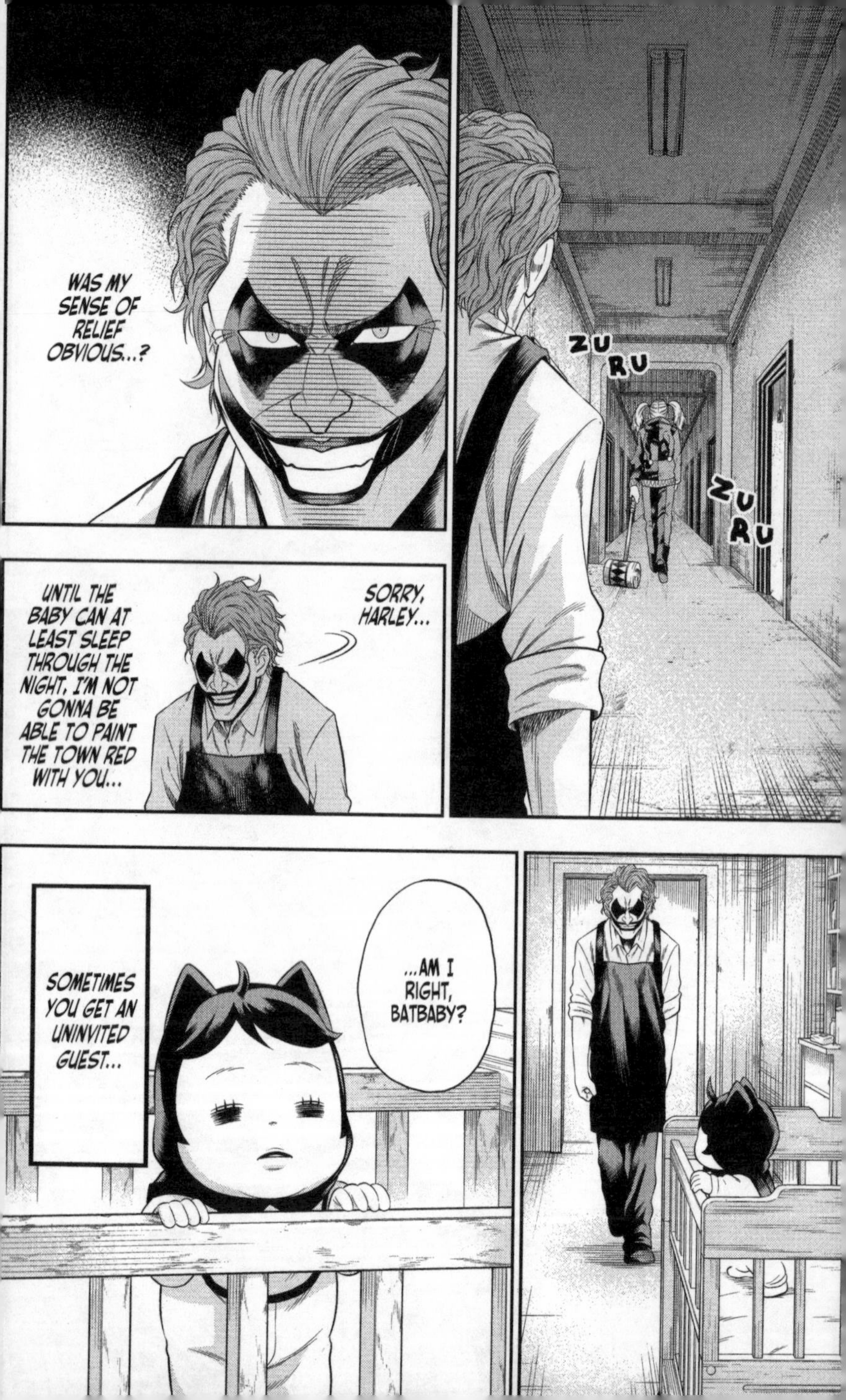
ZURU
ZURU
WAS MY SENSE OF RELIEF OBVIOUS...?
SORRY, HARLEY...
UNTIL THE BABY CAN AT LEAST SLEEP THROUGH THE NIGHT, I'M NOT GONNA BE ABLE TO PAINT THE TOWN RED WITH YOU...
...AM I RIGHT, BATBABY?
SOMETIMES YOU GET AN UNINVITED GUEST...

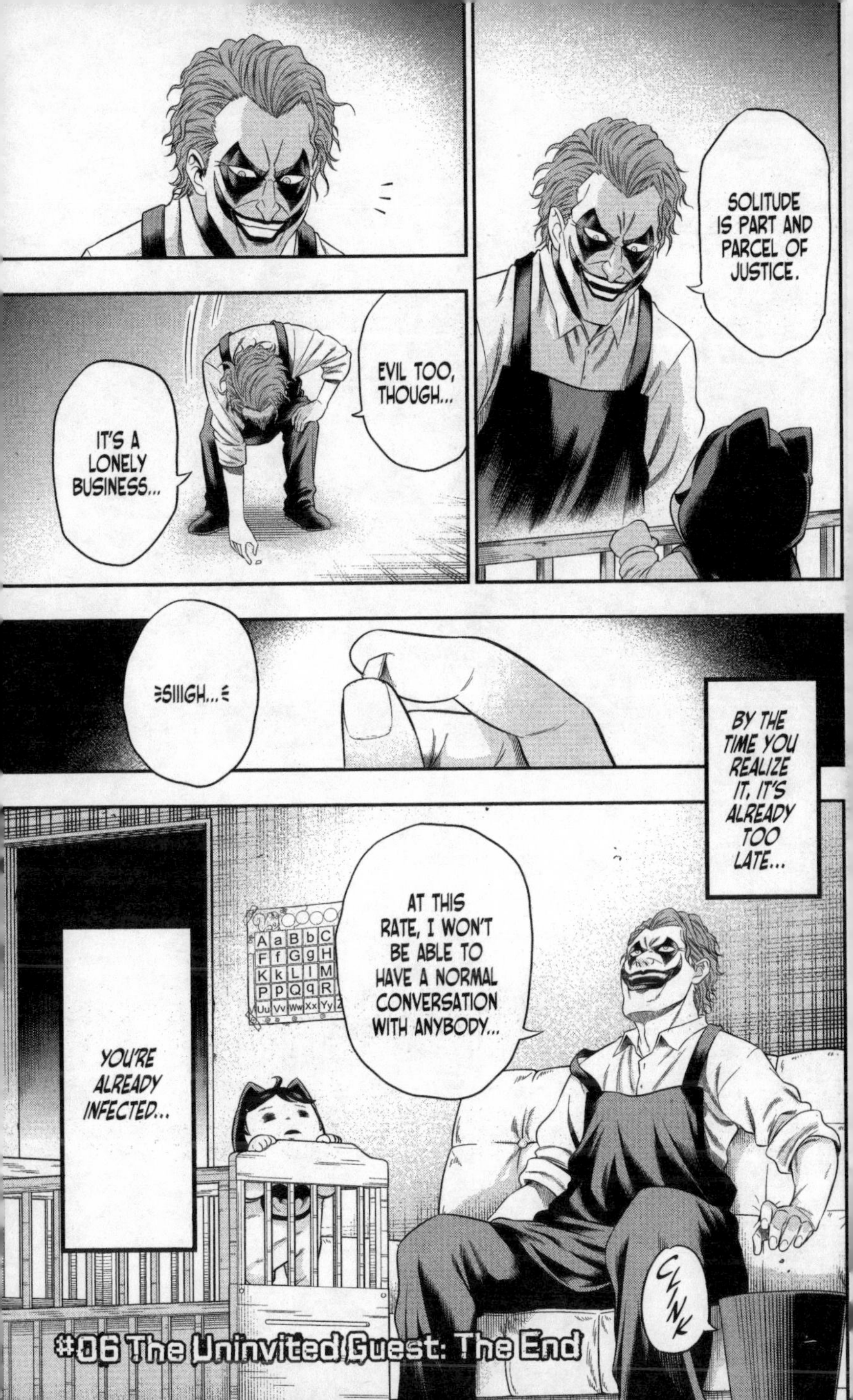
SOLITUDE IS PART AND PARCEL OF JUSTICE.
EVIL TOO, THOUGH...
IT'S A LONELY BUSINESS...
≡SIIIGH...≡
BY THE TIME YOU REALIZE IT, IT'S ALREADY TOO LATE...
AT THIS RATE, I WON'T BE ABLE TO HAVE A NORMAL CONVERSATION WITH ANYBODY...
CLINK
YOU'RE ALREADY INFECTED...
#06 The Uninvited Guest: The End

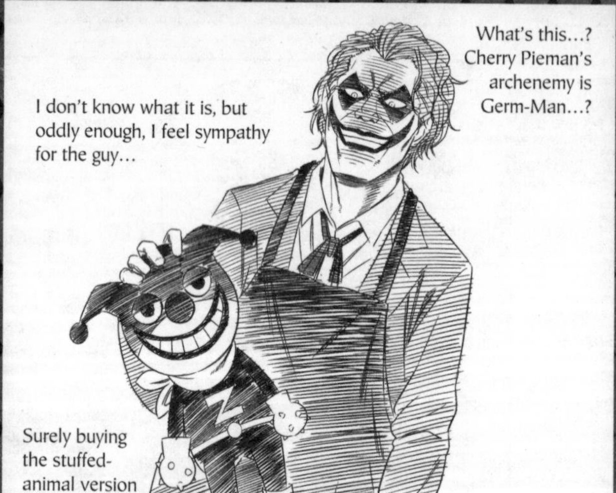
What's this...? Cherry Pieman's archenemy is Germ-Man...?
I don't know what it is, but oddly enough, I feel sympathy for the guy...
Surely buying the stuffed-animal version wouldn't do any harm...

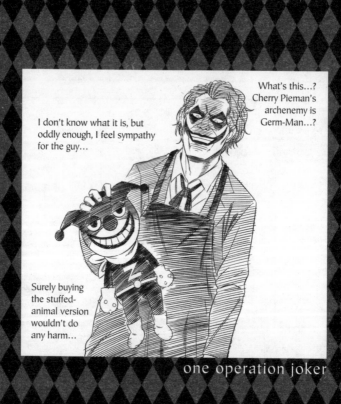

one operation joker

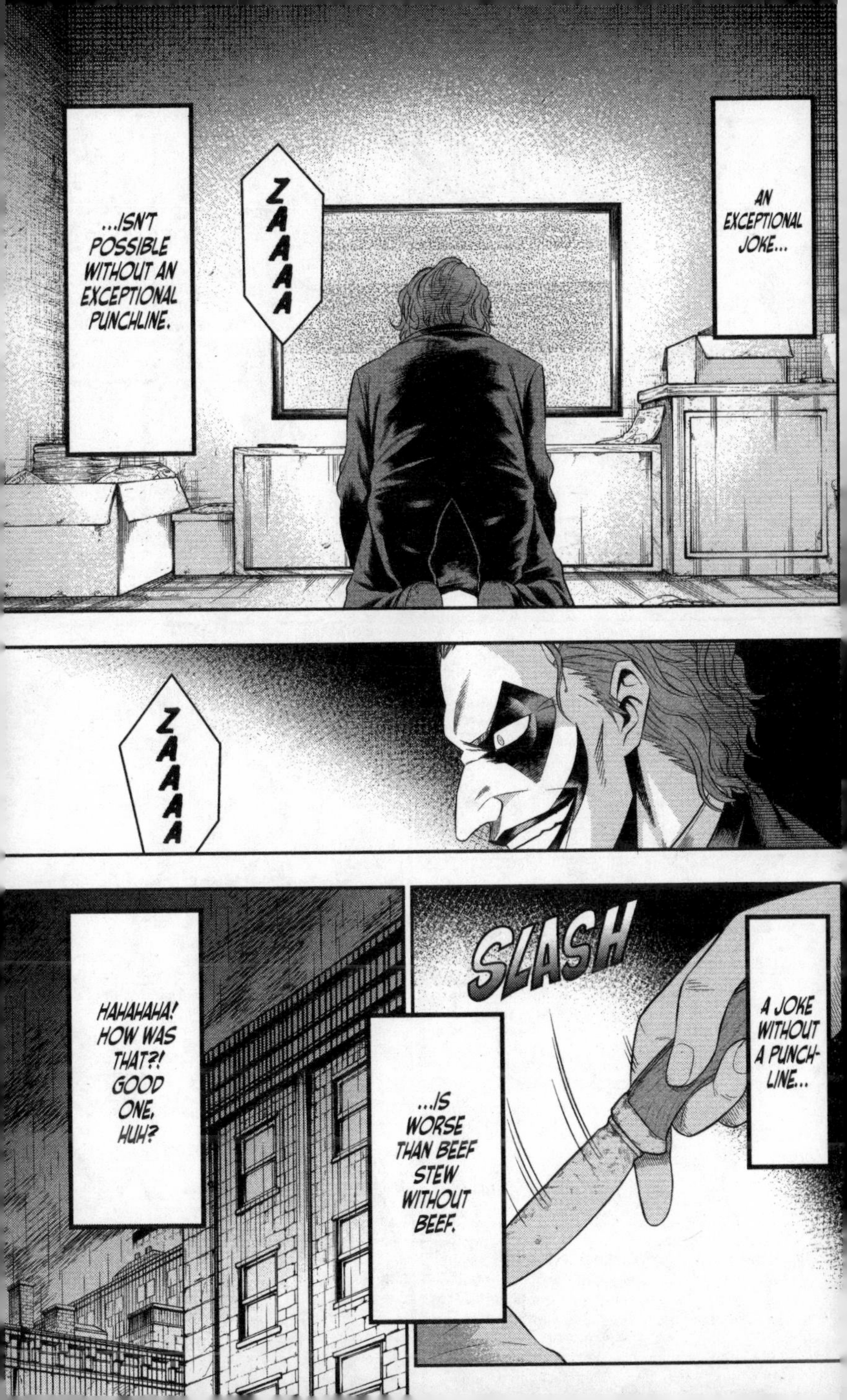
AN EXCEPTIONAL JOKE...
ZAAAA
...ISN'T POSSIBLE WITHOUT AN EXCEPTIONAL PUNCHLINE.
ZAAAA
A JOKE WITHOUT A PUNCH-LINE...
SLASH
...IS WORSE THAN BEEF STEW WITHOUT BEEF.
HAHAHAHA! HOW WAS THAT?! GOOD ONE, HUH?

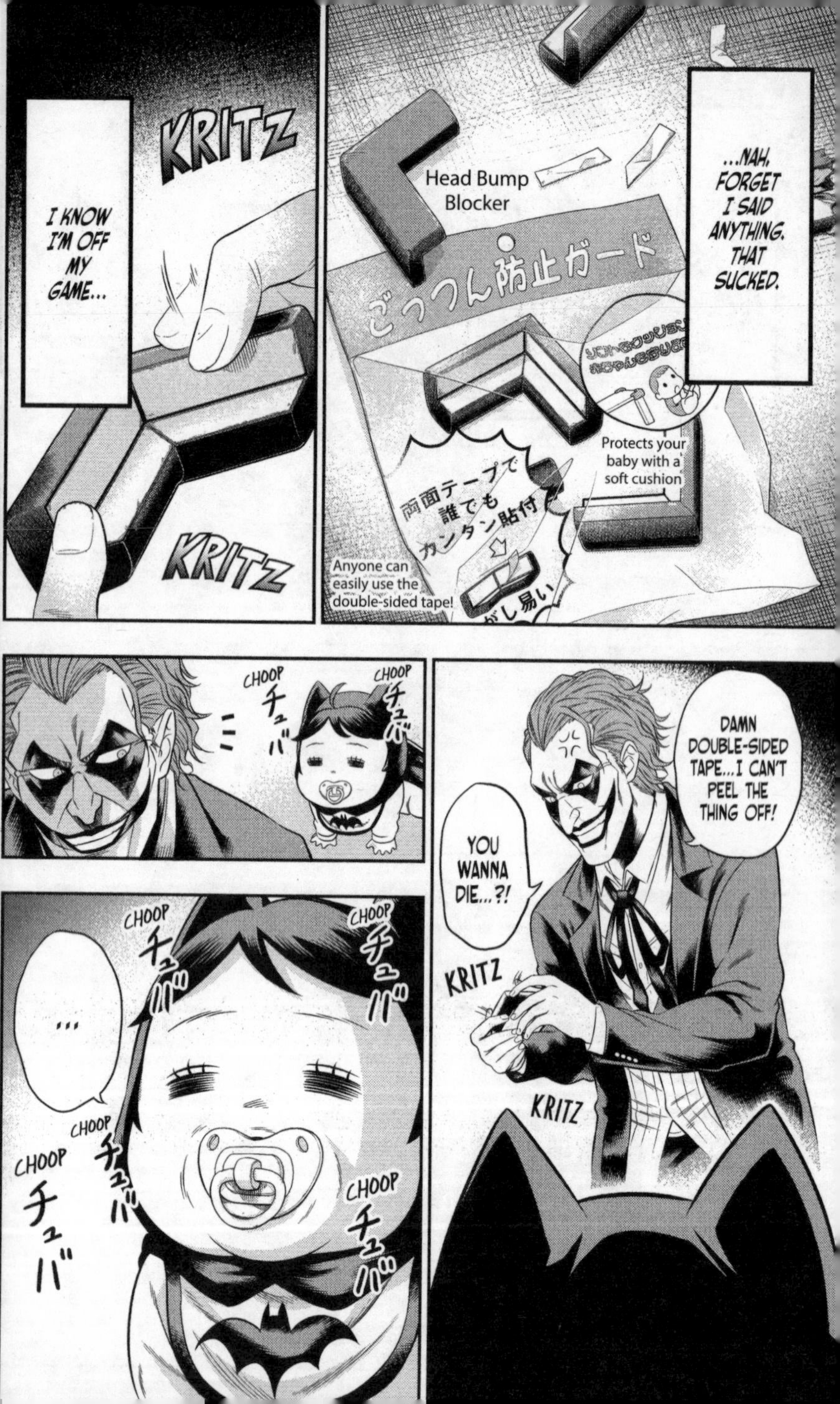

...NAH, FORGET I SAID ANYTHING. THAT SUCKED.
Head Bump Blocker
ごっつん防止ガード
Protects your baby with a soft cushion
両面テープで誰でもカンタン貼付
Anyone can easily use the double-sided tape!
がし易い
KRITZ
I KNOW I'M OFF MY GAME...
KRITZ
DAMN DOUBLE-SIDED TAPE...I CAN'T PEEL THE THING OFF!
YOU WANNA DIE...?!
KRITZ
KRITZ
CHOOP チュバ
CHOOP チュバ
CHOOP チュバ
CHOOP チュバ
...
CHOOP チュバ
CHOOP チュバ
CHOOP チュバ

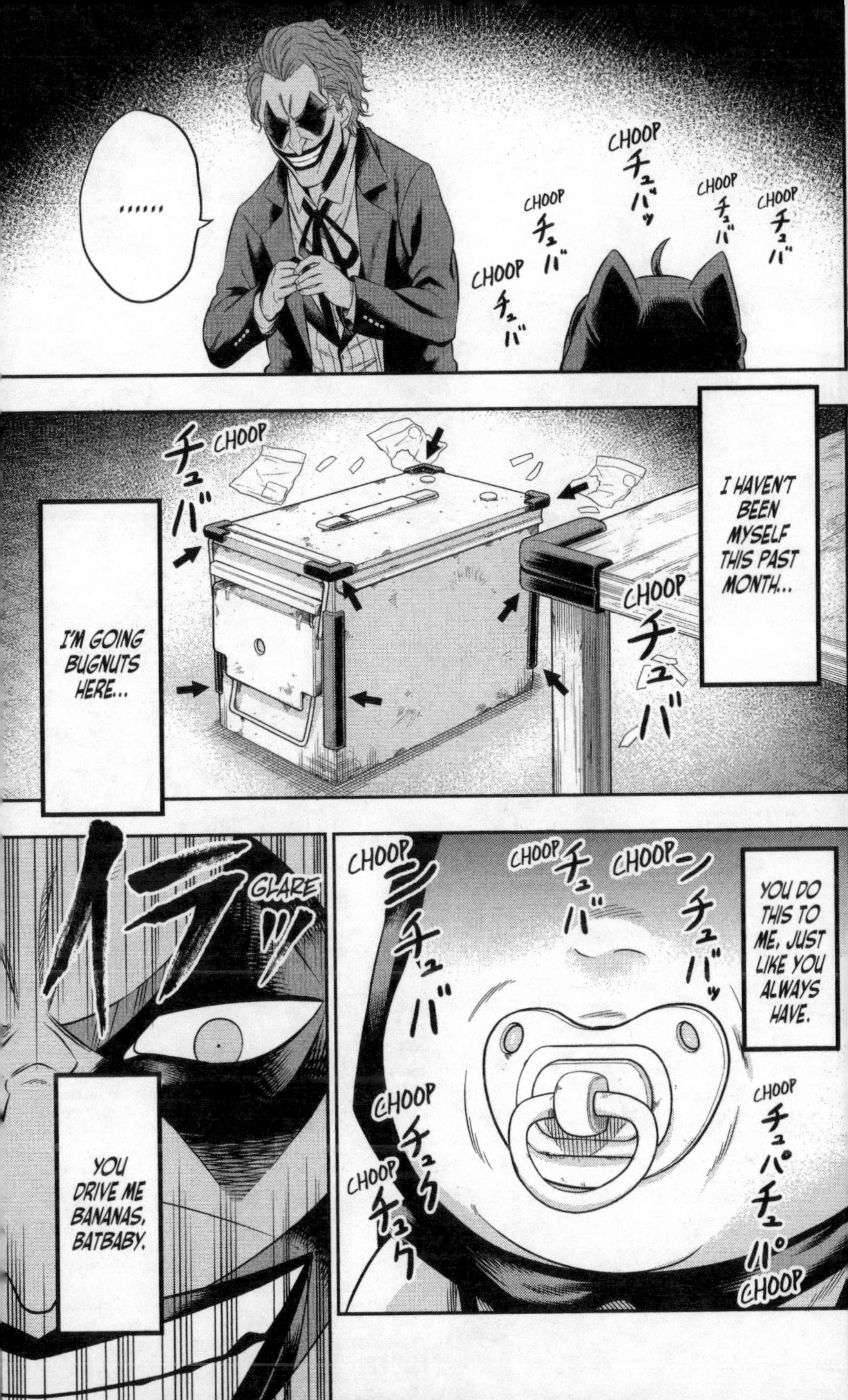
CHOOP チュバ
CHOOP チュバ
CHOOP チュバッ
CHOOP チュバ
CHOOP チュバ
......
I HAVEN'T BEEN MYSELF THIS PAST MONTH...
CHOOP チュバ
CHOOP チュバ
I'M GOING BUGNUTS HERE...
YOU DO THIS TO ME, JUST LIKE YOU ALWAYS HAVE.
CHOOP チュバッ
CHOOP チュバ
CHOOP チュパチュパ CHOOP
CHOOP チュバ
CHOOP チュク
CHOOP チュク
GLARE イラッ
YOU DRIVE ME BANANAS, BATBABY.

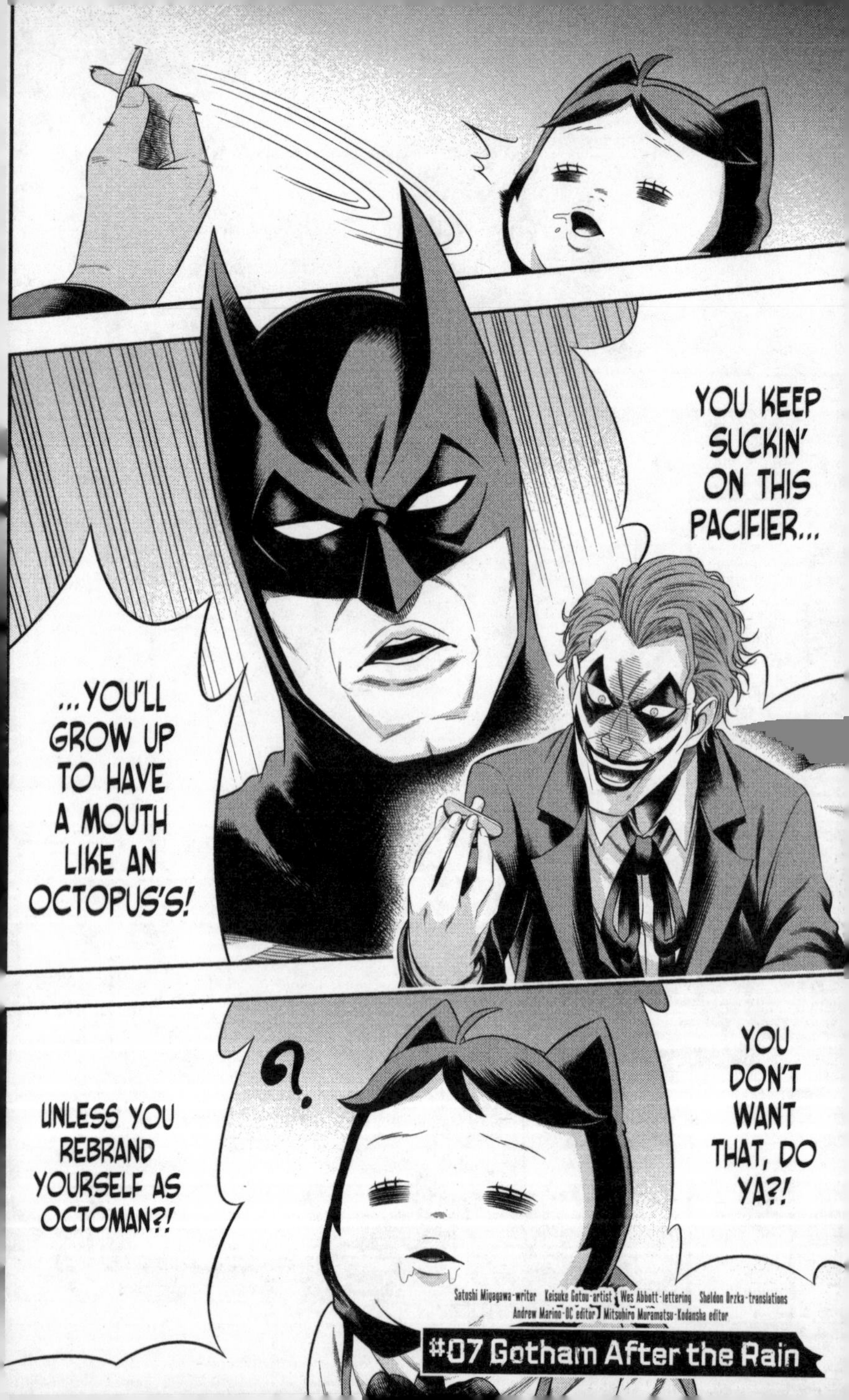
YOU KEEP SUCKIN' ON THIS PACIFIER...
...YOU'LL GROW UP TO HAVE A MOUTH LIKE AN OCTOPUS'S!
YOU DON'T WANT THAT, DO YA?!
?
UNLESS YOU REBRAND YOURSELF AS OCTOMAN?!
Satoshi Miyagawa-writer Keisuke Gotou-artist Wes Abbott-lettering Sheldon Drzka-translations
Andrew Marino-DC editor Mitsuhiro Muramatsu-Kodansha editor
#07 Gotham After the Rain

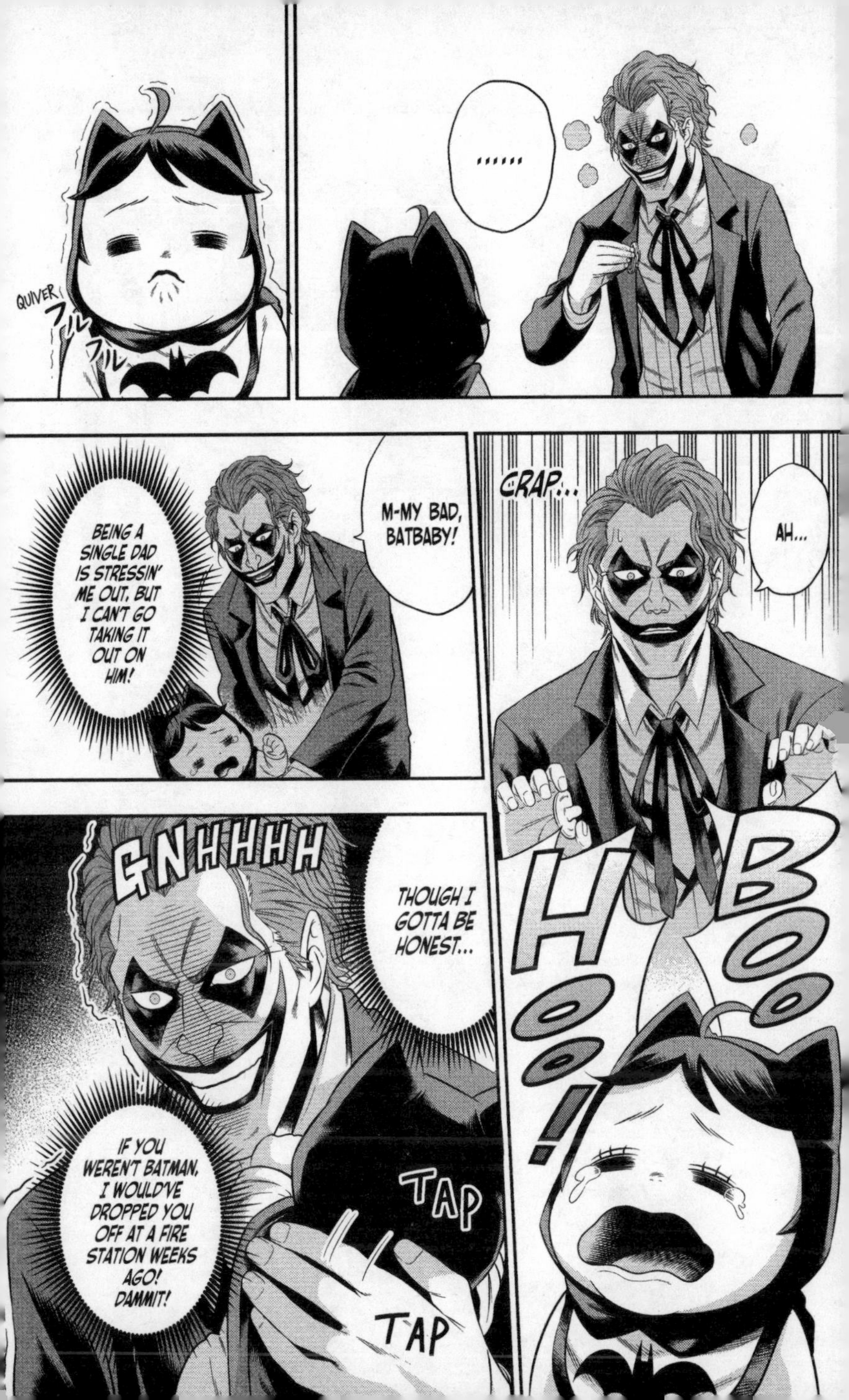
......
QUIVER
フル
フル
AH...
CRAP...
HBOOOOO!
M-MY BAD, BATBABY!
BEING A SINGLE DAD IS STRESSIN' ME OUT. BUT I CAN'T GO TAKING IT OUT ON HIM!
THOUGH I GOTTA BE HONEST...
GNHHHHH
TAP
TAP
IF YOU WEREN'T BATMAN, I WOULD'VE DROPPED YOU OFF AT A FIRE STATION WEEKS AGO! DAMMIT!

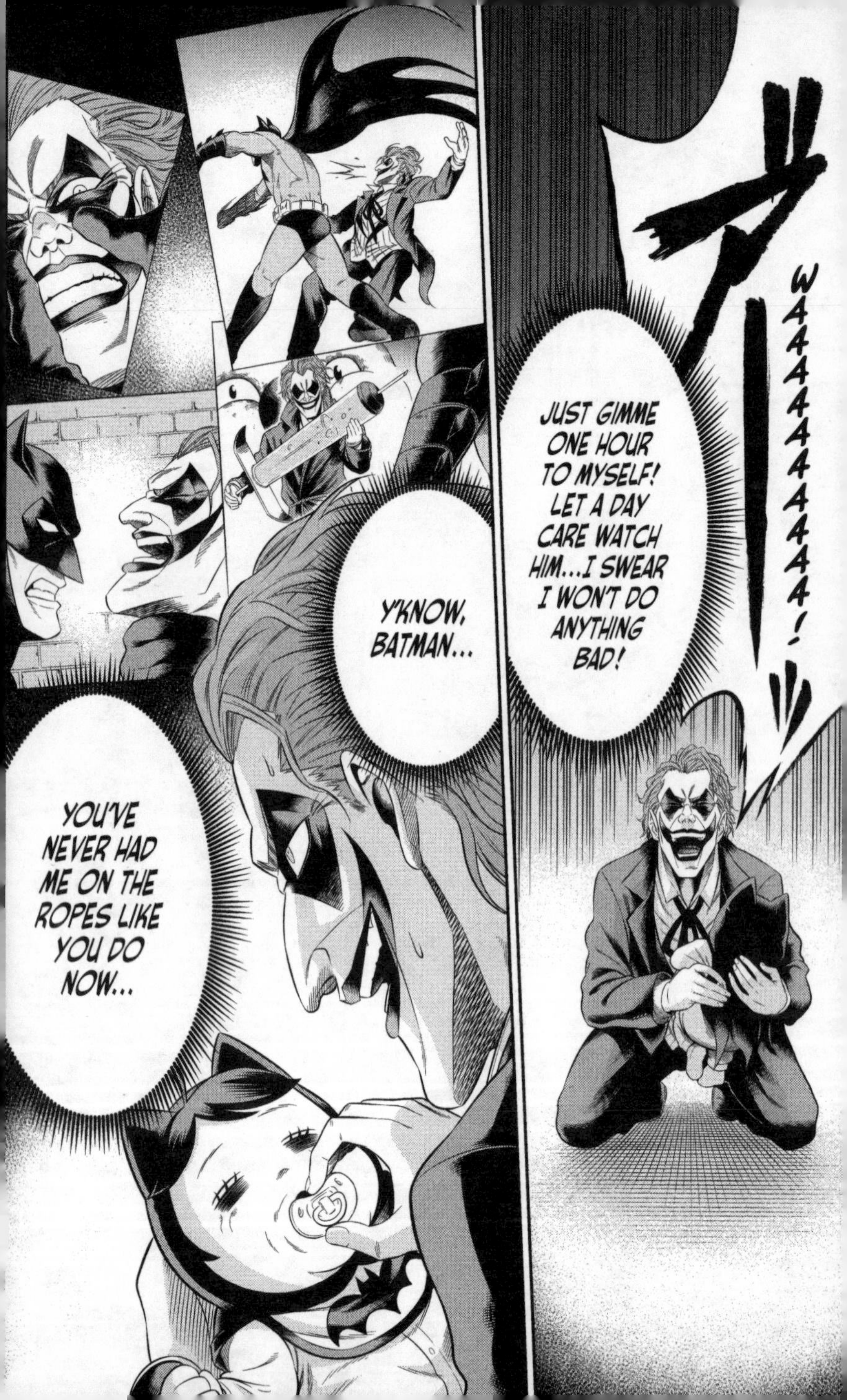
WAAAAAAAAA!
JUST GIMME ONE HOUR TO MYSELF! LET A DAY CARE WATCH HIM...I SWEAR I WON'T DO ANYTHING BAD!
Y'KNOW, BATMAN...
YOU'VE NEVER HAD ME ON THE ROPES LIKE YOU DO NOW...

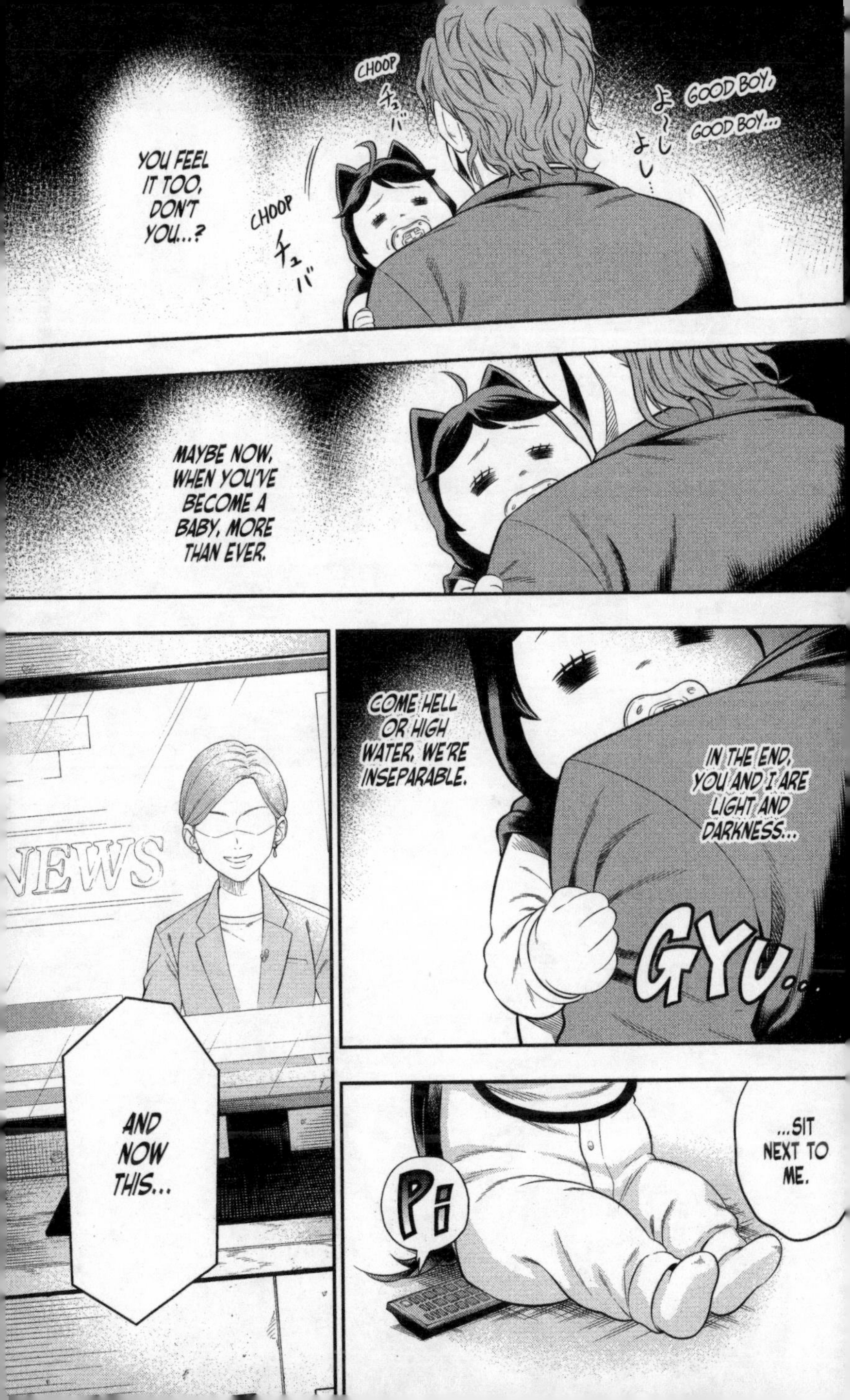
GOOD BOY, GOOD BOY...
よ～しよし…
CHOOP
チュバ
CHOOP
チュバ
YOU FEEL IT TOO, DON'T YOU...?
MAYBE NOW, WHEN YOU'VE BECOME A BABY, MORE THAN EVER.
IN THE END, YOU AND I ARE LIGHT AND DARKNESS...
COME HELL OR HIGH WATER, WE'RE INSEPARABLE.
GYU...
...SIT NEXT TO ME.
Pi
NEWS
AND NOW THIS...

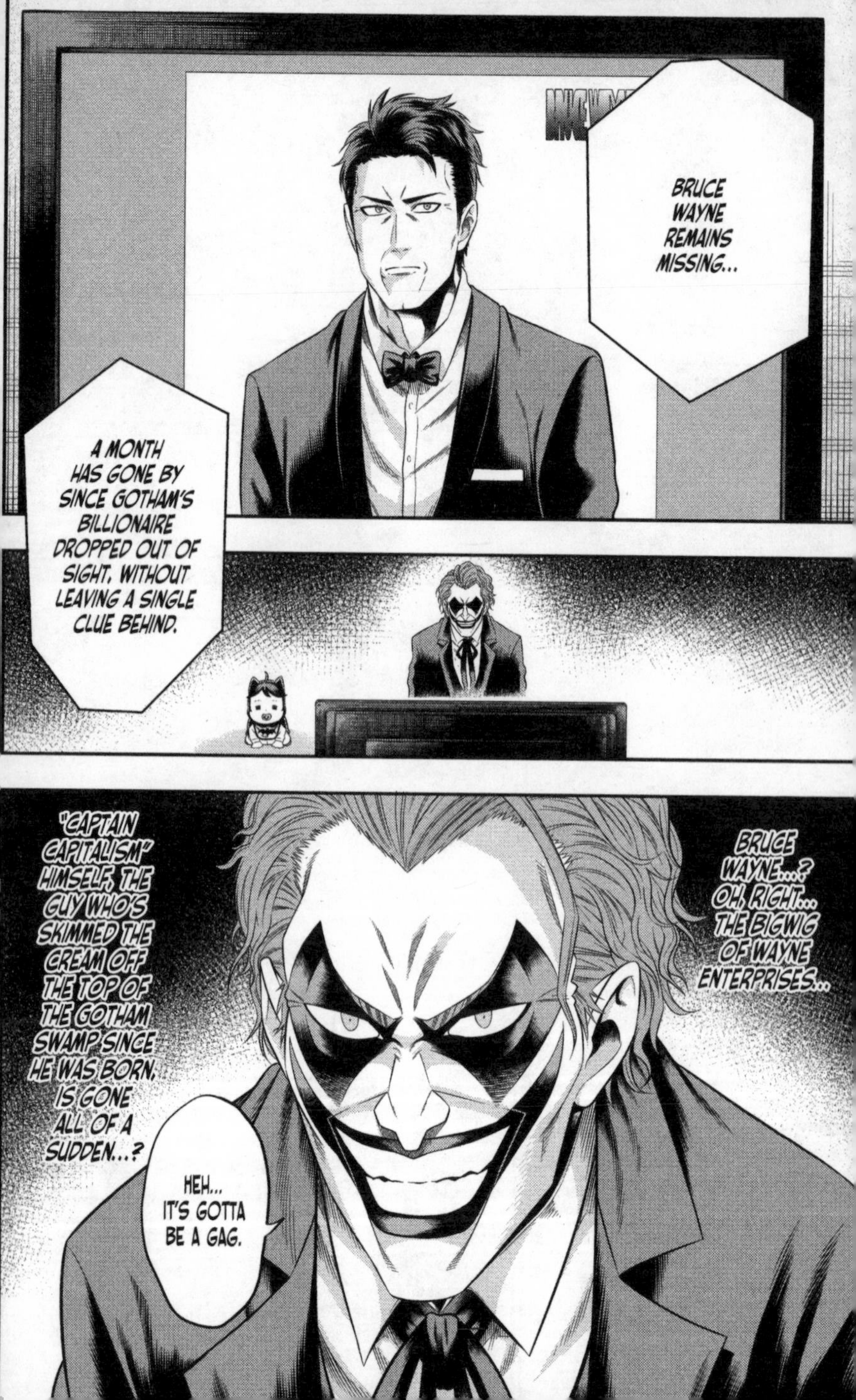
BRUCE WAYNE REMAINS MISSING...
A MONTH HAS GONE BY SINCE GOTHAM'S BILLIONAIRE DROPPED OUT OF SIGHT, WITHOUT LEAVING A SINGLE CLUE BEHIND.
BRUCE WAYNE...? OH, RIGHT... THE BIGWIG OF WAYNE ENTERPRISES...
"CAPTAIN CAPITALISM" HIMSELF, THE GUY WHO'S SKIMMED THE CREAM OFF THE TOP OF THE GOTHAM SWAMP SINCE HE WAS BORN, IS GONE ALL OF A SUDDEN...?
HEH... IT'S GOTTA BE A GAG.

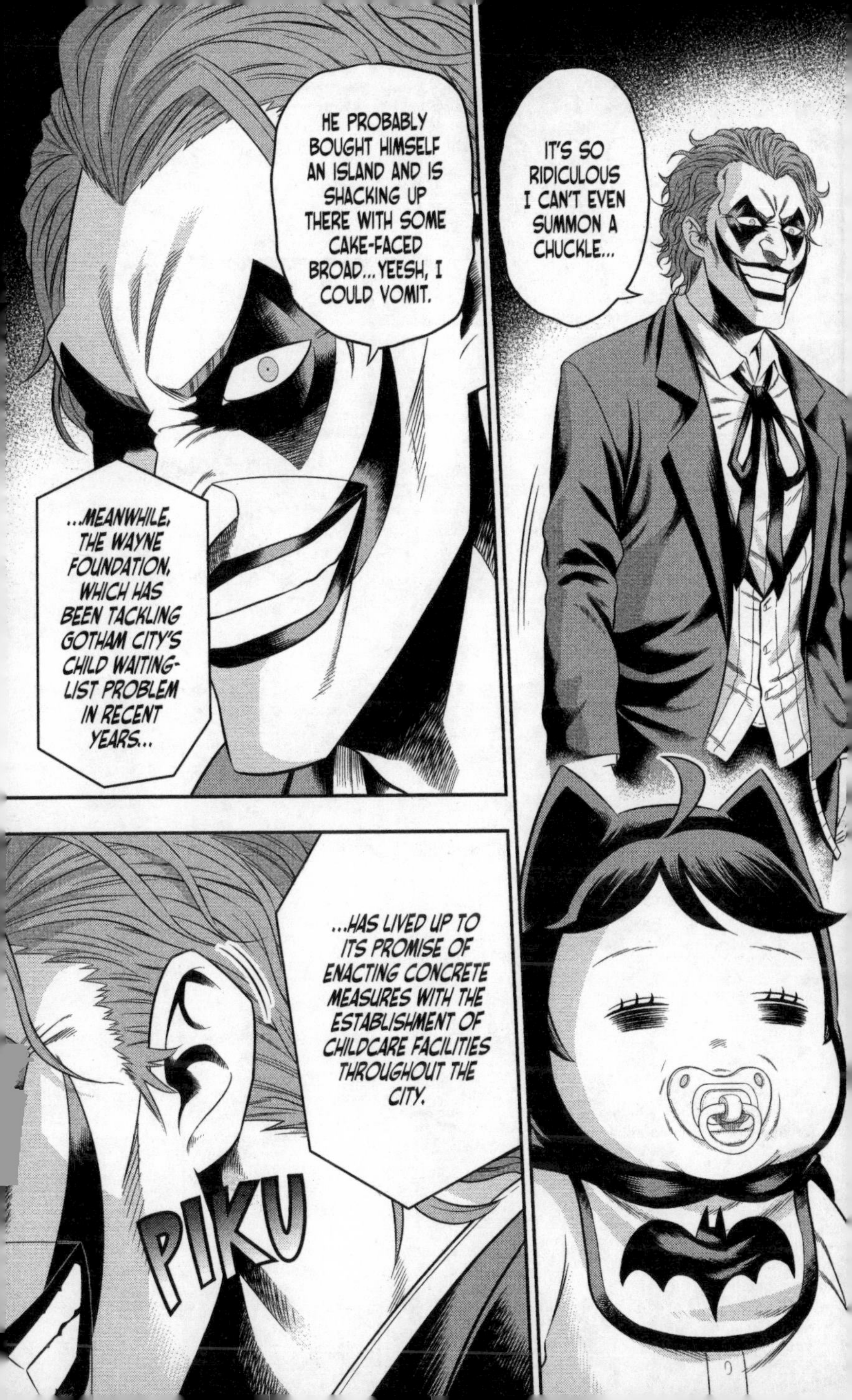
IT'S SO RIDICULOUS I CAN'T EVEN SUMMON A CHUCKLE...
HE PROBABLY BOUGHT HIMSELF AN ISLAND AND IS SHACKING UP THERE WITH SOME CAKE-FACED BROAD... YEESH, I COULD VOMIT.
...MEANWHILE, THE WAYNE FOUNDATION, WHICH HAS BEEN TACKLING GOTHAM CITY'S CHILD WAITING-LIST PROBLEM IN RECENT YEARS...
...HAS LIVED UP TO ITS PROMISE OF ENACTING CONCRETE MEASURES WITH THE ESTABLISHMENT OF CHILDCARE FACILITIES THROUGHOUT THE CITY.
PIKU

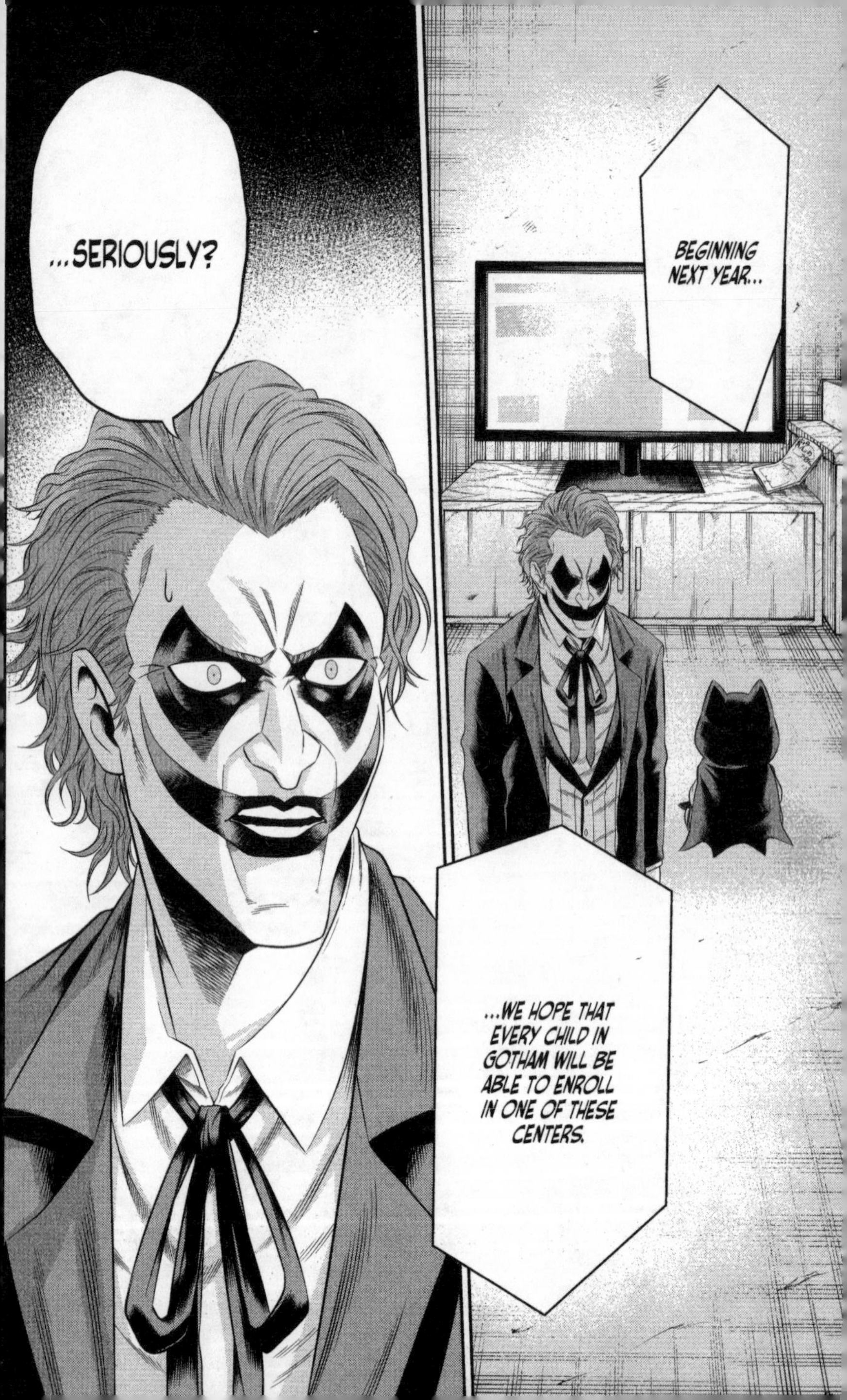
BEGINNING NEXT YEAR...
...WE HOPE THAT EVERY CHILD IN GOTHAM WILL BE ABLE TO ENROLL IN ONE OF THESE CENTERS.
...SERIOUSLY?

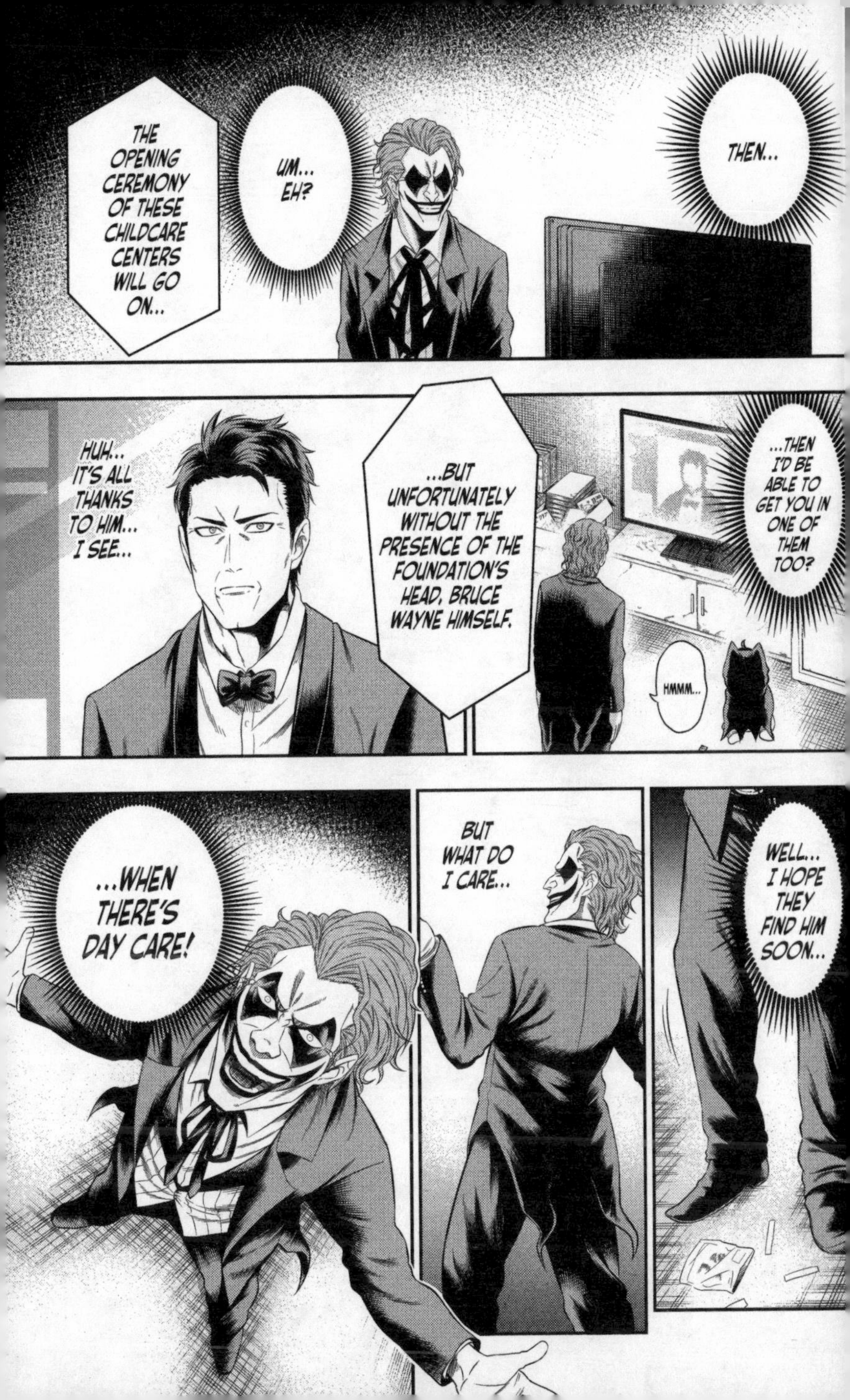
THEN...
UM... EH?
THE OPENING CEREMONY OF THESE CHILDCARE CENTERS WILL GO ON...
...THEN I'D BE ABLE TO GET YOU IN ONE OF THEM TOO?
HMMM...
...BUT UNFORTUNATELY WITHOUT THE PRESENCE OF THE FOUNDATION'S HEAD, BRUCE WAYNE HIMSELF.
HUH... IT'S ALL THANKS TO HIM... I SEE...
WELL... I HOPE THEY FIND HIM SOON...
BUT WHAT DO I CARE...
...WHEN THERE'S DAY CARE!

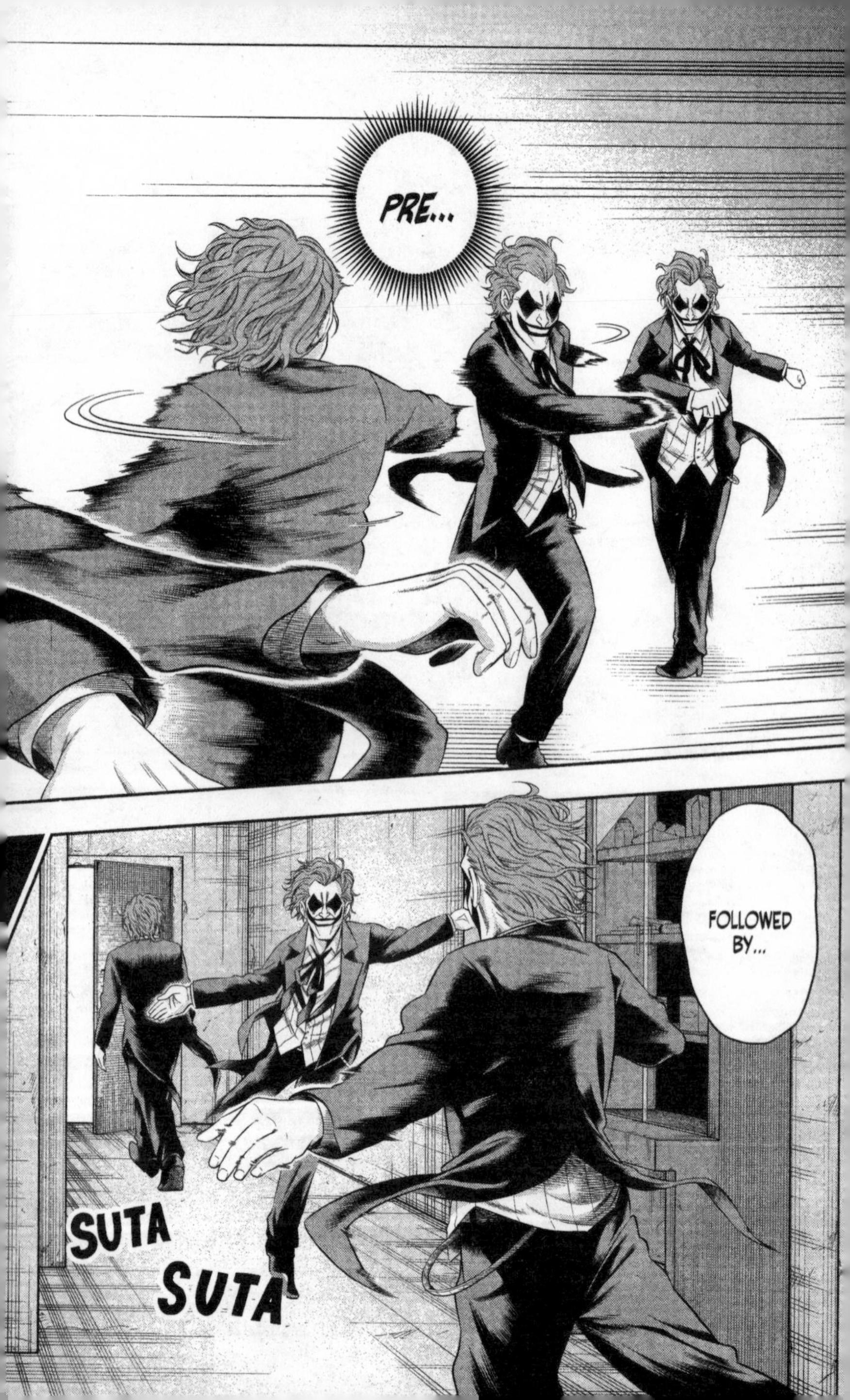
PRE...
FOLLOWED BY...
SUTA SUTA

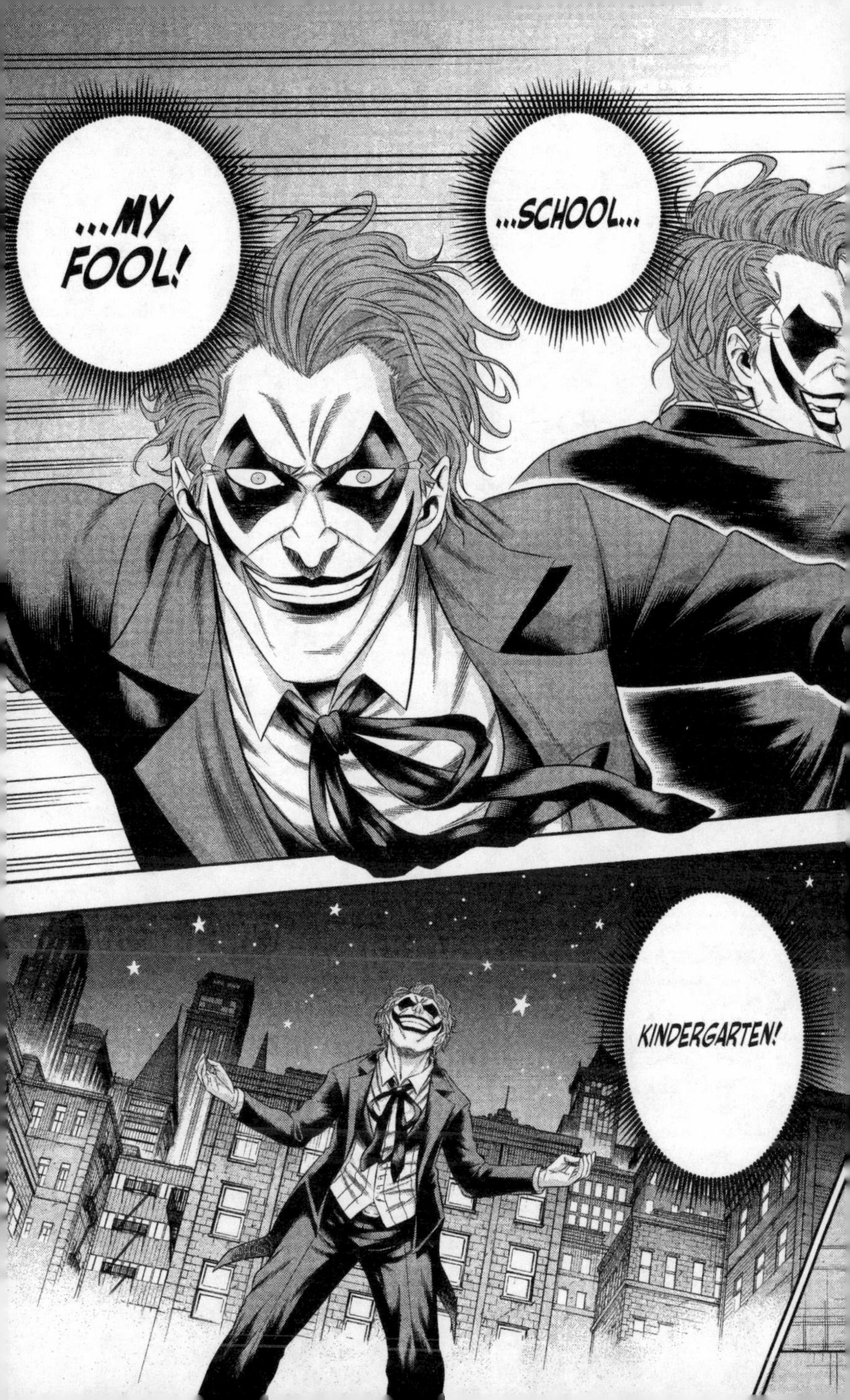
...SCHOOL...
...MY FOOL!
KINDERGARTEN!

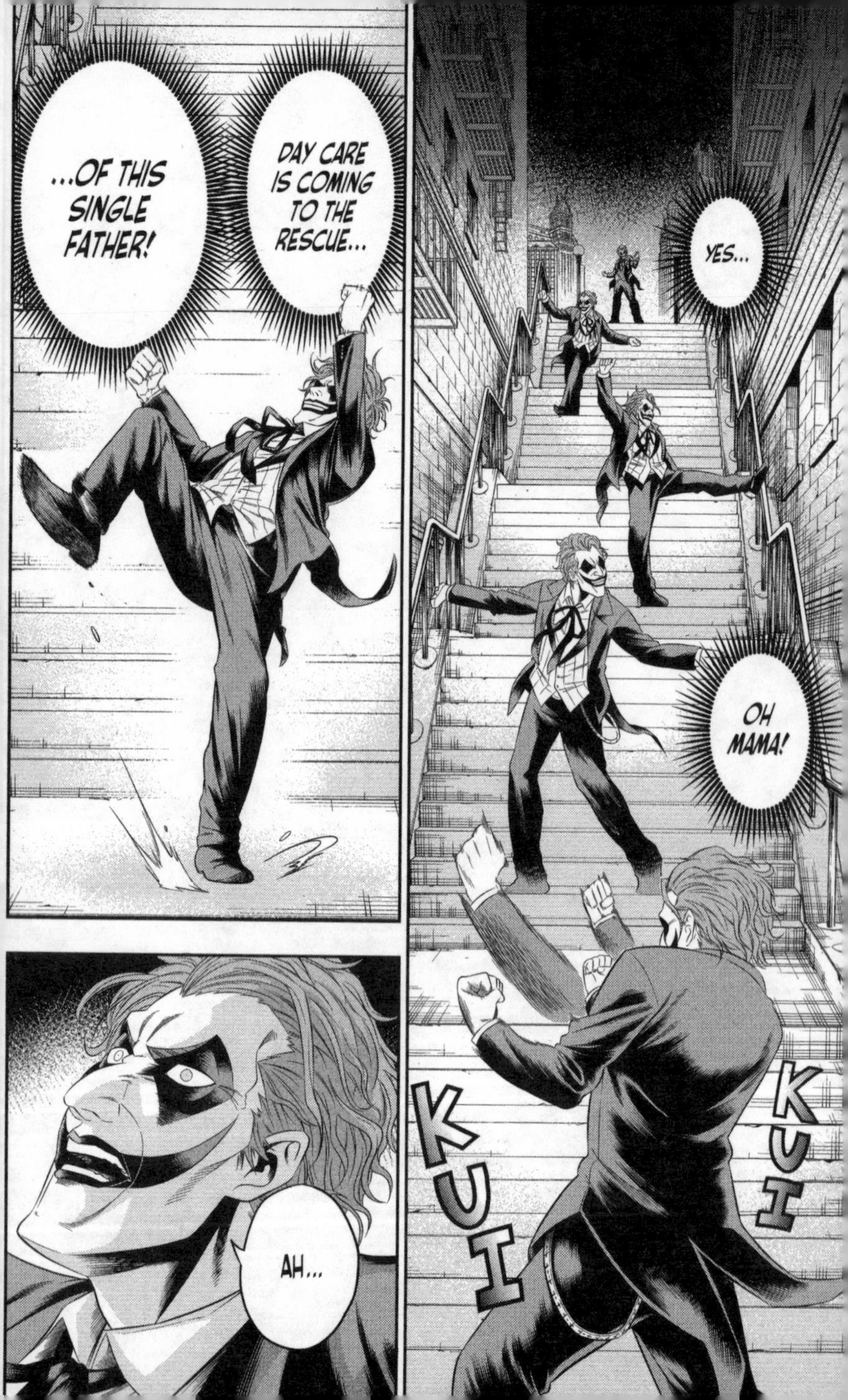
YES...
OH MAMA!
KUI
KUI
DAY CARE IS COMING TO THE RESCUE...
...OF THIS SINGLE FATHER!
AH...

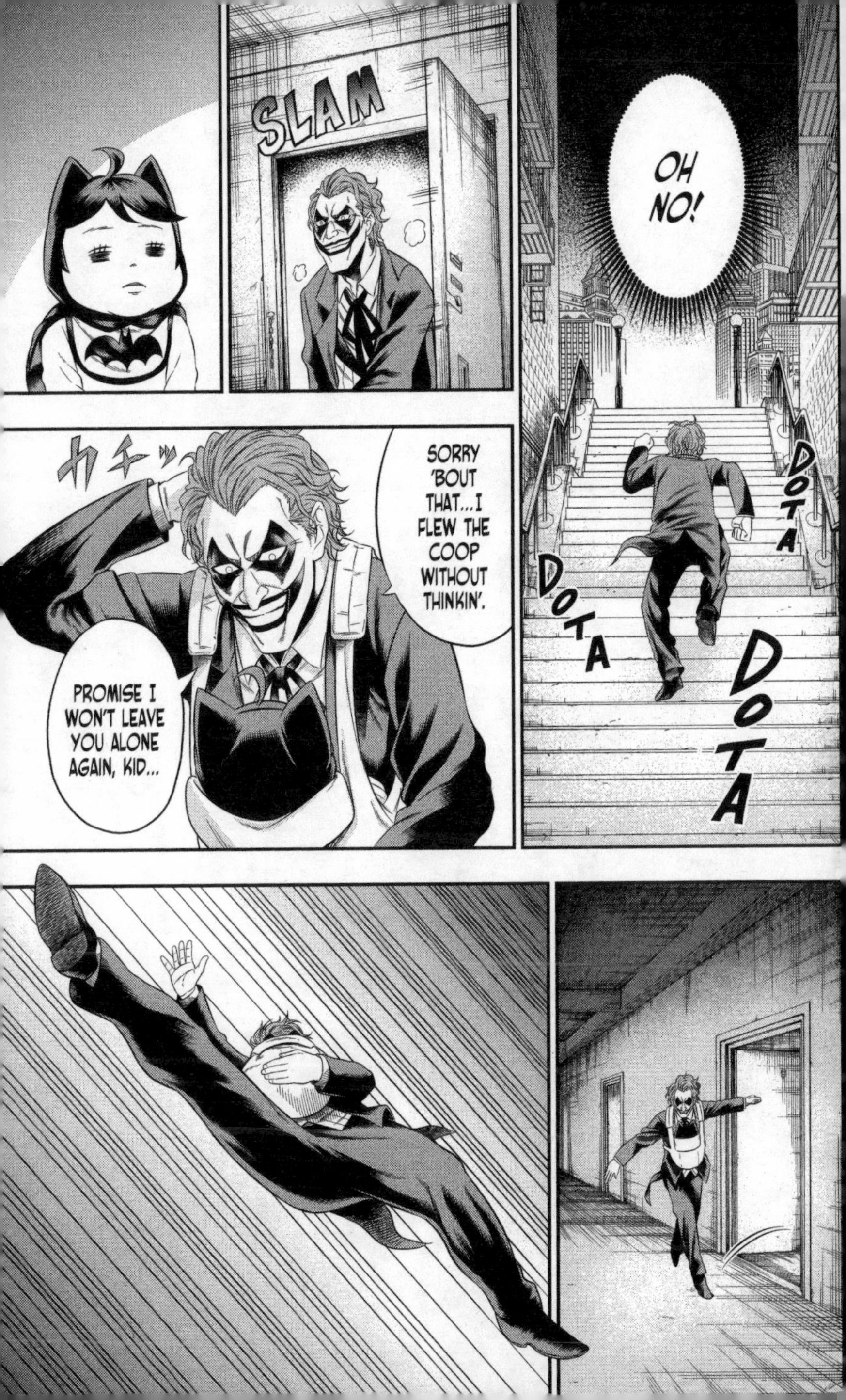
OH NO!
DOTA
DOTA
DOTA
SLAM
カチッ
SORRY 'BOUT THAT...I FLEW THE COOP WITHOUT THINKIN'.
PROMISE I WON'T LEAVE YOU ALONE AGAIN, KID...

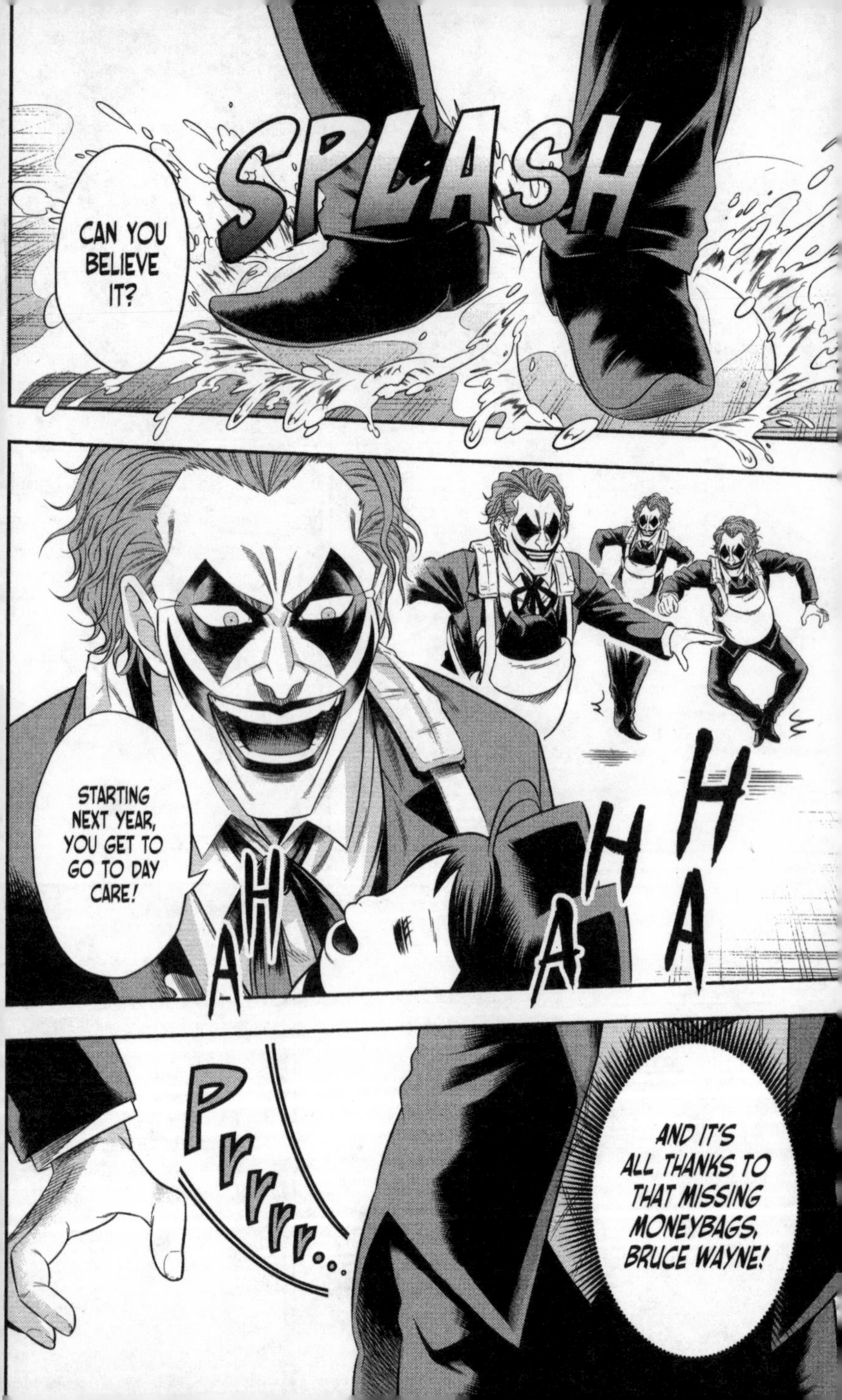
SPLASH
CAN YOU BELIEVE IT?
HA
HA
HA
STARTING NEXT YEAR, YOU GET TO GO TO DAY CARE!
AND IT'S ALL THANKS TO THAT MISSING MONEYBAGS, BRUCE WAYNE!
Prrrr...

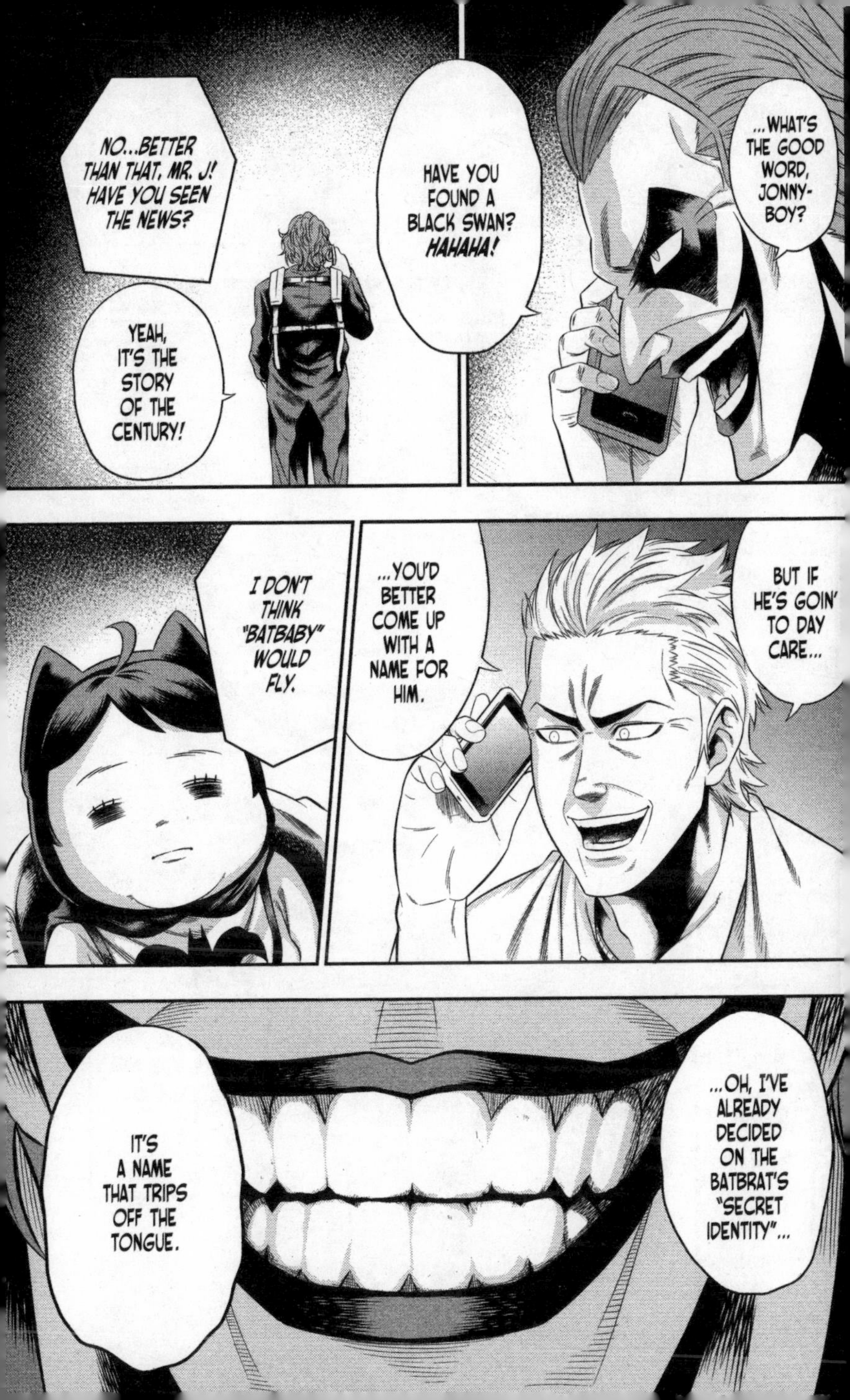
...WHAT'S THE GOOD WORD, JONNY-BOY?
HAVE YOU FOUND A BLACK SWAN? *HAHAHA!*
NO...BETTER THAN THAT, MR. J! HAVE YOU SEEN THE NEWS?
YEAH, IT'S THE STORY OF THE CENTURY!
BUT IF HE'S GOIN' TO DAY CARE...
...YOU'D BETTER COME UP WITH A NAME FOR HIM.
I DON'T THINK "BATBABY" WOULD FLY.
...OH, I'VE ALREADY DECIDED ON THE BATBRAT'S "SECRET IDENTITY"...
IT'S A NAME THAT TRIPS OFF THE TONGUE.

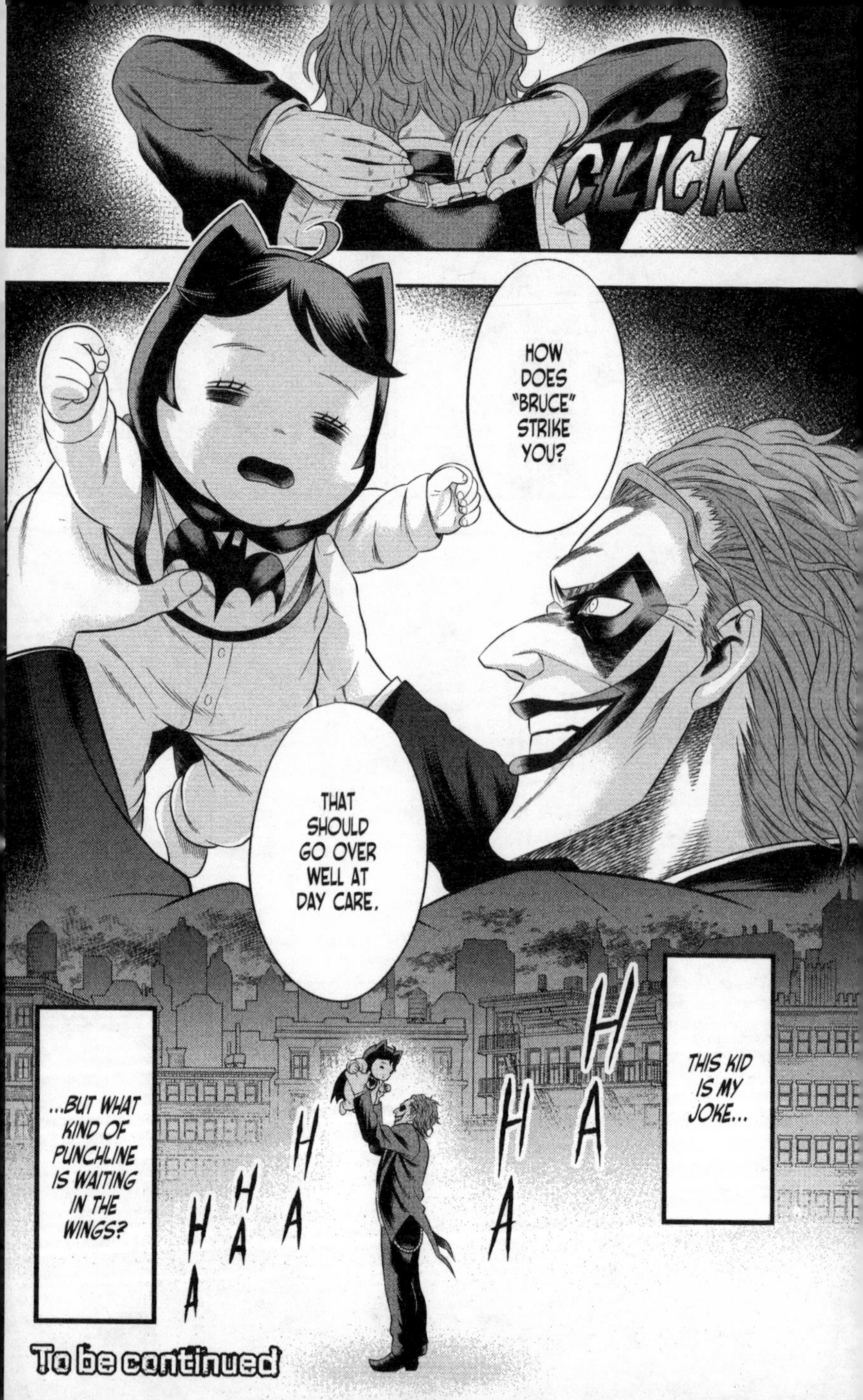
CLICK
HOW DOES "BRUCE" STRIKE YOU?
THAT SHOULD GO OVER WELL AT DAY CARE.
THIS KID IS MY JOKE...
HA
HA
HA
HA
HA
...BUT WHAT KIND OF PUNCHLINE IS WAITING IN THE WINGS?
To be continued

ANDREW MARINO   DC Editor – Original Series & Collected Edition
MITSUHIRO MURAMATSU   Kodansha Editor – Original Series & Collected Edition
STEVE COOK   Design Director – Books
MEGEN BELLERSEN   Publication Design
CHRISTY SAWYER   Publication Production
JODI TONG   Production Artist

MARIE JAVINS   VP – Editor-in-Chief

JIM LEE   President, Publisher & Chief Creative Officer
ANNE DePIES   Senior VP & General Manager
LARRY BERRY   VP – Brand Design & Creative Services
DON FALLETTI   VP – Manufacturing & Production
LAWRENCE GANEM   VP – Editorial Programming & Talent Strategy
NICK J. NAPOLITANO   VP – Publishing & Business Operations
NANCY SPEARS   VP – Sales & Marketing

JOKER: ONE OPERATION JOKER VOL. 1

Publisher: Hiroaki Morita
Publishing House: Kodansha Ltd.
2-12-21 Otowa, Bunkyo-ku Tokyo 112-8001 Japan
DC Comics, 4000 Warner Blvd., Bldg. 700, 2nd Floor,
Burbank, CA 91522
Printed by Solisco Printers, Scott, QC, Canada.
3/29/24. Third Printing.
ISBN: 978-1-77952-311-2

Library of Congress Cataloging-in-Publication Data is available.

STOP!

THIS IS THE END OF THE GRAPHIC NOVEL.
YOU'RE READING IN THE WRONG DIRECTION.
BE SURE TO READ EACH PAGE RIGHT TO LEFT LIKE THE GUIDE BELOW.

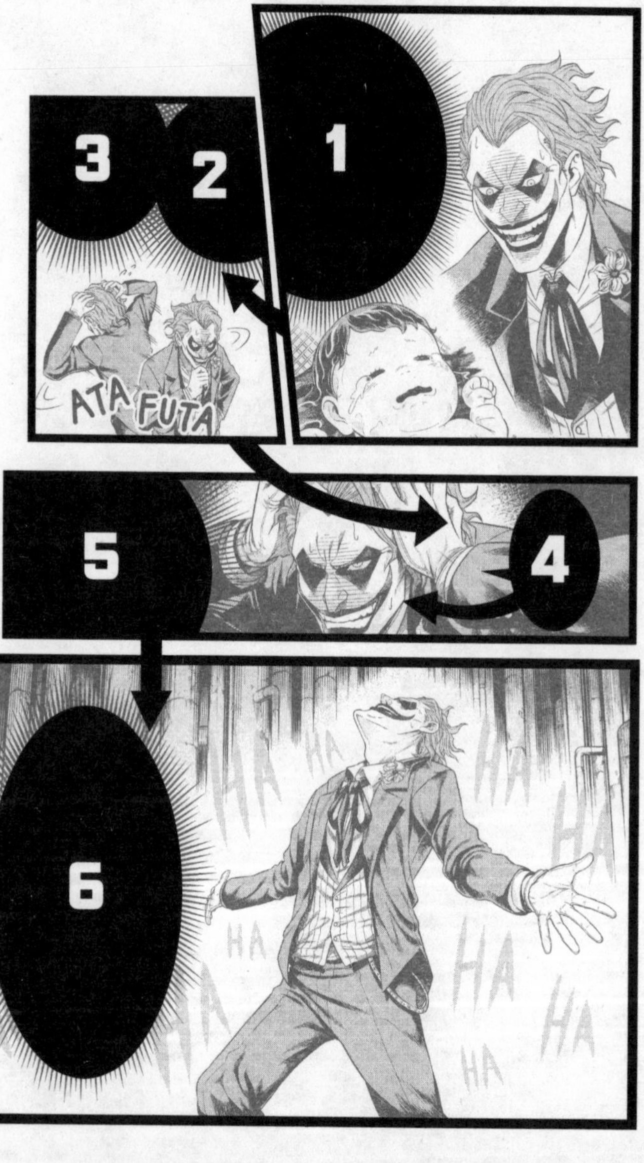
1
2
3
ATA FUTA
4
5
6
HA HA HA HA HA HA HA HA